Democratic Governance

Democratic Governance

Mark Bevir

PRINCETON UNIVERSITY PRESS

PRINCETON AND OXFORD

Copyright © 2010 by Princeton University Press
Requests for permission to reproduce material from this work
should be sent to Permissions, Princeton University Press

Published by Princeton University Press, 41 William Street,
Princeton, New Jersey 08540
In the United Kingdom: Princeton University Press, 6 Oxford Street,
Woodstock, Oxfordshire OX20 1TW

Library of Congress Cataloging-in-Publication Data

Bevir, Mark.
Democratic governance / Mark Bevir.
p.   cm.
Includes bibliographical references and index.
ISBN 978-0-691-14538-9 (hardcover : alk. paper)
ISBN 978-0-691-14539-6 (pbk. : alk. paper)
1. Democracy. 2. Public administration. 3. State, The. I. Title.
JC423.B428 2010   321.8—dc22
2009052058

British Library Cataloging-in-Publication Data is available

This book has been composed in Sabon

Printed on acid-free paper.   ∞

press.princeton.edu

Printed in the United States of America

10 9 8 7 6 5 4 3 2 1

To Harry

Contents

Tables

Preface

DEMOCRATIC GOVERNANCE offers a genealogy of some problems confronting democracy. The genealogy focuses on modernist social science. Modernism has transformed our political practices. New theories of governance have contributed to the rise of new worlds of governance. The new governance challenges democracy. Policy makers have ignored the challenge, or responded to it in terms set by the theories that caused it. Democratic action has lost out to scientific expertise.

While the new theories of governance have roots in the late nineteenth and early twentieth centuries, the new worlds of governance did not appear much before the 1980s. I do not mention the 1980s to support the glib identification of governance with a reified, uniform, and unchanging set of neoliberal policies: the new worlds of governance have always been diverse and contested, and even when governments did adopt neoliberal policies, the policies rarely worked as intended so they have been replaced or supplemented with alternative policies. Instead, I mention the 1980s to suggest the new worlds of governance have coincided with my adult lifetime. When I have written on governance, I have narrated my times.

My narratives are my political action. When we describe the new worlds of governance and explain how they arose, we necessarily approve or critique the ideas embedded in those worlds. Our stories can challenge current ways of acting and suggest alternative possibilities. New stories do not create new practices, but they can prepare the way for them. I tell stories because I have little talent or taste for other forms of political action.

Acknowledgments

I THANK Ben Krupicka, Rod Rhodes, and Frank Trentmann for discussions and collaborations on governance. Sage, Elsevier, and Oxford University Press kindly allowed me to draw on previously published essays: the introductions to M. Bevir, ed., *Public Governance* (Sage, 2007); "Police Reform, Governance, and Democracy," in M. O'Neil, M. Marks, and A-M. Singh, eds., *Police Occupational Culture: New Debates and Directions* (Elsevier, 2007); and "The Westminster Model, Governance, and Judicial Reform," *Parliamentary Affairs* 61 (2008): 559–77. Ian Malcolm of Princeton University Press has been an intelligent and supportive editor. Laura once again did the index, and once again the index is the least of the many things she does for which I am so very grateful.

Abbreviations

AMS	additional member system
COPS	Community Orientated Policing Services
CRA	Constitutional Reform Act
DBERR	Department of Business, Enterprise, and Regulatory Reform
DHS	Department of Homeland Security
DIUS	Department for Innovation, Universities, and Skills
ECHR	European Court of Human Rights
ECJ	European Court of Justice
EU	European Union
GLA	Greater London Authority
HRA	Human Rights Act
MBO	management by objectives
MBR	management by results
NHS	National Health Service
NPM	new public management
NRM	natural resource management
OECD	Organisation for Economic Co-operation and Development
PMCA	Police and Magistrates' Courts Act
PSA	public service agreement
STV	single transferable vote
TQM	total quality management

Democratic Governance

Interpreting Governance

ONCE you start to listen out for the word "governance," it crops up everywhere. The Internet faces issues of Internet governance. International organizations promote good governance. Hospitals are introducing systems of clinical governance. Climate change and avian flu require innovative forms of global and transnational governance. Newspapers report scandalous failures of corporate governance.

Unfortunately, the ubiquity of the word "governance" does not make its meaning any clearer. A lack of clarity about the meaning of governance might engender skepticism about its importance. The lack of clarity lends piquancy to questions such as: How does the concept of governance differ from that of government? Why has the concept of governance become ubiquitous? What is the relationship of governance to democracy? How do policy actors respond to the challenges of governance?

This book attempts to answer these questions. It argues that:

- The concept of governance evokes a more pluralistic pattern of rule than does government: governance is less focused on state institutions, and more focused on the processes and interactions that tie the state to civil society.
- The concept of governance has spread because new theories of politics and public sector reforms inspired by these theories have led to a crisis of faith in the state.
- Governance and the crisis of faith in the state make our image of representative democracy implausible.
- Policy actors have responded to the challenge of governance in ways that are constrained by the image of representative democracy and a faith in policy expertise.

While these arguments might seem straightforward, we will confront a host of complexities along the way. These complexities often reflect the limited extent to which we can expect concepts such as governance to have fixed content. "Governance" is a vague and contested term, as are many political concepts. People hold different theories and values that lead them, quite reasonably, to ascribe different content to the concept of governance. There are, in other words, multiple theories and multiple worlds of governance, each of which has different implications for democracy.

I have responded to this complexity in part by mixing general discussions of the new governance with specific case studies that locate Britain in various comparative and international contexts. In the particular case of Britain, this book argues that:

- The concept of governance evokes a differentiated polity that stands in contrast to the Westminster model.
- The concept of governance has spread because new theories of politics and also public sector reforms inspired by these theories have eroded faith in the Westminster model.
- A shift of perspective from the Westminster model to the differentiated polity poses challenges for the constitution and public administration.
- Policy actors have generally responded to these challenges by promoting reforms that remain constrained by the Westminster model and a faith in policy expertise.

Diagnosis and Prescription

My aims are primarily diagnostic. I identify trends and problems in current democracy. Governance undermines old expressions of representative democracy including the Westminster model. Policy actors typically remain trapped by the image of representative democracy buttressed now by a faith in policy expertise. Their policies restrict democracy. Representative governments struggle to direct the policy process. An illusory expertise crowds out citizen participation.

While this book is mainly diagnostic, it contains prescriptive arguments. Just as the diagnosis points to modernist theories as a source of current problems of democracy, so the prescription involves turning away from these theories. Modernist social science has restricted democracy. Interpretive social science may be a cure.

Interpretive social science certainly shifts our perspective on the relationship of knowledge to the state. Modernist social scientists generally see only how their theories analyze the state. An interpretive approach enables us also to see how social science partly constitutes the state. It may be controversial to argue that social science makes the world as well as analyzing it. But the argument is obvious: if policy actors form policies using formal or folk theories from social science, then social science partly constitutes those policies.

Approaches to social science do not have logically necessary relation-ships to democratic theories and practices. However, my diagnosis sug-gests that historically modernist social science has undermined faith in representative democracy and led policy actors to turn increasingly to an expertise based on modernist social science itself. My prescriptive hope is that an interpretive social science may reveal the limitations of this exper-tise and encourage more pluralist and participatory forms of democracy.

These diagnostic and prescriptive arguments reflect a historical narra-tive about the changing nature of social science and democratic practice. The new theories and worlds of governance are part of a long process of rethinking and remaking the modern state. My diagnosis narrates the shift from developmental historicism to modernism. My prescrip-tion advocates another shift to interpretive social science, dialogue, and participation.

Much of the nineteenth century was dominated by a developmental historicism in which the state appeared as a consummation of the his-tory of a nation that was held together by ties of race, language, charac-ter, and culture. This developmental historicism promoted the following three ideas. First, the state was or at least could be the expression of the common good (or public interest) of a nation (or people) that was bound together by prepolitical ties. Second, social science grasped the character of any particular state as a historical product of a prepolitical nation. Third, representative institutions enabled citizens to elect and hold ac-countable politicians who expressed, acted on, and safeguarded the com-mon good of the nation.

The modern literature on governance rose as developmental histori-cism gave way to modernist social science. Modernist social science undermined older views of the state and nation. Instead the literature on governance exhibits the following three ideas. First, the state is frag-mented, consisting of self-interested actors or complex networks. Second, social science explains policy outcomes by appealing to formal ahistori-cal models, correlations, mechanisms, or processes. Third, representative institutions are at most a small part of a larger policy process in which a range of actors, many of whom are unelected and unaccountable, nego-tiate, formulate, and implement policies in accord with their particular interests and norms.

If the new governance is part of a process of profound historical im-portance, it still remains up to us to make the future out of current cir-cumstances. How should we do so? This book promotes an interpretive theory of governance that promotes the following three ideas. First, the state is fragmented, consisting of complex networks of actors inspired by different beliefs formed against the background of competing traditions. Second, social science can offer us only stories about how people have acted and guesses about how they might act. Third, representative institutions should be supplemented less by appeals to an allegedly formal and ahistorical expertise and more by alternative forms of democracy.

My adherence to an interpretive theory of governance thus leads me to question the wisdom of recent attempts to remake the state. Modernist theories of governance typically suggest that the cracks in representative institutions can be papered over by policy expertise. Rational choice theory and institutionalism often appeal to expert knowledge that promotes nonmajoritarian institutions or networks. In contrast, I adhere to an interpretive theory that undermines the modernist notion of expertise and suggests we should be thinking instead about how to renew democracy.

Clearly my prescription reflects my diagnosis. The appeal to interpretive social science and participatory democracy rests on the account of the way modernist social science influences democratic governance. Equally, however, the diagnosis reflects the interpretive social science I prescribe. Aspects of the prescription are important to a proper understanding of the diagnosis. Thus, this book has a somewhat circular structure. The rest of this chapter introduces the interpretive approach to social science that informs the ensuing diagnosis of problems of democratic governance. The final chapter returns to this interpretive approach and participatory democracy as possible solutions to these problems. Readers who get impatient with philosophy may want to skip directly to the next chapter, avoiding my justification of my approach and going straight to the start of my narrative.

INTERPRETIVE SOCIAL SCIENCE

There are various ways of defining interpretive social science.[1] Sometimes interpretation appears primarily as a matter of method. Interpretive methods contrast with quantitative ones or with both quantitative and qualitative ones. Advocates defend them as superior to these other methods or at least as necessary supplements to these other methods. The argument is often that only methods such as observation, interviewing, and discourse analysis can reveal the rich texture of human life. Interpretive methods are, in this view, the route to a level of factual detail that other methods miss. Advocates defend interpretive studies either as a means of checking and fleshing out broad generalizations or as the only

---

[1] The tension between interpretation as method and philosophy recurs in D. Yanow and P. Schwartz-Shea, eds., *Interpretation and Method: Empirical Research Methods and the Interpretive Turn* (Armonk, NY: M. E. Sharpe, 2006).

way of discovering the facts. Their methodological concept of interpretive social science leads them to spend much time worrying about the objectivity of their data, the rigor of their analyses, and the criteria for evaluating their work.

In my view, however, interpretation is primarily about philosophy. Interpretive social science derives from a historicist philosophy—but a more radical historicism than the developmental one I mentioned earlier. Historicism refers generally to a belief that we can discuss human cultures and practices adequately only as historical objects. Historicist modes of reasoning became commonplace in the nineteenth century. Social scientists conceived of human life as being inherently purposeful and intentional. Yet nineteenth-century historicism remained developmental, conceiving of purposes and intentions as guided by fixed principles. While different social scientists relied on slightly different principles, the most commonly accepted ones included liberty, reason, nation, and state. These principles guided social scientists in selecting the facts to include in their historical narratives. They defined nineteenth-century histories. They inspired a belief in the unity and progressive nature of history.

Radical historicism does away with appeals to principles that lend necessity and unity to history.[2] The result is an emphasis on nominalism and contingency. Nominalism refers here to the idea that universals are just names for clusters of particulars. In social science, aggregate concepts do not refer to natural kinds with essences, but only to a series of particular people and actions. Radical historicists reject uses of concepts that refer to types of state, society, economy, or nation as if they had an essence that defines their boundaries and explains other aspects of their nature or development. They reject reifications. All social life is meaningful activity. Moreover, a rejection of reifications highlights the contingency of social life. Activity is not governed by either formal reified concepts or teleological principles. Social life consists of a series of contingent, even accidental, actions that appropriate, modify, and transform the past to create the present. Radical historicists reject determinism, whether it reduces activity to economic factors or to reified structures and institutions.

An emphasis on nominalism and contingency leads radical historicists to an antinaturalist analysis of social explanation. Radical historicists may accept a naturalist ontology according to which humans are part of nature and no more than part of nature. But radical historicists typically argue that the social sciences require a different form of explanation from the natural sciences. As Clifford Geertz famously claimed, social science

[2] Compare M. Bevir, *The Logic of the History of Ideas* (Cambridge: Cambridge University Press, 1999).

needs to be "not an experimental science in search of law but an interpretive one in search of meaning."[3]

Positivists once defended naturalism by arguing that causal explanations are valid only if they fit observations, and meanings are irrelevant because they are not observable.[4] Today, however, most modernist social scientists accept that actions have meanings for those who perform them, and even that agents act for reasons of their own. The naturalism of these modernist social scientists differs from the antinaturalism of interpretive social science in the role given to meanings in social explanation. Naturalists want meanings to drop out of explanations. They might argue that to give the reasons for an action is merely to redescribe it; to explain an action, we have to show how it—and so perhaps the reason for which the agent performed it—conforms to a general law couched in terms of social facts.

In contrast, radical historicists, emphasizing nominalism, dismiss social facts as reifications. They argue that actions are meaningful and meanings are holistic. They then take holism to entail a distinctive contextualizing approach to social explanation. Social scientists can explain people's beliefs and actions by locating them in a wider context of meanings. Meanings cannot be reduced to allegedly objective facts because their content depends on their relationship to other meanings. Social science requires a contextualizing form of explanation that distinguishes it from the natural sciences. We elucidate and explain meanings by reference to wider systems of meanings, not by reference to reified categories such as social class or institutional position, and not by construing meanings as independent variables in the framework of naturalist forms of explanation.

When modernist social scientists let meanings drop out of their explanations, they are usually hoping at least to point to classifications, correlations, or other regularities that hold across various cases. Even when they renounce the ideal of a universal theory, they still regard historical contingency and contextual specificity as obstacles that need to be overcome in the search for cross-temporal and cross-cultural regularities. Naturalists characteristically search for causal connections that bestride time and space like colossi. They attempt to control for all kinds of variables and thereby arrive at parsimonious explanations.

In contrast, radical historicists, emphasizing contingency, argue that the role of meanings in social life precludes regularities acting as explanations. Radical historicists do not deny that we can make general statements covering diverse cases. They reject two specific features of a naturalist view of generalization. Radical historicists deny, first, that

[3] C. Geertz, *The Interpretation of Cultures* (New York: Basic Books, 1973), 5.

[4] E.g., J. Watson, *Behaviorism* (New York: Norton, 1924).

general statements are a uniquely powerful form of social knowledge. They believe that statements about the unique and contingent aspects of particular social phenomena are at least as apposite and valuable as general statements. Generalizations often deprive our understanding of social phenomena of what is most distinctly and significantly human about them. Radical historicists deny, second, that general statements actually explain features of particular cases. Just as we can say that several objects are red without explaining anything else about them, so we can say that several states are democracies without their being democracies explaining any other feature they have in common.

Radical historicists conceive of human action as inherently particular and contingent. They oppose social explanations that appear to appeal to ahistorical causal mechanisms. Much current philosophy supports their antinaturalist commitment to contextualizing explanations.[5] Today the naturalism of the positivists has been almost entirely replaced by philosophical analyses such as those of Ludwig Wittgenstein and Donald Davidson. Wittgenstein argued that the meaning of a word cannot be elucidated in abstraction from the context in which it is used.[6] Davidson then argued that social science presupposes ideas of choice and contingency that are incompatible with the forms of explanation found in natural science. Actions are explained by reasons in a way that implies actors could have reasoned and acted differently. Actions are products of contingent decisions, not the determined outcomes of lawlike processes.[7]

ON CASES AND GENEALOGIES

A commitment to interpretive social science informs the logical form of my arguments. Many social scientists think in terms of methods, not the logic of arguments. However, just as I argued that interpretive social science is primarily philosophical rather than methodological, so I now want to describe my approach to democratic governance in terms of the logical form of its arguments rather than method. Interpretive social science does not require any particular techniques of data collection. But

---

[5] Yet when modernist social scientists discuss causality and explanation, they typically ignore the resurgence of antinaturalism, discuss only naturalist perspectives, and refer exclusively to works on the philosophy of science and dated ones on the philosophy of social science. E.g., H. Brady, "Causation and Explanation in Social Science," in J. Box-Steffensmeier, H. Brady, and D. Collier, eds., *The Oxford Handbook of Political Methodology*, (Oxford: Oxford University Press, 2008), 217–70.

[6] L. Wittgenstein, *Philosophical Investigations*, trans. G. Anscombe (Oxford: Basil Blackwell, 1972).

[7] D. Davidson, *Essays on Actions and Events* (Oxford: Clarendon Press, 1980).

it does require social scientists to adopt contextualizing and historical forms of explanation. Indeed, radical historicism reminds us that modernist correlations, classifications, and models are not properly speaking explanations; they are just more data that social scientists need to explain using contextualizing and historical narratives. Correlations and classifications become explanations only if we unpack them as shorthand for narratives about how, for example, beliefs fit with other beliefs in a way that made possible certain activity. Models may appeal to beliefs and desires, but they are mere fables; they become explanations only if we accept them as accurate depictions of the beliefs and desires that people really held in a particular case.

The logical form of my arguments differs from modernist social science in the use of case studies and historical context. Interpretive social science challenges the idea that case studies can serve as evidence in favor of formal and ahistorical theories. Modernist social science typically aims at formal theories that describe a social logic or lawlike regularity that follows from the essential properties of a type of actor, institution, or situation. So, for example, social scientists might define governance by reference to one or more essential property, such as multiplying networks. They might argue that this property characterizes all cases of governance. Then they might argue that this property explains other features of governance, such as the state's growing reliance on steering and regulation as opposed to direct oversight and control. The quest for formal theories means social scientists often use cases as systematic evidence. They worry about the selection of their cases. They try to make their cases appropriately systematic, random, similar, diverse, typical, or extreme, according to the content of the formal theory they want to test.[8]

An interpretive approach undermines the very idea of formal theories and so the idea that cases are best conceived as systematic evidence for such theories. An emphasis on nominalism precludes appeals to allegedly essential properties and so comprehensive theories or midlevel hypotheses couched in formal terms. Interpretive social science often aims instead at drawing attention to an aspect of the world that has gone largely unnoticed. Interpretive social science appeals to a case or series of cases to illustrate an aspect of the world rather than as systematic evidence of its extent or inner logic. The result is a new way of seeing—a new picture or concept rather than a new formal theory. Wittgenstein wrote here of using examples to pick out a pattern of family resemblances without appealing to a comprehensive theory.[9] The examples have a range

---

[8] E.g., J. Gerring, "Case Selection for Case-Study Analysis," in Box-Steffensmeier, Brady, and Collier, eds., *Oxford Handbook of Political Methodology*, 645–84.

[9] Wittgenstein, *Philosophical Investigations*, sections 63–69.

of similarities at various levels of detail, but they do not have any one essential property or set of properties in common. We do not master the new concept by discovering a rule that tells us when to apply it. We do not recognize the new pattern by devising a formal theory that explains it. Our grasp of the concept lies in our ability to provide reasons why it applies to one case but not another, and our ability to draw analogies with other cases. We recognize the pattern when we can discuss whether or not it is present in other cases.

Interpretive social science often uses cases as illustrative of patterns rather than systematic evidence of formal theories. There is nothing intrinsically troubling about a rather ad hoc approach to cases. Cases legitimately may be cherry-picked to illustrate the aspect of the world the social scientist wants people to see. In this book, I rely mainly on cases from Britain, but I also add a sprinkling of comparative cases. These comparative cases are not meant to provide systematic and sustained evidence that Britain is somehow representative of a broader social logic. Nor do the comparative cases purport to identify or stay within a specific geographical range within which a social logic operates. Instead, the comparative cases, stretching from police reform to good governance in developing countries and from Australia to Haiti, are an admittedly unsystematic attempt to help us see a picture. They illustrate the presence in various aspects of current policymaking of particular ideas and discourses—a continuing commitment to representative democracy along with forms of expertise associated with modernist social science. I describe this pattern in abstract terms. I use case studies to illustrate it. If readers recognize the pattern, they will be able to draw analogies to other cases, but I hope they will remain nominalists and resist the temptation to treat cases as systematic evidence for a midlevel hypothesis or general theory.

To reject formal theories is not to renounce the ambition to explain. It is just that the emphasis on contingency requires interpretive social scientists to rely on historical explanations rather than formal ones. So, I offer a historicist explanation of the cases of policymaking being influenced by a commitment to representative democracy and forms of expertise associated with modernist social science. Modernist social science and the broader culture associated with it have inspired changes in the state that have weakened democracy. Sometimes I point to the influence of particular social scientists on policy makers. But I am not arguing that politicians or even their advisers are remarkably well-read in social science or even understand and believe the formal theories developed by social scientists. My argument is more about the culture in which we live. The ideas that inspire modernist social science have folk as well as technical forms. As rational choice theorists develop technical models based on assumptions about the self-interested nature of action, so many of us have a folk idea that politicians and even bureaucrats and public sector workers are likely to be trying to increase their pay or shorten their working hours even at the expense of the public good. My narrative thus refers to a general cultural shift. New concepts of rationality both highlighted problems in older democratic theories and encouraged people to respond to these problems by drawing on knowledge and strategies associated with modernist social science.

This historicist explanation of current patterns of democratic governance is, more specifically, a genealogy. The very style of this book resembles other genealogies. I try to offer a bold, sweeping, and provocative argument that relies on historical narratives and illustrative cases to change the way we see current ideals and practices. I try to unsettle without necessarily specifying a detailed alternative. Genealogies denaturalize beliefs and actions that others think are natural. Genealogies suggest that ideas and practices that some people believe to be inevitable actually arose out of contingent historical processes. The critical nature of genealogies consists in their thus unsettling those who ascribe a spurious naturalness to their particular beliefs and actions.

Neither policy makers nor modernist social scientists are much inclined to reflect on the historical sources of their beliefs. Policy makers often suggest their reforms are inherently reasonable at least given the circumstances. Modernist social scientists often portray their formal theories as natural, correct, and applying across time and space. In contrast, my genealogy suggests that the reforms seem reasonable and the formal theories correct only because of a tacit background of assumptions that have contingent historical roots in the late nineteenth and early twentieth centuries. To expose these assumptions is to denaturalize and unsettle current democratic practice and current social science.

A SUMMARY OF THE BOOK

This book offers a genealogy illustrated by specific cases from Britain and elsewhere of the relationship between the new governance and democracy. The general argument is that while the new governance challenges representative democracy, current attempts to deal with this challenge are constrained by the lingering effects of modernist ways of thinking about constitutionalism and public administration. The specifically genealogical argument is that these modernist ways of thinking have contingent historical roots of which their exponents are generally unaware.

Part 1, on the new governance, provides much of the historical background, offering a detailed account of the new theories of governance and the reforms they have inspired. In chapter 2, I discuss the historical emergence of modernist social science and the modern state. Developmental historicism seemed increasingly implausible during the late nineteenth and early twentieth centuries. Social scientists questioned the principles that had guided earlier narratives of the state and nation. Skepticism about these principles left social scientists with facts but no way of making sense of the facts. Social scientists rejected historicist modes of thinking and if only by default turned to formal modes of analysis. Economic and sociological concepts of rationality came to dominate. This shift from developmental to modernist analyses altered the concept of the state and over time the nature of the state. Social scientists increasingly highlighted the role played by factions and special interests in policymaking. Many appealed to a neutral bureaucracy to guard the common good. A hierarchic bureaucracy represented the public interest, scientific expertise, and rationality. Bureaucratic accountability began to replace responsible government as a key conceptual feature of democracy. Yet, by the late 1970s, the modern bureaucratic state was itself in crisis. The new governance of markets and networks has risen as an attempt to resolve this crisis.

Chapter 3 provides a more detailed survey of the main theories of governance. Typically these theories rely on modernist social science to make sense of the crisis of the modern bureaucratic state. The economic concept of rationality spread from neoclassical economics to rational choice theory. Rational choice draws on the assumptions and techniques of neoclassical economics and decision theory to analyze social life more generally. The sociological concept of rationality inspires a range of social theories that attempt to explain actions by reference to reified accounts of social norms or structures. Prominent examples in the study of governance include the new institutionalism (or at least its historical and sociological variants), systems theory, and regulation theory. Chapter 3 also returns to interpretive social science as an alternative to approaches premised on either the economic or the sociological concept of rationality. I look specifically at how interpretive social scientists make sense of the crisis of the state and the rise and nature of the new governance.

In chapter 4, I turn to the new worlds of governance that are associated in various ways with modernist theories. The theories encouraged us to see aspects of governance that were already present. More important for us, the theories also encouraged policy makers to respond to the crisis of the state by introducing reforms that reflected the theories. It is useful here to distinguish between two waves of reform. The first wave was indebted to theories associated with the economic concept of rationality. Neoliberalism and rational choice inspired attempts at privatization and marketization and the spread of new styles of management. The second wave of reforms owed more to theories tied to a sociological concept of rationality. People inspired by institutionalism and systems theory struggled to make sense of the pattern of governance arising out of first-wave reforms. Social scientists increasingly rethought institutional and systems theories in terms of networks. Their understanding of the new governance and their promotion of networks helped inspire a turn to joined-up governance, partnerships, and whole of government agendas. Chapter 4 concludes by drawing on interpretive social science to develop an alternative decentered account of the emergence of new worlds of governance.

Part 1 provides the historical background to cases in which policy actors respond to the new governance by bolstering representative democracy with new forms of expertise. Part 2, on constitutionalism, turns to some of these cases. It examines the challenges the new governance poses to democracy and the ways policy actors have responded to these challenges. The cases focus on the continuing adherence of policy actors to old ideals of representative government.

In chapter 5, I describe some of the problems that the new theories and worlds of governance pose for democratic theory and responses to them. I emphasize that issues of good governance occur for developed countries as well as developing ones. The growth of networks and markets raises questions about the health of democratic institutions in all states. The questions include how to think about and reform public service, representative institutions, accountability, and social inclusion. Different theories of governance usually inspire different responses to these questions. Rational choice theorists with their debt to the economic concept of rationality often play down the need for democratic practices. Some defend the rationality of extending the role of nonmajoritarian institutions to areas that previously were subject to democratic control. Institutionalists and others indebted to the sociological concept of rationality typically cling to the old picture of representative government, attempting to redefine ideals such as accountability to fit the reality of the new governance. Finally, an interpretive social science may encourage us to pay greater attention to participatory innovations as ways of dealing with the problems posed by the new governance.

Chapters 6 and 7 provide more specific case studies of how policy actors are responding to some of the democratic problems raised by the new governance. The cases illustrate my general argument that policy makers are clinging to representative ideals supplemented by modernist forms of expertise. Chapter 6 looks at constitutional reform in Britain. I show how New Labour's reforms remain limited by a preoccupation with representative democracy and even a lingering adherence to the Westminster model. The reforms are all about representative assemblies and elections. They reflect liberal and Fabian traditions of socialism. New Labour has shown little interest in the dialogic and participatory reforms associated with nongovernmental and pluralist traditions of socialism. Chapter 7 turns to judicial reform, concentrating on Britain but also looking at the United States, Europe, and international relations. Judicial reform too reflects New Labour's preoccupation with representative democracy and lingering adherence to the Westminster model. Yet, judicial reform is also generally an attempt to respond to the new governance by increasing the role of legal expertise at the expense of democratic decision making.

Part 1 makes a broad historical argument about the new governance and democracy. Part 2 illustrates the argument with various cases related to constitutional issues. Part 3, on public administration, further illustrates the argument with cases related to public policy. I examine the ways in which the new governance challenges policymaking before showing how attempts to respond to this challenge also rely on old ideas of representative democracy bolstered by modernist forms of expertise. The topics covered—joined-up governance and police reform—are illustrative. They were chosen with an eye on the concept of the state. The state is often conceived as consisting of legislative, judicial, and executive branches and as having a monopoly of legitimate force inside its territorial borders. Part 2 discusses legislatures and the judiciary. Part 3 then looks at joined-up governance because it is a clear attempt to modernize the executive and administrative aspects of government, and policing because it is an obvious example of legitimate force. Collectively parts 2 and 3 cover the main activities of the state in making, implementing, and enforcing law.

In chapter 8 I describe problems that the new theories and worlds of governance pose for public policy and show how responses to these problems typically draw on the new theories of governance. The new governance poses the problem of how the state can implement its policies given a proliferation of markets and networks in the public sector. Once again the different theories of governance typically inspire different responses to this problem. Rational choice theory usually encourages market solutions that reduce the role of the state in implementing policies. Institutionalists are more likely to explore a range of strategies by which they hope the state can manage and promote organizations and networks. Their greater skepticism about market rationality also leads to greater emphasis on regulation and policy learning. Finally, interpretive social science may promote an alternative that gives pride of place to dialogic approaches to public policy.

Chapters 9 and 10 provide more specific case studies of how policy actors are responding to some of the administrative problems raised by the new governance. The cases illustrate my general argument that policy makers often draw on modernist forms of social science to respond to the new governance. Public policies reflect neoliberalism, rational choice, institutionalism, and network theory with their advocacy of markets and networks. Chapter 9 tackles the spread of joined-up governance and whole of government agendas. I trace New Labour's debt to institutionalism and network theory, showing how this debt appears in the attempt to modernize governance. I trace a similar pattern in Australia's whole of government agenda, Homeland Security in the United States, and the efforts of the international community to intervene in fragile states. Chapter 10 looks specifically at police reform in Britain and the United States. I trace the fortunes of a neoliberal narrative associated with the economic concept of rationality and a community narrative associated with the sociological concept of rationality. I argue that the role of expertise in police reform helps explain its failings. The fallacy of expertise bedevils public policy.

The concluding chapter returns to the themes of this introduction. It begins by summarizing my diagnosis of the historical roots of some contemporary problems of democracy. Thereafter I offer some prescriptive reflections. With social science, I place hope in an interpretive approach that replaces economic and sociological concepts of rationality with one of local reasoning. With democratic practice, I place hope in greater participation and dialogue as alternatives to, respectively, representation and expertise. No doubt my recommendations for democratic practice will disappoint some readers by being too vague. My recommendations are limited in part because of lack of space—a normative theory of democracy would require another book. But they are also vague because, as should by now be clear, I do not believe in the kind of expertise offered by modernist social science. If we reject the mantle of expertise, we may admit to not being able to say that such and such an approach to policymaking will solve our problems. If we advocate democratic participation, we may also want to argue that citizens, not social scientists, should decide how we try to solve our problems and what forms of participation to adopt. Let me put the point more starkly than I feel committed to: social scientists should limit themselves to diagnosis and critique, leaving prescription and decision making to participants in the relevant democratic practices.

PART I

The New Governance

CHAPTER TWO

The Modern State

MUCH OF THIS BOOK provides a particular perspective on current practices and problems of democratic governance. The new governance seriously questions and erodes representative ideals and institutions. Policy actors still cling to representative ideals and institutions, trying to patch up the erosion by introducing modernist forms of expertise. As well as defending this perspective on democratic governance, I provide a historical explanation of it. The new governance rose because new modernist theories led us to see the world differently and even to make the world anew. Policy actors have responded to the new governance in limited ways because of their attachment to both old democratic ideals and folk versions of these new modernist theories. These historical explanations are critical genealogies because they denaturalize theories and practices that modernist social scientists and policy actors usually take for granted.

Part 1 develops the historical explanation of current practices and problems of democratic governance. This chapter and the next two trace the rise of modernist forms of social science and their impact on the changing nature of governance. This chapter describes the emergence of modernist social science and the modern bureaucratic state followed by the crisis of the state and, as we will see later, the rise of a new governance. Chapter 3 shows how modernist social science has inspired many of the theories of governance by which people make sense of the crisis of the bureaucratic state. Then chapter 4 considers the ways these new theories altered not only the way we understand governance but also the policies by which governance has been remade to create new worlds.

Analytically we can distinguish between three aspects of the new governance. The first is the rise of new forms of policy production and implementation. The new public management, marketization, and various forms of cogovernance have risen alongside if not in place of centralized bureaucracies. A second feature of the new governance is the expansion of public discussion and action to include new social actors. Policy networks may be more extensive and widespread. Many state actors consciously try to involve new actors in policy processes. These two aspects of the new governance are well recognized and widely discussed. The third is not. My argument is that these two aspects of the new governance are constituted in part by the third. The third aspect is a broader historic shift in knowledge production from developmental historicism to a modernist social science based on formal economic and sociological concepts of rationality. The new governance is in large part about the rise of new forms of knowledge and expertise. So, this chapter tracks the rise of modernist social science and the next chapter shows how modernist social science inspires new theories of governance. Only in chapter 4 do I then look at the new forms of policy production and implementation and public discussion and action associated with these theories.

MODERNIST SOCIAL SCIENCE

So, the general argument of this book is embedded in a historical narrative that begins at the turn of the twentieth century when developmental historicism gave way to those modernist modes of knowledge that led to the long, drawn-out rethinking of the state.[1] Table 2.1 provides a quick overview of the rise and varieties of modernism. The narrative will end, in the final chapter, with the suggestion that modernism itself should now give way to an interpretive social science that shifts attention from policy expertise to democratic theory.

The Rise of Modernism

In the late nineteenth century the study of politics was dominated by a diverse and evolving stream of comparative-historical scholarship that had emerged in the mid-nineteenth century and that persisted well into the early decades of the twentieth century. This developmental historicism inspired grand narratives centered on the nation, the state, and freedom. In Britain it included Whig history, idealist philosophy, and evolutionary theorizing. As early as the late nineteenth century, however, an evolutionary positivism, associated with Auguste Comte and Herbert Spencer, began to give way to a neopositivism that in time would come to exert a major influence on modern social science, especially in the United States.

The distinctiveness of American political science in the twentieth century should not be overplayed. The most significant feature of early-twentieth-century social science was the nearly ubiquitous rise of modernist modes of knowledge that atomized the flux of reality and deployed

---

[1] See M. Bevir, "Prisoners of Professionalism," *Public Administration* 79 (2001): 469–89; and, more recently, M. Bevir, "Political Studies as Narrative and Science, 1880–2000," *Political Studies* 54 (2006): 583–606; and R. Adcock, M. Bevir, and S. Stimson, eds., *Modern Political Science: Anglo-American Exchanges since 1880* (Princeton: Princeton University Press, 2007).

TABLE 2.1.
The Rise and Varieties of Modernism

	Developmental historicism	Modernism	
		Government	The new governance
Concept of rationality	Civilizational	Economic and sociological	New theories of governance—rational choice and new institutionalism
State formation	Nation and/or imperial state	Corporate and/or welfare state	Neoliberal and/or network state
Public sector	Civil service	Bureaucracy	New worlds of governance—markets and networks
Mode of accountability	Responsible government	Procedural accountability	Performance accountability

new approaches to gather, summarize, and analyze data. Modernist social science broke with developmental historicism's reliance on national
narratives that situated the study of particular political events and institutions within a larger order of developmental continuity.

The modernist break with developmental historicism had formal and
substantive aspects. In formal terms modernist social science turned from
historical narratives to a range of more ahistorical techniques.[2] The modernists appealed to models, correlations, and classifications that held
across time and place. They explained outcomes by reference to the functional requirements of systems, psychological theories or types, a general
human rationality, and formal analyses of process. In substantive terms
modernist social science overlapped with a pluralist challenge to the state
as conceived by developmental historicists. New topics came to the fore
including political parties, interest groups, and policy networks. These
new topics helped to inspire pluralist theories of the state and democracy.[3]
The substantive and formal aspects of modernist social science could reinforce one another: the new techniques made it possible or at least easier

[2] Compare W. Everdell, *The First Moderns* (Chicago: University of Chicago Press,
1997); T. Porter, *Trust in Numbers: The Pursuit of Objectivity in Science and Public Life*
(Princeton: Princeton University Press, 1995); D. Ross, *The Origins of American Social
Science* (Cambridge: Cambridge University Press, 1991), chaps. 8–10; and M. Schabas, *A
World Ruled by Number: William Stanley Jevons and the Rise of Mathematical Economics*
(Princeton: Princeton University Press, 1990).

[3] E.g., A. Bentley, *The Process of Government* (Chicago: University of Chicago Press,
1908). On the later interactions of pluralism and democratic theory, see J. Gunnell, *Imagining the American Polity: Political Science and the Discourse of Democracy* (University Park:
Pennsylvania State University Press, 2004).

to study some of the new topics, and the new topics sometimes appeared to require new techniques for gathering and arranging data.

One reason to highlight the rise of modernist social science is to draw attention away from the more usual focus on the behavioral revolution of the 1950s. This focus obscures the fact that many of the topics and techniques associated with behavioralism arose far earlier, spread far more extensively outside the United States, and persisted far longer than is usually recognized.[4] The main innovation associated with the behavioral revolution was an aspiration to craft a universal empirical theory. When later social scientists repudiate behavioralism, they often reject the aspiration to a universal theory while remaining wedded to modernist topics and modernist techniques.

Contemporary social science is dominated by two varieties of modernism, both of which stand in contrast to the nineteenth-century understanding of history as progressive and rational. But they rely on different formal, ahistorical concepts of rationality, which are associated with different forms of explanation, and, as we will see later, with different analyses of governance and democracy. On the one hand, the economic concept of rationality privileges utility maximization; it arose with neoclassical theorists and today has spread to rational choice theory. On the other hand, the sociological concept of rationality privileges appropriateness in relation to social norms; it arose with functionalism and today has spread to network theory and communitarianism.

Economic Rationality

The social sciences have long debated the concept of rationality. Today the concept is associated most closely with neoclassical economics and its extensions in rational choice theory. Yet the economic concept of rationality found in neoclassical theory is just one of several alternatives, and one, moreover, that has a distinctive history. For much of the nineteenth century, economists themselves merged types of analysis pioneered by Adam Smith with organic and historical themes. When, in the mid-nineteenth century, John Stuart Mill renounced the wages-fund theory and so the classical theory of distribution, a range of voices sought to rethink the study of economics: historical, positivist, and moral economics all flourished.[5]

---

[4] Compare R. Adcock, "Interpreting Behavioralism," in Adcock, Bevir, and Stimson, eds., *Modern Political Science*, 180–208.

[5] J. S. Mill, "Thornton on Labour and its Claims," in *Collected Works of J. S. Mill* (Toronto: University of Toronto Press, 1963–91), vol. 5, 631–68. For a survey of the varied

Neoclassical economics established its growing dominance only as the nineteenth century turned into the twentieth, and it did so in the context of a broad intellectual shift away from romanticism (with its emphasis on the organic and development) and toward modernism (with its emphasis on atomization and analysis). Neoclassical economics did not completely obliterate other traditions of economic knowledge. Alternative traditions, such as historical and institutional economics, still thrived, especially on the European continent where economists remained divided about the relevance of utility theory as late as the 1930s. Nonetheless, the spread of modernism saw diachronic narratives of the development of economies, states, and civilizations give way to synchronic models and statistical correlations.

Neoclassical economics instantiates a concept of rationality suited to the modernist emphasis on atomization, deductive models, and synchronic analysis. Economic rationality is a property of individual decisions and actions; it is not tied to norms, practices, or societies save insofar as these are to be judged effective or ineffective ways of aggregating individual choices. In addition, economic rationality is postulated as an axiom on the basis of which to construct deductive models; it is not deployed as a principle by which to select or interpret facts that are discovered through inductive, empirical research. Finally, the models derived from the axioms of economic rationality are typically applied to general patterns irrespective of time and space; they do not trace the particular evolution of individuals, practices, or societies.

While a modernist view of knowledge set the scene for the economic concept of rationality, the concept acquired much of its content from utility maximization.[6] In neoclassical economics individuals act in order to maximize their personal utility, where utility is defined as a measure of the satisfaction or happiness that they gain from a commodity, service, or other outcome. Critics complain that this assumption is tantamount to saying that individuals are inherently self-interested. But it would be more accurate to recognize that neoclassical economics strives to remain agnostic on the question of what constitutes happiness. Neoclassical economics asserts that people act in accord with their preferences, but it does not necessarily assume that these preferences are selfish ones. To the

---

voices, see the oft-maligned but still useful T. Hutchison, *A Review of Economic Doctrines, 1870–1929* (Oxford: Clarendon Press, 1953). For an example of their debating public policy, see United Kingdom, *Royal Commission on the Depression of Trade and Industry, Final Report*, c. 4893/1886.

[6] On the history of rational choice theory, see S. Amadae, *Rationalizing Capitalist Democracy: The Cold War Origins of Rational Choice Liberalism* (Chicago: University of Chicago Press, 2003).

contrary, neoclassical economics treats preferences as being revealed by people's actions: we deduce or know the nature of people's preferences from the fact that they purchase, or otherwise seek to attain, the particular commodities, services, or outcomes they choose.

I would suggest, however, that rational choice theorists in particular can apply their models to social and political life only if they are willing to assume that the relevant people's preferences stand in relation to one another as the model suggests, and, to do this, they have to make further assumptions about the actual content of these preferences. Typically they assume not only that people are self-interested but also that people's interests can be reduced to wealth, power, and status. To put my suggestion another way: although a concept of revealed preference enables neoclassical economists to avoid a naïve instrumentalism, it does so at the cost of leaving them able only to explain the consequences of actions (not the actions themselves), and this cost leaves their theory a long way short of a full-fledged account of governance. Besides, even if neoclassical economists try to remain agnostic about the content of preferences, they still make clear assumptions about the structure of an individual's set of preferences. They assume that any preference set is reflexive, transitive, and complete. While neoclassical economists sometimes grant that these assumptions about preferences (and actions) are simplistic and even unrealistic, they justify such oversimplification as the necessary cost of building the kinds of models and aggregate theories at which—at least according to a modernist view of knowledge—the social sciences should aim.

Sociological Rationality

The most prominent alternatives to the economic concept of rationality are sociological ones. Many sociologists replace instrumentality with appropriateness. Sociological rationality is about acting in accord with appropriate social norms so as to fulfill established roles in systems, processes, institutions, or practices. Some sociologists argue that even modern individuals are best conceived not as instrumental actors but as following established social norms and roles. Emile Durkheim and Pierre Bourdieu have been influential exponents of this argument. Other sociologists express fear over the almost totalitarian spread of selfish, acquisitive, and instrumental norms and roles in modern, capitalist, consumerist societies. Max Weber and Herbert Marcuse have expressed this fear. These two strands of modernist sociology are sometimes brought together in broad condemnations of modernity, capitalism, or consumerism for spreading selfish and instrumental norms and thereby wrecking older forms of solidarity and community. Recently, communitarians have made much of the idea that the spread of instrumental rationality, a rights mentality, and consumerism has undermined community and democracy.[7]

It is worth noting that these sociological traditions with their alternative concepts of rationality often date, like neoclassical economics, from the broad intellectual shift away from a developmental historicism that emphasized diachronic forms of analysis toward modernism with its emphasis on synchronic forms of analysis. The commonalities of the economic and sociological concepts of rationality are just as important as are their differences. Both modernist economists and modernist sociologists compartmentalize aspects of social life so as to manage and explain facts. They seek to make sense of the particular not by locating it in a temporal narrative but by reducing it to formal midlevel or universal generalizations that hold across time and space. Sociologists might eschew deductive models, but they also reject narratives; they prefer formal classifications, correlations, functions, systems, and ideal types. While we can trace functionalist themes back to the nineteenth century, these sociological forms of explanation flourished only with the rise of modernist modes of knowing. It was Durkheim and Bronislaw Malinowski, not Comte or Spencer, who distinguished functional explanations that refer to the synchronic role of an object in a system or social order (a type of explanation that they considered to be scientific) from both the psychological question of motivation and the historical question of origins.

The reliance on modernist modes of knowledge means that sociologists often have problems allowing adequately for agency. Classifications, correlations, and functions generate forms of explanation that reduce individual choices and actions to social facts. When sociologists appeal to rationality as appropriateness, they usually argue that individual actions are governed by social norms in a way that appears to downplay agency.[8] Crucially, if norms or roles explain people's actions, the implication is that norms or roles somehow fix the content of peoples' preferences, beliefs, or reasoning: if norms or roles did not fix such content, we would presumably need to explain people's actions by reference to their beliefs, preferences, or reasoning, and not norms and roles.

---

[7] Examples include A. Etzioni, *The Spirit of Community: Rights, Responsibilities, and the Communitarian Agenda* (New York: Crown, 1993); R. Putnam, *Bowling Alone: The Collapse and Revival of American Community* (New York: Simon and Schuster, 2000); and M. Sandel, *Democracy's Discontent* (Cambridge: Harvard University Press, 1996).

[8] Consider J. March and J. Olsen, *Rediscovering Institutions: The Organizational Basis of Politics* (New York: Free Press, 1989).

THE MODERNIST STATE

The shift from developmental historicism to modernist modes of knowledge altered the concept and nature of the state. As modernists placed less emphasis on historical narratives, so they displaced the concept of the state as arising out of a nation or people bound together by a common language, culture, or past. In the wake of World War One, modernists in Britain and the United States derided this concept of the state as an invention of German thinkers and as one of the causes of the war. Modernists turned instead to formal patterns, regularities, or models of action and institutions across space and time. Sometimes they turned away from a substantive focus on the state toward topics such as political parties, interest groups, and policy networks, where these substate institutions were themselves studied less as expressions of the particular history of a particular nation than in terms of laws or regularities derived, for example, from their functions in abstract systems. Even when modernists continued to study the state, they increasingly portrayed it as fragmented into factional interests associated with different classes or parties; occasionally they even portrayed the state as beset by collective irrationalities.

Corporatism and the welfare state arose in part as bureaucratic arrangements to overcome such factionalism and irrationality. Within corporatism the bureaucracy reached out to organized interests and brokered their disputes.[9] The corporatist state gave particular associations a privileged status as the representatives of social and economic groups. The privileged associations were involved in the formulation of public policy, and in return they helped to ensure the implementation of those policies. So, for example, in the 1970s many European states used corporatist arrangements to try to develop a stable incomes policy: they tried to control inflation by brokering wage agreements between business and trade unions.

The bureaucracy also reached out to individual citizens, assuming greater responsibility for their welfare.[10] The welfare state took control of the individual's interests in education, pensions, and unemployment

---

[9] P. Schmitter, and G. Lehmbruch, *Patterns of Corporatist Policy Making* (London: Sage, 1982).

[10] Diverse patterns of welfare are discussed in G. Esping-Andersen, *Three Worlds of Welfare Capitalism* (Princeton: Princeton University Press, 1990). For discussions of the growing role of expertise from the nineteenth century to the early spread of social welfare, see R. MacLeod, ed., *Government and Expertise: Specialists, Administrators, and Professionals, 1860–1919* (Cambridge: Cambridge University Press, 1988).

insurance. It developed policies not only to redistribute resources but also to ensure that these resources were used rationally to meet the real, long-term needs of citizens.

The Bureaucratic Narrative

Modernist social science undermined the concept of the state as an expression of a people or nation who shared a common good. Modernism thus made it difficult to conceive of the state as a consummation of the history of a nation. Likewise, modernism challenged the idea that representative democracy was a way of electing and holding to account politicians who would act in accord with the nature or common good of a nation. Representative democracy, we might suggest, was in danger of losing much of its legitimacy. Yet modernist modes of knowledge opened up new ways of making and legitimating public policy in representative democracies. In particular, modernist social science inspired a new belief in formal expertise. Public policy could be legitimate if it were based on the formal knowledge of modernist social science. Elected representatives no longer needed to express a national character or good. Rather, they could define policy goals and check the activity of experts. Social scientists, professionals, and generalist civil servants would use their expertise to devise rational, scientific policies in accord with these goals. Modernist social science thus helped to create the conditions not only for the welfare state but also for the bureaucratic narrative.

One important justification for the creation of an increasingly insulated and centralized bureaucracy was the need to deal with abuses and irrationalities in democratic processes.[11] Modernist social scientists often highlighted the threat of such abuses and irrationalities. Social scientists such as Mosei Ostrogrorski, Graham Wallas, and W. F. Willoughby drew attention to the factionalism, propaganda, and financial extravagances to which democratic governments were prone. The bureaucratic narrative thus arose in part as a response to fears similar to those that have led more recently to a crisis in that narrative. Many modernist social scientists believed that an insulated and centralized bureaucracy could act as a counter to the collective irrationalities of the electorate. Many of them also believed that an insulated and centralized bureaucracy could prevent strong, organized interests from taking control of state policy. In their view, a permanent and neutral bureaucracy promised to divide politics

[11] Compare L. Lynn, "The Myth of the Bureaucratic Paradigm: What Traditional Public Administration Really Stood For," *Public Administration Review* 61 (2001): 144–60.

from policy or, more accurately, to divide decisions about what polices to adopt from decisions about how to implement those policies.

Bureaucracy was evoked as a means of preserving democracy while removing its worst features—instability, irrationality, and factionalism—from the day-to-day activities of governing. Of course, policy can never be separated entirely from politics, and, doubtless, when public officials implement a policy they necessarily help to determine its political content. Nonetheless, when modernist social scientists championed the bureaucratic narrative, they rarely meant it to be a literal description of how public servants would operate. The bureaucratic narrative arose, rather, as an ideal type based on a commitment to certain values.[12] Exponents of the bureaucratic narrative associated the civil service with public spirit and scientific neutrality defined in stark contrast to the self-interest and factionalism that they found in the democratic process. Some of them also associated bureaucracy with efficiency; it was a rational form of organization that facilitated specialization according to function. Others mentioned various inefficiencies and problems associated with bureaucracy but dismissed these as a price worth paying for the benefits of a neutral, civic-minded administration.

Even today the conflict between the bureaucratic narrative and its critics often focuses on public spirit and scientific neutrality.[13] Advocates of the new theories of governance, especially those associated with the economic concept of rationality, often dismiss the concept of a public service ethic as a utopian fiction. Those who remain attached to the bureaucratic narrative often worry that public sector reforms—especially those associated with the promotion of markets and a private sector ethos—have eroded the values of the public sector. Perhaps the lure of the private sector has tempted reformers to hand tasks to that sector without asking whether doing so is in accord with democratic values. Perhaps public officials were less results-oriented than their private sector counterparts because of the values that are appropriate to each sector. Perhaps a focus on immediate, short-term results entails a neglect of equally important, if less visible, goals. Some critics fear that the new theories of governance denigrate the public sector and worship the private sector in mistaken ways. Critics certainly complain that these theories encourage false stereotypes that promote a neglect of important civic values. Of course, to retain faith in the historic values of the public sector is not necessarily

---

[12] On the nature, role, and social context of these values, see especially J. Harris, *Private Lives, Public Spirit: A Social History of Britain, 1870–1914* (Oxford: Oxford University Press, 1993).

[13] E.g., M. Brereton and M. Temple, "The New Public Service Ethos: An Ethical Environment for Governance," *Public Administration* 77 (1999): 455–74.

to deny that reforms were needed in the late twentieth century, but it is at the very least to set up a normative yardstick by which such reforms might be judged.

The Crisis of the State

The new governance arose in large part out of a crisis in the modernist state. Oversimplifications will abound in any attempt to differentiate the plethora of ideas that fed into narratives about the crisis of the state in the late twentieth century. Nonetheless, one way of approaching these narratives is to see them as attacks on the main forms of expertise embedded in the postwar state. These narratives undermined faith in the expertise of bureaucrats, Keynesians, and social-welfare officials. In the first place, various commentators suggested that there was something obsolete about bureaucratic institutions. They argued that the state faced new and complex demands such as those associated with information technology and a global economy, and that these demands could be met only by competitive, flexible, and entrepreneurial organizations. In the second place, various commentators suggested that Keynesianism led to unacceptable levels of inflation. They argued that the state had to adopt a tighter monetary policy in order to keep inflation down and provide a stable macroeconomic environment for the private sector. Finally, various commentators suggested that the state could no longer cope with the demands for welfare that its citizens placed on it. They argued that the welfare state had become too expensive: too high a proportion of gross national product went to the public sector.

Ironically the most prominent early narratives of the crisis of the state challenged bureaucracy, Keynesianism, and social welfare by appealing to the alternative expertise offered by monetarism and rational choice theory. The microlevel assumptions of rational choice theory informed, for example, narratives that purported to show that fiscal crises were a pathology built into the welfare state. These narratives generally took the following course.[14] As rational actors, citizens act to maximize their short-term financial interests; they privilege welfare policies that are of benefit to them as individuals over the long-term, cumulative, and shared effects of rising state expenditure. Similarly, as rational actors, politicians act to maximize their short-term electoral interests; they promote policies that will gain the votes of these rational citizens rather than pursuing fiscal responsibility. Narrow political considerations thereby trump economic imperatives. Groups of voters demand more and more welfare

---

[14] E.g., A. King, "Overload: Problems of Governing in the 1970s," *Political Studies* 23 (1975): 284–96.

benefits, and politicians constantly pass welfare legislation on behalf of these voters. Thus an ever-growing proportion of the national product goes into welfare, and so a fiscal crisis becomes inevitable. These narratives of state overload and state crisis pointed to a particular solution. The remedy lay with fiscal austerity, monetary control, and a rolling back of the state. But these narratives also suggested that the public would not like this remedy since they had become used to short-term payouts from the state. Perhaps the remedy would have to be imposed upon them against their will. Alternatively, perhaps the crisis would become so bad that the public would accept the remedy.

While rational choice assumptions form the foundation for the early formal narratives of the crisis of the state, other narratives highlighted alleged changes in the world. These other narratives implied that the state had to change in response to international and domestic pressures. Internationally, the increased mobility of capital made it more difficult for states to direct economic activity. The state could not go it alone but rather had to pursue coordination and regulation across borders. Industries that had operated in the domain of the state became increasingly transnational in their activities. The increasing number and prominence of transnational corporations raised problems of coordination and questions of jurisdiction. There was a gap between the national operation of regulatory structures and an increasingly international economy. Domestically, the state confronted the rising demands of its citizens. These demands arose from popular discontent with the state's handling of the economy and with its apparent unresponsiveness. Many states were saddled with large debts. Globalization provoked anxieties about competitiveness and wages. Sections of the public worried that the state had lost control. Equally, state actors often found that they were subject to varied and even contradictory demands from the public. Voters wanted better services and lower taxes. They wanted a more effective state but also a more transparent and accountable one. They wanted decisive leaders and yet more popular participation.

Many narratives of the crisis of the state denigrated bureaucracy as cumbersome and inefficient. Numerous popular satires derided the state, especially its bureaucratic agencies, for their layers of procedure and their endless red-tape. Likewise, rational choice theorists developed models of bureau shaping that suggested public officials acted in their own interests (often to enlarge their personal fiefdoms) rather than for the public good: public officials allegedly focused on expanding budgets, payroll, jurisdiction, and their own job satisfaction, not public goods. The narratives of crisis often condemned the mindset of public officials. They defined this mindset as overly preoccupied with inputs, procedures, and bureaucratic turf-wars. Some of them contrasted this mindset and its consequences unfavorably with a private sector in which the pressures of competition were thought to ensure a greater focus on the efficient use of resources and customer satisfaction.

THE NEW GOVERNANCE

The new governance consists of the interconnected theories and reforms by which people conceived of the crisis of the state and responded to it. These theories and reforms rejected the expertise associated with the postwar state. But instead of challenging the very idea of applying scientific expertise to social life, they turned to alternative modernist modes of knowing to sustain new forms of expertise.

Chapter 3 explores the new theories of governance. These theories often refer to all patterns of rule, including the kind of hierarchic state that is often thought to have existed prior to the public sector reforms of the 1980s and 1990s. Typically theorists use "governance" in a general, abstract way to refer to any pattern of rule or coordinated order. This abstract concept of governance enables theorists to explore general questions about the construction of social coordination and social practices irrespective of their specific content. Theorists can divorce such abstract analyses from specific questions about the state, the international system, or the corporation.

"Governance" is also used as a specific term to describe the new governance associated with changes in the state following the public sector reforms of the 1980s and 1990s. Chapter 4 explores these reforms. Typically the reforms are said to have led to a shift from a hierarchic bureaucracy toward a greater use of markets, quasi-markets, and networks, especially in the delivery of public services. The effects of the reforms were intensified by global changes, including an increase in transnational economic activity and the rise of regional institutions such as the European Union (EU). So understood, the new governance expresses a widespread belief that the state increasingly depends on other organizations to secure its intentions, deliver its policies, and establish a pattern of rule.[15] Chapter 4

---

[15] By analogy, governance also can be used to describe any pattern of rule that arises either when the state is dependent upon others or when the state plays little or no role. For example, the term "international governance" often refers to the pattern of rule found at the global level where the United Nations is too weak to resemble the kind of state that can impose its will upon its territory. Likewise, the term "corporate governance" refers to patterns of rule within businesses—that is, to the systems, institutions, and norms by which corporations are directed and controlled. So understood, governance expresses a growing awareness of the ways in which diffuse forms of power and authority can secure order even in the absence of state activity.

suggests that the new governance has arisen through two waves of public sector reform inspired by new theories of governance. The first wave of reforms is associated with neoliberalism and rational choice theory. The second wave is associated with the Third Way (or at least a revival of social democratic and center left politics) and institutionalist social science.

Neoliberalism

Neoliberals argue that the state is inherently inefficient when compared with markets. They believe that the postwar state cannot be sustained any longer, especially in a world that is now characterized by highly mobile capital and vigorous economic competition between states. Hence they attempt to roll back the state. They often suggest, in particular, that the state should concentrate on making policy decisions rather than on delivering services. They want the state to withdraw from the direct delivery of services, making way for an entrepreneurial system based on competition and markets. For example, David Osborne and Ted Gaebler distinguish between making policy decisions, which they describe as steering, and delivering public services, which they describe as rowing.[16] They argue that bureaucracy is bankrupt as a tool for rowing, and they propose replacing bureaucracy with an "entrepreneurial government," based on competition, markets, customers, and measurement of outcomes.

Because neoliberals deride government, many of them look for another term to describe the kind of entrepreneurial pattern of rule they favor. Governance offers them such a concept. It enables them to distinguish between "bad" government (rowing) and necessary governance (steering). The early association of governance with a minimal state and the spread of markets thus arose from neoliberal politicians and the policy wonks, journalists, economists, and management gurus who advised them.

The advisers to neoliberals often drew on rational choice theory. Rational choice theorists influenced neoliberal attitudes toward governance in large part by way of a critique of the concept of public interest. Their insistence that individuals, including politicians and civil servants, act in their own interest undermines the idea that policy makers act benevolently to promote a public interest. Indeed, their reduction of social facts to the actions of individuals casts doubt on the very idea of a public interest over and above the aggregate interests of individuals. More specifically, rational choice theorists provide neoliberals with a critique of bureaucratic government. Often they combine the claim that individuals act on their preferences with an assumption that people prefer to maxi-

---

[16] See D. Osborne and T. Gaebler, *Reinventing Government: How the Entrepreneurial Spirit is Transforming the Public Sector* (Reading, MA: Addison-Wesley, 1992).

mize their personal wealth or power. They argue that bureaucrats act to optimize their power and career prospects by increasing the size of their fiefdoms even when doing so is unnecessary. This argument implies that bureaucracies have an inherent tendency to grow even when there is no good reason for them so to do.

Because rational choice theory privileges microlevel analysis, it might appear to have peculiar difficulties explaining the rise of institutions and their persistent stability. Microeconomic analysis has long faced this issue in the guise of the existence of firms. Once rational choice theorists extend such micro analysis to government and social life, they generally face the same issue with respect to all kinds of institutions, including political parties, voting coalitions, and the market economy itself. The question is: if individuals act according to their preferences, why don't they break agreements when these agreements no longer suit them? The obvious answer is that some authority would punish them if they broke the agreement, and they have a preference for not being punished. But this answer assumes the presence of a higher authority that can enforce the agreement. Some rational choice theorists thus began to explore how they might explain the rise and stability of norms, agreements, or institutions in the absence of any higher authority. They adopted the concept of governance to refer to norms and patterns of rule that arise and persist even in the absence of an enforcing agent.

The Third Way

The neoliberal concept of governance as a minimal state conveys a preference for less government. Arguably, it often does little else, being an example of empty political rhetoric. Indeed, when social scientists study neoliberal reforms of the public sector, they often conclude that these reforms have scarcely rolled back the state at all. They draw attention instead to the unintended consequences of the reforms. According to many social scientists, the neoliberal reforms fragmented service delivery and weakened central control without establishing proper markets. In their view, the reforms have led to a proliferation of policy networks in both the formulation of public policy and the delivery of public services.

The 1990s saw a massive outpouring of work that conceived of governance as a proliferation of networks.[17] Much of this literature explores the ways in which neoliberal reforms created new patterns of service delivery based on complex sets of organizations drawn from all the public, private, and voluntary sectors. It suggests that a range of processes—

[17] E.g., R. Rhodes, *Understanding Governance: Policy Networks, Governance, Reflexivity, and Accountability* (Buckingham: Open University Press, 1997).

including the functional differentiation of the state, the rise of regional blocs, globalization, and the neoliberal reforms themselves—have left the state increasingly dependent on other organizations for the delivery and success of its policies. Although social scientists adopt various theories of policy networks, and so different analyses of the new pattern of rule, they generally agree that the state can no longer command other policy actors. In their view, the new governance is characterized by networks in which the state and other organizations depend on each other. Even when the state remains the dominant organization, it and the other members of the network are now interdependent in that they must exchange resources if they are to achieve their goals. Many social scientists argue that this interdependence means that the state now has to steer other organizations instead of issuing commands to them. They also imply that steering involves a much greater use of diplomacy and related techniques of management by the state. Some social scientists also suggest that the proliferating networks have a considerable degree of autonomy from the state. In this view, the key problem posed by the new governance is that it reduces the ability of the state not only to command but even to steer effectively.

Social scientists have developed a concept of governance as a complex and fragmented pattern of rule composed of multiplying networks. They have done so in part because of studies of the impact of neoliberal reforms on the public sector. But two other strands of social science have also given rise to this concept of governance. First, a concept of governance as networks arose among social scientists searching for a way to think about the role of transnational linkages within the EU. Second, a concept of governance as networks appeals to some social scientists interested in general issues about social coordination and interorganizational links. These latter social scientists argue that networks are a distinct governing structure through which to coordinate activities and allocate resources. They develop typologies of such governing structures—most commonly bureaucracies, markets, and networks—and they identify the characteristics associated with each such structure.[18] Their typologies often imply that networks are preferable, at least in some circumstances, to the bureaucratic structures of the postwar state and also to the markets favored by neoliberals. As we will see in chapter 3, this positive valuation of networks led to what we might call a second wave of public sector reform.

[18] E.g., G. Thompson et al., eds., *Markets, Hierarchies, and Networks: The Coordination of Social Life* (London: Sage, 1991). For a still more baroque classification, see T. Malone, "Modelling Coordination in Organizations and Markets," *Management Science* 33 (1987): 1317–32. These classifications even haunt studies that come close to suggesting that the categories rarely fit the world: e.g., J-F. Hennart, "Explaining the Swollen Middle: Why Most Transactions Are a Mix of Market and Hierarchy," *Organization Science* 4 (1993): 529–47.

DEMOCRATIC GOVERNANCE

The new theories and worlds of governance raise issues for democracy. The increased role of nonstate actors in the delivery of public services has led to a desire to improve the ability of the state to oversee these other actors. The state has become more interested in various strategies for creating and managing networks and partnerships. It has set up all kinds of arrangements for auditing and regulating other organizations. In the eyes of many observers, there has been an audit explosion.[19] In addition, the increased role of unelected actors in policymaking suggests that we need to think about the extent to which we want to hold them democratically accountable and about the mechanisms by which we might do so. Similarly, accounts of growing transnational and international constraints upon states suggest that we need to rethink the nature of social inclusion and social justice. Political institutions such as the World Bank and the EU now use terms such as "good governance" to convey their aspirations for a better world.

Many of the issues confronting democratic governance date back to the rise of modernist social science. The collapse of developmental historicism undermined many of the assumptions that had long accompanied representative democracy. No longer could the state be viewed as the expression of the common interests of a people or nation. No longer could one assume that responsible politicians and officials would act in accord with a common good. The problem of ensuring that representatives were responsible gave way to that of making them accountable. Yet even as modernism revealed cracks in representative democracy, so it papered over them by appeals to an apparently neutral expertise. The new governance has done much the same. The main change has been the content of the expertise. Today's wallpaper is a blend of rational choice theory and the new institutionalism.

From Responsibility to Accountability

For developmental historicists, representative democracy was a historical achievement. The civil society (or stage of civilization) that was needed to sustain representative democracy served to promote moral ideals and behavior such as those that made for responsible government. Responsibility referred as much to the character of politicians and officials as to their relationship to the public. Politicians and officials had a duty to respond to the demands, wishes, and needs of the people. To act respon-

---

[19] M. Power, *The Audit Explosion* (London: Demos, 1994).

sibly was to act so as to promote the common good rather than to seek personal advantage. It was to pursue national interests and thereby overcome petty factionalisms. Words and concepts akin to responsibility were equally prominent in other European languages, as with *verantwoordelijkheid* (Dutch), *responsabilité* (French), *verantwortlichkeit* (German), *responsabilità* (Italian), and *responsabilidad* (Spanish). In stark contrast, "accountability" rarely appeared in dictionaries or encyclopedias before the twentieth century.

The concept of accountability rose alongside modernism. On one hand, modernism was associated with a loss of faith in the principles that had sustained belief in the progress of nations toward statehood, liberty, and representative and responsible government. Modernists increasingly portrayed the nation itself as fragmented, and so democracy seemed less a means of expressing a common good and more a contest among factions or classes. On the other hand, modernism gave rise to new forms of apparently neutral social science. Social science appeared to provide a neutral expertise that might guide policymaking. Social science could show us what policies would best produce whatever results or values our democratic representatives decided upon. Modernism thereby helped sustain the now classic distinction between politics and administration. The political process generates values or political decisions for which ministers then are the spokespeople. Public officials provide the politically neutral expertise that formulates and implements policies that are in accord with these values or political decisions. In this context, responsibility, as conceived by developmental historicists, becomes less relevant than the accountability of public officials to their political masters and the accountability of politicians to the electorate.

The intimate connection between accountability and bureaucratic expertise appears in the content of the former. The theory, if not the practice, of accountability applies much more firmly to public officials than it does to politicians.

Politicians are held accountable through the institutions of representative democracy. Legislators are accountable to the voters who periodically decide whether or not to return them to office. The executive, especially presidents in political systems with a strong separation of powers, might also be directly accountable to the electorate. Alternatively, the executive, notably prime ministers and cabinets, might be held accountable by a legislature that can revoke the authority of the government. Modernist theories often suggested that these forms of political accountability are fairly weak. While politicians and governments can be voted out of office, they often control knowledge, agendas, and resources in ways that make them more powerful than those who might seek to hold them to account.

Besides, even when politicians and governments are voted out of office, it often seems that their fall owes less to their conduct in office than to broad political and social trends.

The mechanisms for holding public officials accountable appear much more firm. Administrative accountability occurs in bureaucratic hierarchies. Bureaucratic hierarchies are meant clearly to define a specialized, functional division of labor. They are meant to specify clear roles to individuals in the decision-making process, thereby making it possible to identify who is responsible for what. Typically individual officials are thus directly answerable to their superiors (and ultimately their political masters) for their actions. In addition, administrative accountability has increasingly been supplemented by a range of ombudsmen and other judicial means for investigating maladministration and even corruption.

Rethinking Accountability

While administrative accountability appeared firmer than did political accountability, it was arguably a rather blunt instrument.[20] Administrative accountability provided a theoretical account of how to apportion blame and seek redress in cases of maladministration. But critics of the bureaucratic narrative complained that it did not provide a way of assessing and responding to different levels of performance. The new theories of governance, including rational choice theory and organization or network theory, often highlighted concerns that overlapped with the question of the performance of the public sector. The result has been a shift from procedural accountability, of the sort we have just discussed, to performance accountability.[21]

Rational choice theory recast accountability as the principal-agent problem. The postulate of rational, self-interested actors undermined the idea that public officials could generally be relied on to act selflessly for the public good. The problem was not to check on how they behaved, but rather to create a framework in which their interests were aligned with those on behalf of whom they acted. Instead of thinking about how to make agents (politicians or public officials) accountable to their principals (the electorate and ministers, respectively), rational choice theorists suggested that the question was how to get agents to act in the interests of

---

[20] Compare A. Dunsire, *Control in a Bureaucracy* (Oxford: St Martin's, 1978).

[21] Compare L. DeLeon, "Accountability in a 'Reinvented Government'," *Public Administration* 76 (1998): 539–58. For a plea to restrict accountability to procedure, not performance, see R. Mulgan, "Accountability: An Ever Expanding Concept," *Public Administration* 78 (2000): 555–73.

principals, and they answered this question largely in terms of the provision of suitable incentives for the agents.[22]

Organization theory, and its impact on institutional and network theories, revealed a world in which decision making was a more complex process involving diverse policy actors in networks. This complexity suggested that there was something illusory, and even unfair, about the assumption that people further up the bureaucratic hierarchy could be accountable for the decisions and actions of their subordinates.[23] Administrative and political roles and decisions could rarely be distinguished from one another. Ministerial responsibility became too obvious a myth to be taken seriously. Procedural accountability appeared inappropriate, and also too limited, especially when conceived as reactive to decisions that already had been made.

Even as the new theories of governance undermined the forms of expertise and accountability associated with the bureaucratic narrative, so they promoted new forms of expertise that pointed to new approaches to democracy in general and accountability in particular. The main concern of this book is with the democratic theories and practices associated with the new governance. Chapters 5 and 8 offer general overviews of the new theories of governance and the way they conceive of democracy and participation within constitutional arrangements and public policy. Chapters 6, 7, 9, and 10 offer detailed case studies of the rise of new forms of expertise and democratic governance in, respectively, constitutionalism, the judiciary, joined-up governance, and policing. For now, one key point is that the rise of the new governance has been linked to concepts of accountability that emphasize not procedure but performance.

Performance accountability identifies legitimacy primarily with stakeholder satisfaction with outputs. It thereby sidesteps the problems that the new theories of governance associated with procedural accountability. For a start, if the state is judged by its performance or outputs, there is less need to cling to the mythical distinction between the administrative

---

[22] For the importance of incentives, rather than procedural accountability, see, e.g., D. Sappington, "Incentives in Principal-Agent Relationships," *Journal of Economic Perspectives* 5 (1991): 45–66.

[23] There is a vast literature on the illusory nature of the distinction between politics and administration and the fact that it nonetheless continues to exercise a powerful influence on the policy process. See B. Peters, *The Politics of Bureaucracy* (New York: Longman, 1995). Some authors have suggested recently that the distinction persists because it is constitutive of representative democracy. See E. Sørensen, "Democratic Theory and Network Governance," *Administrative Theory and Praxis* 24 (2002): 693–720. My suggestion, in contrast, is that the distinction is constitutive of modernist approaches to representative democracy, but not to those concepts of representative democracy associated with developmental historicism or the new theories of governance.

and political domains. In addition, performance accountability makes it less important that the actions of the agent or subordinate be directly overseen and judged by the principal.

One way of conceiving of performance accountability is in quasi-market terms. The citizens act as customers, and they express their satisfaction by buying or selecting services delivered by one agency rather than another. Yet, public agencies often lack the kind of pricing mechanisms, profit levels, and hard budgets that are thought to make the market an indicator of customer satisfaction. Thus an alternative way of conceiving of performance accountability is in terms of measurements of outputs. Targets, benchmarks, and other standards and indicators provide a basis for monitoring and auditing the performance of public agencies. Finally, performance accountability can be embedded in horizontal exchanges among a system of actors.[24] Whereas procedural accountability privileged vertical relationships such as that of public officials to their political masters, performance accountability is equally at home within horizontal relationships in which various actors provide checks and balances to one another. Each actor can call into question the performance of another.

Conclusion

The new governance replaces one type of modernism with another. Out go the bureaucratic narrative, the neutral expertise of the professions, and procedural accountability. In come markets and networks, rational choice theory and network institutionalism, and performance accountability. The changes have been dramatic. The principal aim of this book is to explore how some of those changes have influenced democracy. Equally, however, this book locates the changing nature of democracy in a broader historical narrative. This narrative suggests that the new governance, as theory and as practice, is still part of a modernism that has long been struggling with the demise of nineteenth-century understandings of the state. The concluding chapter will explore the possibility of moving beyond such modernism. Instead of modernist approaches to economic and sociological rationality, might we conceive of social life in terms of more contingent forms of local reasoning? Instead of moving from procedural to performance accountability, might we bolster procedural ac-

---

[24] G. O'Donnell, "Horizontal Accountability in New Democracies," in A. Schedler, L. Diamond, and M. Plattner, eds., *The Self-restraining State: Power and Accountability in New Democracies* (Boulder: Lynne Rienner, 1999), 29–51.

countability, and, in doing so, make it less a matter of reacting to decisions that already have been made and more a matter of citizens holding people accountable during the processes of decision making? Such questions open up the possibility of more direct involvement and control by citizens throughout the formation and implementation of policies. They point toward more plural and participatory concepts of democracy.

CHAPTER THREE

New Theories

NEW THEORIES and new worlds of governance pose problems for representative democracy. Representative democracy was firmly entrenched within the developmental narratives of the nineteenth century. Typically these narratives relied on principles such as liberty, state, and nation to tame contingency and contestation. The principle of liberty suggested that democracy was something like the teleological outcome of history. The principle of the nation suggested that the citizens of a democratic polity had a common good that would guide their public life. The principle of the state suggested that it was the expression of this common good. Collectively these principles contributed to a theory of politics in which representative democracy appeared as the perfect expression of the common good of a nation as established within a state.

Developmental historicism collapsed in the early twentieth century. In its wake there arose a range of new theories of politics. Even before World War One, modernist empiricists such as Graham Wallas had begun to champion a shift of focus to the study of political behavior.[1] After the war political scientists increasingly studied political parties, interest groups, and bureaucracies as sources of public policy. Their work generally pointed to a pluralist analysis of the state. Another type of pluralism inspired socialists and others who emphasized conflicts in civil society such as that between classes.[2] The spread of these pluralisms challenged the idea that the state expressed the common good of a largely uniform nation. Although some institutionalists continued to defend an emphasis on the formal institutions of the state, they increasingly appeared to be old-fashioned adherents of a decaying paradigm. This appearance has become even more marked following the rise of rational choice theory. The microlevel foundations of rational choice theory again exposed the unjustified nature of assumptions about the unity of institutions, nations, and states. Rational choice theory implies that individuals act in accord

[1] See M. Wiener, *Between Two Worlds: The Political Thought of Graham Wallas* (Oxford: Clarendon Press, 1971).

[2] See A. Wright, *G.D.H. Cole and Socialist Democracy* (Oxford: Clarendon Press, 1979).

with their private interests, and it thereby challenges the assumption that state actors pursue the common good of a uniform nation. The rise of rational choice theory helps to explain why most institutionalists have effectively redefined their theory of politics so as to break with developmental historicism.[3]

Few political scientists now adhere to the developmental narratives in which representative democracy used to be so entrenched. They are the heirs of a range of new theories of politics. This chapter explores some of these new theories of governance. An economic concept of rationality inspires rational choice theory. The sociological concept of rationality inspires the new institutionalism, systems theory, and regulation theory. Finally, I turn again to the alternative of an interpretive social science.

The new theories have a dual relationship to the new worlds of governance. On one hand, the new governance has been a spur to many of these theories: the changing nature of the state has inspired attempts to develop more general accounts of political order that place less emphasis on formal authority and formal institutions. On the other hand, the new worlds of governance can be seen as products of some of these new theories: policy makers drew on theories such as rational choice and new institutionalism in their attempts to reform the state. In this respect, the new governance is not the natural development it sometimes can appear to be. Changes in governance have arisen not only as pragmatic responses on the ground, but also as a result of sustained theoretical (even ideological) advocacy by intellectuals and policy makers. The purpose of this chapter is thus both to examine the theories by which we might make sense of the new governance, and to introduce some ideas that have inspired the formation of the new governance. Table 3.1 provides a quick overview of the main theories.

RATIONAL CHOICE THEORY

Rational choice theory attempts to explain all social phenomena by reference to the micro level of rational individual activity.[4] It unpacks social facts, institutions, and patterns of rule entirely by analyses of individuals acting, and it models individuals acting on the assumption that they adopt the course of action most in accord with their preferences. Sometimes, rational choice theorists require preferences to be rational: preferences

---

[3] Compare R. Adcock, M. Bevir, and S. Stimson, "Historicizing the New Institutionalism(s)," in Adcock, Bevir, and Stimson, eds., *Modern Political Science*, 259–89.

[4] For a historical perspective, see S. Amadae, *Rationalizing Capitalist Democracy*.

TABLE 3.1.
Theories of Governance

	Rational choice theory	Institutionalism	Systems theory	Regulation theory
Concept of rationality	Economic	Sociological	Sociological	Sociological
Source of coordination	Preferences and incentives	Rules and norms	Autopoesis	Temporary effect of regime of regulation
Explanation of the new governance	Electoral competition and/or bureau shaping	Social learning and/or policy transfer	Functional differentiation	Post-Fordism
Network analysis	Actor-centered	Power dependence	Self-organizing system	Dialectic (strategic-relational)
Examples				
1. general	1. Hardin	1. March and Olson	1. Luhmann	1. Boyer
2. the new governance	2. Dowding et. al.	2. Greener	2. Kooiman	2. Jessop

are assumed to be complete and transitive. Sometimes they also make other assumptions, most notably that actors have complete information about what will occur following their choosing any course of action. At other times, however, rational choice theorists try to relax these unrealistic assumptions by developing concepts of bounded rationality. They then attempt to model human behavior in circumstances where people lack relevant information.

The Problem of Governance

A microlevel emphasis on individual rationality leads to a broad acceptance of the efficiency of the market as a form of coordination and even as a way of allocating resources.[5] However, markets can operate only in a context of suitable norms and laws, including those that enforce contracts. Many rational choice theorists thus conceive of the problem of governance in terms of explaining the emergence of suitable norms and laws. The dominance of the micro level in rational choice theory makes it difficult to take for granted the origins, persistence, and effects of norms and laws. One abstract difficulty is how to explain the rise and stability of a pattern of rule in the absence of any higher authority. Rational choice theorists generally conclude that the absence of any effective higher authority means that such institutions must be self-enforcing. A more specific issue is how to model those weakly institutionalized environments in which the absence of a higher authority leads people to break agreements and so create instability. Examples of weak institutions include the inter-

[5] Compare M. Allingham, *Theory of Markets* (London: Macmillan, 1989).

national system and also nation states in which the rule of law is fragile. Rational choice theorists explore self-enforcing agreements, the costs associated with them, and the circumstances in which they break down.

Rational choice theorists attempt to explain forms of governance (patterns of order) by reference to microlevel analyses in which actions are driven by individuals' calculation of their interests. At an abstract level, rational choice theorists must explain the stability of a social and political order given that their micro theory implies that people will break up such an order whenever it is in their interests to do so. One explanation is that a higher authority creates incentives and disincentives so that people have an interest in sustaining a stable order. But this explanation leaves unanswered the question of how orders can be stable in the absence of a higher authority, which leads to the question of how such a higher authority might arise in the first place. Rational choice theorists thus confront issues about governance at a high level of abstraction. They hope to reconcile self-interest with the existence of coordination in the absence of any enforcement mechanism. They explore the possibility of individuals obeying norms and rules despite the absence of a higher authority (and when self-interest at least appears to give no reason for such obedience).

The Danger of Free-riding

For many rational choice theorists, the problem of securing compliance in the absence of a higher authority has policy implications. They worry that a failure to secure compliance leads to free-riding and even a tragedy of the commons.[6] Free-riding is a rational strategy when people have an interest in a common or public good but can allow others to do the work of providing that good. Free-riding works for individuals because public goods are such that nobody is excluded from them once they are provided. When individuals successfully free-ride, they benefit from a public good without bearing any of the costs of providing it. A "tragedy of the commons" arises when everybody involved seeks to free-ride so that a public good is not provided even though it benefits everyone. The phrase "tragedy of the commons" originates from the example provided by ranchers grazing their animals on a common field.[7] The ranchers all

[6] For classic explorations of the theory and implications of the issues, see M. Olson, *The Logic of Collective Action* (Cambridge: Harvard University Press, 1965); and G. Hardin, *Collective Action* (Baltimore: Johns Hopkins University Press, 1982).

[7] See especially G. Hardin, "The Tragedy of the Commons," *Science* 162 (1968): 1243–48.

have an interest in restricting grazing in order to maintain the fertility of the field. But each individual rancher hopes that the others restrict grazing while they themselves add further animals. Thus, each rancher seeks to avoid the shared costs of restricting grazing while reaping the individualized benefits of adding more animals. As a result, the field loses fertility. The ranchers behave rationally as individuals, but the result is tragic social irrationality.

Rational choice theorists argue that the state faces a myriad of problems related to free-riding. Prominent examples include Malthusian population worries, a vast number of environmental problems, and pollution issues. Many rational choice theorists believe that only a higher authority can resolve the problems of free-riding. In this view, coercion, or the threat of coercion, is often the only viable option. Garrett Hardin argues that societies can persist only because they curtail freedoms—such as (he hopes) the freedom to breed—using coercive force or, possibly, just education. He holds out the hope that education might make people aware of the long-term negative consequences (tragedies of the commons) that arise from people acting to maximize their individual utility. He hopes that education and the more general promotion of appropriate social norms might lead people to modify behavior. Yet, as he continues, the danger remains that even if some members of society complied with social norms that were not in their individual interests, others might not do so. There thus arises a double bind even for those inclined to comply with the norms. First, individuals would worry about the shame and guilt associated with a failure to comply. Second, they would worry that if they did comply, they would seem moronic, given that so many others would not be doing so. Faced with this double bind, even those inclined to comply might not do so. Rational choice theorists such as Hardin often conclude, therefore, that the only way to prevent tragedies of the commons is to establish a system of mutually accepted coercion. Coercion, whether overt or a tacit possibility, acts here as something like a corrective feedback mechanism to ensure honesty throughout the population. Even if coercion restricts freedom, and even if the coercion is not just and equitable, coercion is (or so the argument goes) the only alternative to societal instability and eventual ruin.

Rationality and Institutions

Some rational choice theorists believe that there can be self-enforcing patterns of order. They elucidate and defend forms of governance that fall outside the dichotomy between, on one side, freedom and the market (with the threat of a tragedy of the commons) and, on the other side, the coercion associated with hierarchy and the state. Typically they defend the possibility of self-enforcing networks emerging from the actions of utility maximizers.

Oliver Williamson, for example, has explored how transaction costs influence what kinds of organization it is most efficient to establish and maintain under different circumstances.[8] Transaction costs are all the costs that arise from an economic exchange. They include the difficulties of bargaining and the time spent on administering goods. Transaction cost economics is about identifying what system of governance—market, network, or hierarchy—best suits a particular exchange.

Williamson does not argue that one system of governance is inherently superior to all others. On the contrary, he argues that the efficiency of different organizational forms in facilitating exchange depends on the nature of the transaction. In his view, three criteria define the contexts in which different institutions, agreements, laws, and contracts will be found to be efficient. These criteria are: the level of uncertainty, the frequency of the transactions, and the idiosyncrasy of the investment. According to Williamson, these three characteristics of exchange determine which system of contractual governance is the most appropriate.

Yet, Williamson also argues that as societies grow increasingly complex, and as transactions become increasingly uncertain, so relational contracts become more appropriate. He argues that classic contract law is efficient in structuring recurrent and nonspecific transactions, while neoclassical approaches are best suited to the governance of infrequent transactions, but neither is well suited to the frequent idiosyncratic transactions that are increasingly common in modern complex societies. It is only slightly oversimplifying his views to say that these frequent idiosyncratic transactions require relational contracting (or networks) as opposed to both classic contract law (or hierarchy) and the neoclassical approach (or markets).

Williamson defines relational contracting in terms of a pattern of governance based on a history of regular interactions between actors. The past interactions dictate how transactions occur in the system, with relatively little attention being paid to the original contract. Williamson then identifies two main structures of relational contracting. Bilateral structures create incentives for actors to deny opportunistic urges that otherwise might destroy the system. Unified structures integrate transactions vertically under one owner so as to eliminate the threat of self-interest leading to breakdown. In both cases, relational contracting is a viable alternative to coercion as a way of avoiding tragedies of the commons.

[8] O. Williamson, "Transaction-Cost Economics: The Governance of Contractual Relations," *Journal of Law and Economics* 22 (1979): 233–61.

Explaining the New Governance

While rational choice theory is often rather abstract, it has been used to examine more concrete policies and changes associated with the new governance. For example, Keith Dowding and his coauthors run through many of the arguments we have discussed in their study of the governance of London.[9] They too show how rational choice raises the problem of collective action, that is, the problem of addressing free-riding so as to avoid the tragedy of the commons. They too suggest that rational choice can help us to understand the ways in which agents overcome antagonistic cooperation. They too pay particular attention to the possibility of achieving coordination through networks. They argue that the state can eliminate the negative externalities that erode cooperation if it fosters coalitions and networks from which all the actors benefit. According to Dowding and his coauthors, state actors still often have greater resources than do other policy actors. State actors are thus able to play a crucial role in structuring and prioritizing the payoffs and interests of other societal actors. However, Dowding and his coauthors allow that even state actors confront considerable difficulties in building cooperation in highly fragmented systems. They argue that fragmented systems render hierarchical forms of governance far less appropriate. Decentralization and division lead rational actors to shift their efforts at coordination from hierarchies to networks. Dowding and his coauthors conclude, therefore, that because the new public management (NPM) eroded the place of the state in the implementation of policy, and especially the delivery of services, it led to the spread of networks. The rise of networks in urban governance was, in their view, a product of reforms that dramatically increased, albeit inadvertently, the mutual dependence of public and private actors.

THE NEW INSTITUTIONALISM

An institutional approach dominated the study of the state, government, public administration, and politics up until the 1940s.[10] Political scientists focused on formal rules, procedures, and organizations, including consti-

---

[9] K. Dowding et al., "Understanding Urban Governance: The Contribution of Rational Choice," in G. Stoker, ed., *Power and Participation: The New Politics of Local Governance* (London: Macmillan, 2000), 91–116.

[10] On institutionalism, its dominance, and its relation to the new institutionalism, see Adcock, Bevir, and Stimson, "Historicizing the New Institutionalism(s)"; and Rhodes, *Understanding Governance*, chap. 4. On the loosely parallel case of economics, see M. Rutherford, *Institutions in Economics: The Old and New Institutionalism* (Cambridge: Cambridge University Press, 1994).

tutions, electoral systems, and political parties. Although they sometimes emphasized the formal rules that governed these institutions, they also paid attention to the behavior of actors within them. This institutional approach was challenged in the latter half of the twentieth century by a series of attempts to craft universal theories: behavioralists, rational choice theorists, and others attempted to explain social action with relatively little reference to specific institutional settings. The new institutionalism is conventionally seen as a restatement of the older institutional approach in response to these alternatives. The new institutionalists retain a focus on rules, procedures, and organizations: institutions are composed of two or more people; they serve some kind of social purpose; and they exist over time in a way that transcends the intentions and actions of specific individuals. But the new institutionalists adopt a broader concept of institution that includes norms, habits, and cultural customs alongside formal rules, procedures, and organizations. In this conventional view, the new institutionalism focuses on the persistence and effects of institutions, as opposed to the microlevel studies of rational choice theory, and yet it understands institutions in terms of norms, culture, and habits, as opposed to the more formal and legalistic studies of older institutionalists. New institutionalists often imply that this less formal definition of "institution" leads to a greater emphasis on change, history, and dynamics, especially through an appreciation of the potential for adjustment and feedback among actors and institutions.

An Amorphous Concept

The conventional understanding of the new institutionalism is problematic. For a start, attempts to pin down the distinction between a new contemporary institutionalism and an older institutionalism rely on caricatures of the old institutionalism. In addition, far from a homogenous new institutionalism arising as a reaction to rational choice theory, one part of it is a "rational choice institutionalism" inspired by the work of Williamson and others.[11] These kinds of problems have inspired attempts to distinguish several species of the new institutionalism. The leading varieties are rational choice institutionalism, historical institutionalism, and sociological institutionalism.[12]

[11] For an overview by one of the main political scientists involved, see K. Sheplse, "Studying Institutions: Some Lessons from the Rational Choice Approach," in J. Farr, J. Dryzek, and S. Leonard, eds., *Political Science in History: Research Programs and Political Traditions* (New York: Cambridge University Press, 1995), 276–95.

[12] The two key works that served to demarcate institutionalisms as alternatives to rational choice were P. Hall and R. Taylor, "Political Science and the Three Institutionalisms," *Political Studies* 44 (1996): 936–57; and K. Thelen and S. Steinmo, "Historical Institution-

Rational choice institutionalists are interested mainly in the effects of norms, laws, and institutions on individuals' actions. They argue that institutions structure people's strategic interactions: stable institutions influence individuals' actions by giving them reasonable expectations about the outcomes of the varied courses of action from which they might choose. Rational choice institutionalists examine how institutions create expectations about the likely consequences of given courses of action and thereby shape the behavior of actors.

Historical institutionalists focus on the ways in which the legacy of past institutional arrangements continues to shape contemporary politics. They argue that past outcomes become embedded in institutions that lock states and other actors into particular paths of development. Historical institutionalists thus concentrate on comparative studies of welfare and administrative reform across states in which the variety of such reforms is explicable in terms of path dependency.

Sociological institutionalists focus on values, identities, and the ways in which these shape actors' perceptions of their interests. They argue that informal sets of ideas and values constitute policy paradigms that shape the ways in which organizations think about issues and conceive of political pressures. They adopt a constructivist approach to governance that resembles the interpretive theories that I will discuss later in this chapter. Sociological institutionalists thus concentrate on studies of the ways in which norms and values shape what are often competing policy agendas of welfare and administrative reform.

Institutions as Actors

Most institutionalists want to claim that institutions are actors in their own right. Institutions are not just the products of interactions between rational actors, nor are they merely the structured environments in which actors decide upon rational strategies by which to pursue their interests, which is loosely the position adopted by rational choice institutionalists. James March and Johan Olsen are leading exponents of the kind of institutionalism associated with historical and sociological perspectives, and

---

alism in Comparative Politics," in S. Steinmo, K. Thelen, and F. Longsttreth, eds., *Structuring Politics: Historical Institutionalism in Comparative Analysis* (New York: Cambridge University Press, 1992), 1–32. Recently some lists of "new institutionalisms" have included a constructivist, discursive, or ideational strand that includes (or perhaps domesticates) the interpretive theory to which we will turn later. See J. Campbell and O. Pederson, eds., *The Rise of Neoliberalism and Institutional Analysis* (Princeton: Princeton University Press, 2001); and R. Rhodes, S. Bender, and B. Rockman, eds., *The Oxford Handbook of Political Institutions* (Oxford: Oxford University Press, 2006).

especially organizational theory.[13] They explicitly define their position in contrast to rational choice. Like many institutionalists, they criticize rational choice as a reductionist approach to the study of politics—an approach in which social facts are reduced to aggregations of numerous microlevel interactions. Again, like many institutionalists, they argue that behavior cannot be grasped adequately as a purely utilitarian attempt to maximize the interests or satisfaction of the actor. Perhaps we should not be surprised, therefore, that March and Olsen describe their new institutionalism as the study of social facts and symbolic action. They want to draw our attention to the relationships among institutions, the inefficiencies of history, and the complexities created by evolving conceptions of meanings and symbolic action.

Institutions are actors primarily, it seems, in that they consist of the rules and norms by which policy is developed and implemented. Institutions contain the residual meanings of political life that then shape the very preferences and behavior of actors. March and Olsen argue, for instance, that institutions shape people's social values and belief systems by means of establishing historical, temporal, endogenous, normative, demographic, and symbolic orders. Institutions thereby construct the heuristics and norms that individuals rely upon in order to define the meanings and myths of political life, where these meanings and myths are in turn what shape societal behavior. Although March and Olsen use vague concepts, and often in somewhat different ways, their overall message is clear. Like most institutionalists, they insist on the vital and autonomous role played by institutions in shaping every aspect of governance from the state down to the individual citizen.

Explaining the New Governance

The amorphous nature of the new institutionalism appears again when we consider its application to the new governance. In particular, we need to distinguish between approaches to institutions that echo rational choice theory as found in the work of social scientists such as Williamson and approaches that embody looser theories and concepts akin to those found in the work of March and Olsen.

Rational choice institutionalism. Many rational choice institutionalists approach the new governance as a response to the problems of coordination that have arisen in the context of those global forces that con-

[13] See J. March and J. Olson, "The New Institutionalism: Organisational Factors in Political Life," *American Political Science Review* 78 (1984): 734–49. The original article was expanded into March and Olson, *Rediscovering Institutions.*

tinue to erode state capacity. Rational choice institutionalists often seem to think of these global forces as more or less inexorable products of a social logic of specialization: as society becomes more complex, reciprocal independence becomes the most common relationship among actors. Fritz Scharpf argues, for example, that the new governance has arisen because state actors are increasingly unable to act unilaterally.[14] As state actors become dependent on other actors, they are pressed to abandon hierarchical approaches to coordination in favor of networks. Scharpf helpfully distinguishes between hierarchical coordination and hierarchical organization, and he is thereby able to recognize, as we surely should do, that vertical organizations such as ministerial departments remain not only common but also useful ways of enforcing agreements. Nonetheless, Scharpf argues that there has been a shift in governance from hierarchical to horizontal coordination. He suggests that even hierarchical organizations now rely increasingly on negotiated forms of coordination, where negotiated coordination is understood as a horizontal system in which no actor has the power to impose its will on the others. Today the state is thus less likely to impose explicit coercive force through binding accords, and it is more likely to rely on networks based on partnerships among diverse actors.

Scharpf's work includes an analysis of the nature and origins of various types of network. The term "network" is commonly used to refer both to "types of interactions" and "more permanent structures." Again, networks can be formed informally as a result of repeated interactions or formally through legislative and administrative fiat. In either case, there are questions about how iterated exchange systems then alter the institutional frameworks in which actors achieve coordination. Scharpf argues here that the history of interactions is crucial for understanding why actors choose not to defect and cheat. In his view, repeated interactions build trust thereby eliminating uncertainty and so facilitating coordination and stability even in the absence of a higher authority. If actors know that the pursuit of their short-term interests will damage future relations and so their long-term interest in future exchanges, then, especially in the context of stable relations based on trust, they will be willing to forgo their short-term interests to secure the cooperation they need to secure long-term gains. Thus, although trust is difficult to achieve, especially in contexts characterized by incomplete information, it can be highly beneficial. Yet, Scharpf continues, mutual trust often requires actors to put others' interests first. To put others first is, as Scharpf shows, especially

[14] F. Scharpf, "Co-ordination in Hierarchies and Networks," in F. Scharpf, ed., *Games in Hierarchies and Networks: Analytical and Empirical Approaches to the Study of Governance Institutions* (Frankfurt: Campus, 1993), 125–65.

difficult for actors in networks with many different partners. The worry here is that actors will find themselves, albeit inadvertently, in situations where they have to decide which of several partners' interests they should put first. In strong cooperative networks, multiple allegiances will often force actors to privilege one partner over another.

Historical and sociological institutionalisms. The conceptual vagueness of much historical and sociological institutionalism makes it hard to tie it to a particular analysis of the new governance. Historical institutionalists typically seek to study contemporary behavior against the background of past interactions. They justify doing so by appeals to path dependency. Although the precise analysis of "path dependency" remains a topic of much controversy, the broad claim is clearly that the past decisions or actions of institutions press them to follow a specific future path. The cost of an alternative becomes increasingly difficult to bear until some point of crisis (a critical juncture) is reached. Clearly path-dependent arguments reduce change, at least implicitly, to relatively rare moments: dramatic policy changes reflect specific moments when events and problems in a political environment come together to open a window in which entrepreneurial actors are able to shift institutions onto different paths.

We might get a better sense of what these vague concepts mean by focusing on an example. Ian Greener has explored changes in the National Health Service (NHS) by combining path dependency with themes from sociological institutionalism.[15] Greener argues, in effect, for the reconciliation of historical and sociological approaches to the study of institutions. He suggests that we can avoid depicting institutions as unchanging structures if we draw on ideas of "social learning" and "policy transfer." Social learning refers to the way in which policy goals and programs develop gradually as and when actors explicitly evaluate and respond to past outcomes; most accounts of social learning thus imply that significant changes in policy occur only infrequently within long histories of relative stability. Policy transfer refers to the dynamic process by which policy goals and programs are exported from one country to another through a range of interactions. Greener argues here that the concept of "path dependency" helps us to understand why changes in policy are as infrequent as the literature on social learning suggests, and under what circumstances the policies developed in one country are likely to be picked up in another. In this view, historical institutionalism helps to

---

[15] I. Greener, "Understanding NHS Reform: The Policy-Transfer, Social-Learning, and Path Dependency Perspectives," *Governance* 15 (2002): 161–83.

explain why social learning and policy transfer are constrained by the legacy of the past.

Greener uses NHS reforms to illustrate how we might combine path dependency with policy transfer and social learning. In his opinion, the social learning and policy transfer approaches can explain why Britain's internal market reforms occurred when they did under Thatcher, and also much of the content and significance of these reforms. A social learning approach explains, in particular, how policy makers adapted various ideas following their previous experience with education reform. A policy transfer approach draws attention to the importance of the individual actors who shaped NHS reform on American models. Nonetheless, neither social learning nor policy transfer by itself can account for the difficulties that confronted the attempts to change a deeply entrenched system of health care. Greener argues that this part of the story of NHS reform becomes clearer if we draw on the idea of path dependency. In his view, timing is fundamentally important to policy analysis, and timing requires an examination of how conjunctures in the political environment influence the development of policy. Policy formation only matters when there are opportunities for advancing and implementing the relevant policy, and these opportunities arise only when there are "critical junctures" and "structural holes" of the type postulated by historical institutionalists.

SYSTEMS THEORY

Institutionalism is amorphous and often based on vague concepts. It has thus been combined with various more precise theories. We have already come across such a combination in rational choice institutionalism. Systems theory is another theory that has been combined with institutionalism; it overlaps in particular with a sociological institutionalism that draws on organizational theory.

The Concept of a System

A system is the pattern of order that arises from the regular interactions of a series of interdependent elements. Systems theorists suggest that these patterns of order arise from the functional relations and interactions among the elements. These relations and interactions involve a transfer of information. This transfer of information leads to the self-production and self-organization of the system even in the absence of any center of control. Systems theorists thus echo various institutionalists, such as March and Olson, in arguing that the interactions of organizations and other actors create social objects that have causal properties of their own. Yet, systems theorists often complain that the new institutionalism does not pay enough attention to the ways in which the different actors and elements of a system interact with and transform one another. They emphasize the self-organizing and self-producing properties of systems.

Niklas Luhmann, a particularly prominent systems theorist, certainly argued that all social interactions are intimately connected to the overall shape of a system.[16] Some of his followers, notably Marleen Brans and Stefan Rossback, argue that this view corrects an imbalance in the dominant forms of institutionalism.[17] In their view, institutionalists typically go astray when they present internal hierarchical exchanges as determining the development of a system. Institutionalists do not adequately consider the impact of the horizontal and exogenous interactions of an institution with its social environment. For Brans and Rossback, classic institutionalists, including Max Weber, are thus associated with idealized bureaucratic command-and-control models that are unable to explain the impact of aberrations from social norms. Systems theory, in contrast, is supposed to be able to explain just such aberrations by portraying them as furthering the development of the system.

The New Governance as a System

Several systems theorists argue that Luhmann offers an especially apt way of thinking about governance or patterns of order that develop in the absence of any clear center or sovereign entity capable of guiding the whole process. Brans and Rossback commend Luhmann's autopoietic theory for its ability to analyze how a system of ordered norms responds to and reformulates complex environments. The system plays a crucial role in the reduction and simplification of issues that arise from the environment. For example, the nation state, a subsystem of society as a whole, defines citizenship according to specific criteria, thereby minimizing the number of problems and issues it must address. Even more generally, Brans and Rossback commend Luhmann's autopoietic theory as a way of grasping how systems rely on reflexivity and self-organization. Luhmann

---

[16] N. Luhmann, *Social Systems*, trans. J. Bednarz Jr. with D. Baecker (Stanford: Stanford University Press, 1995).

[17] M. Brans and S. Rossbach, "The Autopoiesis of Administrative Systems: Niklas Luhmann on Public Administration and Public Policy," *Public Administration* 85 (1997): 417–39. The same broad argument has been made with particular reference to the EU by M. Albert, "Governance and Democracy in European Systems: On Systems Theory and European Integration," *Review of International Studies* 28 (2002): 293–309. For a rather different take on what systems theory brings to institutionalism, see J. Stewart and R. Ayres, "Systems Theory and Policy Practice: An Exploration," *Policy Sciences* 34 (2001): 79–94.

argues that autopoiesis occurs when a system produces and reproduces the elements of which it is composed. Although the wider environment has an impact on the system, it is the system itself that ultimately determines how exogenous forces are interpreted and applied.

The concept of governance as a socio-cybernetic system highlights the limits to governing by the state. It implies that there is no single sovereign authority. Instead there is a self-organizing system composed of interdependent actors and institutions. Systems theorists often distinguish here between governing, which is goal-directed interventions, and governance, which is the total effect of governing interventions and interactions. In this view, governance is a self-organizing system that emerges from the activities and exchanges of actors and institutions. Again, the new governance has arisen because we live in a centerless society, or at least a society with multiple centers. Order arises from the interactions of multiple centers or organizations. Here, the role of the state is not to create order but to facilitate sociopolitical interactions, to encourage varied arrangements for coping with problems, and to distribute services among numerous organizations.

Steering Systems

An emphasis on the self-referential and closed nature of autopoietic systems raises the question of whether a system can actually be consciously governed or steered by the state. There are three main approaches to steering self-governing systems.[18] The first approach is Luhmann's analysis of autopoietic systems structured along principles of self-organization and self-production.[19] Luhmann's analysis implies that actors other than the system itself cannot steer or govern it. Autopoietic systems develop and regulate the elements within them through closed-off and self-referential processes. Perhaps subsystemic actors can influence systems through communication with one another. Even so, Luhmann's analysis ultimately leads to pessimism about the state's ability (as a subsystem) to steer networks and implement its policies.

A second approach to the possibility of steering self-governing systems is an actor-oriented one. Systems theorists often associate this approach with rational choice institutionalism and especially the work of Scharpf.[20]

---

[18] Compare J. Kooiman and M. van Vliet, "Self-Governance as a Mode of Societal Governance," *Public Management* 2 (2000): 359–77.

[19] See N. Luhmann, "Limits of Steering," *Theory, Culture, and Society* 14 (1997): 41–57.

[20] For Scharpf's rational choice institutionalism, see F. Scharpf, *Games Real Actors Play: Actor-Centered Institutionalism in Policy Research* (Boulder: Westview, 1997). On steering, also see F. Scharpf, "Politische Steuerung und Politische Institutionen," *Politisches Vierteljahresschrift* 30 (1989): 10–21.

The actor-orientated approach depicts the new governance as dependent on a constellation of different societal actors who come together in policy networks. It thus conceives of steering as possible but difficult. The state's difficulty consists in finding a balance among the various societal actors who otherwise might resist its attempts at steering the relevant network.

The final approach to steering self-governing systems is the interactionist approach of Jan Kooiman.[21] This approach views governance as a product of the interactions in the system being governed. It highlights the impact of relationships between governors and those being governed, between public and private actors, and between institutions and the social forces they regulate. All these interactions offer sites at which the state, and also societal actors, might intervene in order to steer self-governing systems. In this view, recognition of the importance of interactions explains how steering is possible. Kooiman disaggregates his concept of sociopolitical governance into a number of modes.[22] The modes are chaotic self-governance (as in autopoietic systems), cogovernance through horizontal cooperation (as in networks, public-private partnerships, communicative governing, or responsive regulation), and hierarchical governance. Although Kooiman describes all three modes as distinct methods of governance, he concludes that mixed-mode governing often will develop as the most appropriate one.

REGULATION THEORY

Regulation theory is another example of how an amorphous institutionalism can combine with other theories. Some prominent regulation theorists fuse a Marxist analysis of capitalism with institutionalist themes.

The Marxist Background

Karl Marx took very different views of the prospects for revolution at different times in his life.[23] Up until the end of the First World War, however, Marxists commonly believed that the workers revolution would come soon. By the 1920s, the prospects for revolution looked far bleaker. The call to war had found the workers not uniting to overthrow capi-

---

[21] See J. Kooiman, ed., *Modern Governance: New Government-Society Interactions* (London: Sage, 1990).

[22] J. Kooiman, "Societal Governance: Levels, Modes and Orders of Political Interaction," in J. Pierre, ed., *Debating Governance: Authority, Steering, and Democracy* (Oxford: Oxford University Press, 2000), 138–64.

[23] See the warm and enjoyable biography by F. Wheen, *Karl Marx* (London: Fourth Estate, 1999).

talism but rallying to nationalist causes. Even the Russian Revolution had failed to spark similar uprisings in the more advanced economies of Western Europe.

Much twentieth-century Marxism can be read as an attempt to explain the absence of revolution and the persistence of capitalism. One well-known explanation was formulated by Antonio Gramsci, an Italian Marxist imprisoned under Mussolini. Gramsci argued that the bourgeoisie had established an ideological hegemony; the bourgeoisie had propagated an ideology that dominated throughout society and lent a spurious legitimacy to the capitalist social order.[24] Although the concept of hegemony certainly offered one way of explaining the persistence of capitalism, it did so by emphasizing the role of culture and ideas—an emphasis that inspires the critical, Marxist strains in interpretive theories of governance—in a way that broke somewhat with the more orthodox, economic strands of Marxist thought. Regulation theory tried to explain the persistence of capitalism in terms closer to Marx's economic writings.

The earliest exponents of regulation theory are called the New French School or, more commonly, the Parisian school.[25] They explained the temporary stability of various types of capitalism by reference to economic institutions. This emphasis on institutions means that their work is sometimes assimilated to broader institutionalist challenges to neoclassical economics. Yet, their institutionalism remained firmly located in a Marxist theory according to which capitalism inherently suffered from both unstable development (crises of overaccumulation) and unstable social relations (the class struggle). They thus concentrated on the ways in which institutional arrangements managed to persist in spite of such instabilities.

The main institutional arrangements studied by the Parisian school were regimes of accumulation and regimes of regulation. The regime of accumulation refers to the institutions or regularities that facilitate a stable and proportional distribution of capital across departments of production. It includes norms for the organization of work and production, the relationship between branches of the economy, modes of industrial and commercial management, and the norms that govern the division of income among wages, profits, and taxation. The regime of regulation refers to the legal and political institutions that enable capitalist societies, and so regimes of accumulation, to persist over time. It includes laws, industrial codes, styles of negotiation, state policies, political practices,

[24] A. Gramsci, *Selections from the Prison Notebooks*, ed. and trans. Q. Hoare and G. Nowell Smith (London: Lawrence and Wishart, 1971).

[25] See more generally R. Boyer, *The Regulation School: A Critical Introduction*, trans. C. Charney (New York: Columbia University Press, 1990).

and patterns of consumption. As a rough guide we might almost say that regimes of accumulation mask the instabilities associated with the over-accumulation of capital, while regimes of regulation mask instabilities associated with the class struggle.

Fordism and After

Typically regulation theorists locate the new governance in relation to a broader socioeconomic shift from Fordism to post-Fordism. Fordism refers to a combination of "intensive accumulation" and "monopolistic regulation"—a combination associated with the mass production pioneered by Henry Ford in the 1920s. Intensive accumulation rested on processes of mass production such as mechanization, the intensification of work, the detailed division of tasks, and the use of semiskilled labor. Monopolistic regulation involved monopoly pricing, the recognition of trade unions, the indexing of wages to productivity, corporatist tendencies in government, and monetary policies to manage the demand for commodities. According to regulation theorists, intensive accumulation and monopolistic regulation temporarily created a virtuous circle: mass production created economies of scale, thereby leading to a rise in productivity; increased productivity led to increased wages and so greater consumer demand; the growth in demand meant greater profits due to the full utilization of capacity; and the increased profits were used to improve the technology of mass production, creating further economies of scale and so starting the whole circle going again.

Regulation theorists ascribe the end of Fordism to various causes. Productivity gains decreased because of the social and technical limits to Fordism. Globalization made the management of national economies increasingly difficult. Increased state expenditure produced inflation and state overload. Competition among capitalists shifted the norms of consumption away from the standardized commodities associated with mass production. All these causes contributed to the end not only of Fordism but also of the bureaucratic, Keynesian, welfare state associated with it. Although regulation theorists can be reluctant to engage in speculations about the future, they generally associate the new post-Fordist era with the globalization of capital, neoliberal politics, contracting-out, public-private partnerships, and the regulatory state.

State Theory

Although regulation theorists appeal to underlying contradictions in capitalism, they give considerable scope to the political and social institutions that attempt to manage these contradictions in various ways. It is no wonder, therefore, that many of them echo the institutionalist critique of neoliberalism and rational choice. Regulation theorists too reject the idea that the rational actions of atomized individuals determine economic exchange.[26] They too highlight the institutionalized nature of the economy. Indeed, although regulation theorists have inherited the Marxist emphasis on contradictions and crises and change, they now stress the importance of embedded social institutions and the ways in which these regularize economic interactions so as to establish stable patterns over time.

Bob Jessop in particular points here to the potential relevance of the state for regulation theory.[27] He argues that the state itself is an important source of the regularity and normalization that arises in capitalist economies. The state is intimately involved in the promotion of stability in economic exchanges, as increasingly under post-Fordism are international regimes. The state remains a central actor, nationally and internationally, for the increase in global capital flows and transnational externalities requires governmental regulation.

According to regulation theorists such as Jessop, the state has changed along with the shift from Fordism (with its Keynesian welfare state) to a type of post-Fordism (which includes a Schumpeterian workfare regime). The new governance has risen, in other words, as part of changes in capitalism. The Keynesian state's commitment to demand side growth and labor market maximization has been abandoned. The emerging post-Fordist state supports supply-side interventions while disavowing many labor and social policies on the grounds that they inhibit the flexibility that is said to be vital to competitiveness within the new global economy.

Jessop himself highlights three large trends in the transformation of the state.[28] First, there has been a denationalization of the state: the state has been hollowed out as its capacity and power have moved down to actors in civil society and up to international and transnational organizations. Second, there has been a destatization of politics: the state is increasingly being replaced by networks and public-private partnerships in the making and especially implementation of public policy—

---

[26] Jessop even seems to suggest that rational choice is especially inappropriate given the growth of uncertainty, conflict, and complexity under post-Fordism. See B. Jessop, "Governance and Meta-Governance: On Reflexivity, Requisite Variety, and Requisite Irony," in H. Bang, ed., *Governance as Social and Political Communication* (Manchester: Manchester University Press, 2003), 101–16.

[27] See B. Jessop, *State Theory: Putting the Capitalist State in Its Place* (Cambridge: Polity, 1990); B. Jessop, *The Future of the Capitalist State* (Cambridge: Polity, 2002); and B. Jessop and N-L. Sum, *Beyond the Regulation Approach: Putting the Capitalist State in Its Place* (Cheltenham: Edward Elgar, 2006).

[28] For a short summary, see B. Jessop, "The Regulation Approach: Implications for Political Theory," *Journal of Political Philosophy* 5 (1997): 287–326.

the state is increasingly limited to issues of metagovernance, notably the creation and management of self-organizing networks. Finally, there has been an internationalization of policy regimes: the post-Fordist state finds its policy choices and strategies restricted by the global spread of neoliberalism.

INTERPRETIVE THEORIES

Most theories of governance draw on the economic and sociological concepts of rationality. In contrast, as we saw in chapter 1, this book draws on and promotes an interpretive social science. Interpretive theories of governance typically reject the idea that patterns of rule can be properly understood in terms of a historical or social logic attached to capitalist development, functional differentiation, institutional settings, or utility maximization. Instead they emphasize the meaningful character of human action. Because people act on meanings (beliefs or ideas, conscious or not), we can explain their actions properly only if we grasp the relevant meanings. The older interpretive approaches suggested that meanings are more or less uniform across a culture or society. They inspired studies of the distinctive patterns of governance associated with various cultures. In contrast, more recent interpretive approaches, from postmodernism to decentered theory, highlight the contested nature of meanings.[29] They promote studies of the different traditions and discourses of governance that are found in a particular society.

Against Positivism

Interpretive theorists resist attempts to reduce governance, and changes in governance, to allegedly fixed properties of systems, capitalism, institutions, or rationality. Typically they regard such reductions as a legacy of a mistaken positivism that encouraged social scientists to elide contingency behind allegedly objective social categories.[30] Positivism suggested that

[29] For my initial presentation of decentered theory, see M. Bevir, "A Decentered Theory of Governance," in Bang, ed., *Governance as Social and Political Communication*, 200–21. For the attempts to apply it in which I have been involved, see M. Bevir and R. Rhodes, *Interpreting British Governance* (London: Routledge, 2003); M. Bevir and R. Rhodes, *Governance Stories* (London: Routledge, 2006); M. Bevir, R. Rhodes, and P. Weller, eds., *Traditions of Governance: History and Diversity*, a special issue of *Public Administration* 81/1 (2003); M. Bevir and F. Trentmann, eds., *Governance, Consumers, and Citizens* (Basingstoke: Palgrave, 2007); and M. Bevir and D. Richards, eds., *Decentring Policy Networks*, a special issue of *Public Administration* 87/1 (2009).

[30] On the philosophical arguments that decisively undermined such positivism as long ago as the 1960s, see R. Bernstein, *The Restructuring of Social and Political Theory* (Philadelphia: University of Pennsylvania Press, 1976).

social scientists should look for laws, regularities, or models in which meanings could be ignored, or at least taken for granted given social and economic facts. Most interpretivists argue, in contrast, that meanings constitute webs, discourses, or paradigms such that we can properly grasp them only if we consider them as a whole. So, for example, far from taking people's beliefs for granted given social facts about them, we can explain their actions only by reference to the theories or discourses in terms of which they experience the facts.

Although interpretive theorists analyze governance in terms of meanings, there is little agreement among them about the nature of meanings. The meanings of interest to them are variously described as intentions or beliefs, conscious or tacit knowledge, a substratum of subconscious or unconscious assumptions, a system of signs, or discourses and ideologies. Interpretive theorists often explore these varied types of meanings both synchronically and diachronically. Synchronic studies analyze the relationships between a set of meanings abstracted from the flux of history. They reveal the internal coherence or pattern of a web of meanings: they make sense of a particular belief, concept, or sign by showing how it fits in such a web. Diachronic studies analyze the development of webs of meaning over time. They show how situated agents modify and transform webs of meaning as they use them in particular settings.

In contrast to positivism, many interpretivists believe that experiences are always laden with prior theories. People with different background theories (discourses, webs of belief, or paradigms) experience the world differently. People are likely to form different beliefs and perform different actions even if they occupy the same social or institutional location. Thus interpretivists typically argue that we should rethink institutionalism and rational choice in order to disaggregate governance: we should rethink institutions as the sites of contingent, open-ended struggles over meaning, rather as the fixed embodiments of rules or norms; and we should rethink rational choice theory to give far greater scope to empirical studies of the actual beliefs of the actors who are of interest to us. We should develop a more dynamic account of governance that allows for its contested and disparate nature. For interpretivists, the new governance consists of meaningful practices that change over time as a result of political contests.

Constructing the New Governance

Interpretive approaches conceive of the new governance as meaningful practices. Their emphasis on meanings typically constitutes a form of social constructivism. It is important, however, to be clear about what is and what is not entailed by constructivism. There are different ways of unpacking constructivism, and we should distinguish between them.

A general version of constructivism insists that we make parts of the social world by our intentional actions. People act for reasons that they adopt in the light of beliefs and tacit knowledge that they acquire in part through processes of socialization. For example, when shopkeepers price goods, they make an aspect of the social world in accord with their beliefs about how to make a profit. Other aspects of the social world then arise as the unintended consequences of such intentional actions. For example, if a shopkeeper prices her goods higher than her competitors, and if potential customers buy goods at the lower prices available elsewhere, she will go bust irrespective of whether or not anybody intended or foresaw that outcome.

All kinds of social scientists allow that we make the world through our intentional actions. Often they seek to explain actions in terms of allegedly social or natural facts about institutions, social class, gender, or a universal human rationality. In contrast, constructivists usually argue that the intentions of actors derive in part from traditions, discourses, or systems of knowledge that are also social constructs. Interpretive theory overlaps with this linguistic social constructivism. It implies not only that we make the social world by acting on certain beliefs and meanings, but also that we make the beliefs and meanings on which we act. In this view, our concepts are contingent products of particular discourses and practices; they are not natural or inevitable ways of conceiving and classifying objects. Our concepts are the artificial inventions of particular languages, cultures, and societies.

Is Governance Real?

Interpretive theory implies that traditions or cultures may categorize objects very differently. It is a commonplace, for example, that the Inuit have words for different types of snow, or that the people of the Kalahari Desert have words that distinguish various shades of red. Most interpretive theories are, therefore, antiessentialist. They suggest that our social concepts do not refer to essences. Our concepts do not discern core, intrinsic properties that are common to all the things to which we might apply them and that explain the other facets and behavior of those things. It is certainly possible that none of our social concepts refer to essences, especially if we define a social concept as one that cannot be unpacked solely in terms of our bodies, their movements, and their reactions.

Critics sometimes confuse interpretive theorists' antiessentialism with antirealism. In contrast, we would do well to distinguish between pragmatic, critical, and antirealist forms of antiessentialism. Sometimes antiessentialism inspires a pragmatic account of social concepts. In this view, social concepts are vague; they capture family resemblances; they are conventional ways of dividing up continuums rather than terms for discrete chunks of experience. Yet, although pragmatic concepts do not refer to essences, they do refer to groups of objects, properties, or events. Social factors determine pragmatic concepts because there are innumerable ways in which we can classify things, and because it is our purposes and our histories that lead us to adopt some classifications and not others. Nonetheless, the role of social factors in determining pragmatic concepts does not mean that these concepts have no basis in the world. To the contrary, we might justify adopting the particular pragmatic concepts we do by arguing that they best serve our purposes, whether these purposes are descriptive, explanatory, or normative; we might justify a pragmatic concept such as the new public management on the grounds that its content derives from family resemblances between recent public sector reforms; we might defend ascribing particular content to concepts such as neoliberalism on the grounds that doing so best explains the resemblances between public sector reforms; and we might adopt a particular concept of democratic accountability on the grounds that it best captures those patterns of rule that we should regard as legitimate given our normative commitments.

Critical constructivism arises when we want to suggest that a concept is invalid. In such cases, we might argue that the concept is determined by social factors and that it fails to capture even a group. For example, we might reject the concept of new public management as unfounded, especially if it is meant to refer to a global trend. We might argue that different states introduced very different reforms with widely varying results, and we might add that the reforms drew on and resembled each state's own traditions of administration far more than they did some common neoliberal blueprint. In such cases, we dismiss concepts as unfounded by arguing that there is no fact of the matter—neither an essence nor a group—that they accurately pick out.

Antirealism consists of a kind of global critical constructivism applied to all our concepts. While it is unlikely that interpretivists want to adopt such antirealism, some of them do gesture toward it. At times interpretivists suggest that the role of prior theories and traditions in constructing our experiences precludes our taking experiences to reflect a world independent of us. They suggest that we have access only to our world (things as we experience them), not the world as it is (things in themselves), and they conclude that we have no basis on which to treat our concepts as true to the world. Most interpretive theorists eschew such antirealism, however. They take a pragmatic view of the social concepts they think are valid and a critical view of those they think dominate discourses but are invalid.

RETHINKING THE STATE

While the new theories of governance clearly differ considerably from one another, we should not allow the differences to obscure the extent to which they mark a collective departure from the concept of the state associated with developmental historicism. Early political scientists told narratives about the development of the state in accord with principles such as nationality, liberty, and community. These principles enabled them to treat the state as an organic or historical unity or at least a unity in the making. The concept of the state as a unity was vehemently challenged by the rise of studies of behavioral topics during and after World War One. By the time of the behavioral revolution of the 1950s, various pluralisms were at least as widespread in political science as the older vision of the unified state. The new theories of governance all offer ways of thinking about the state as composed of diverse groups, organizations, or individuals combined in policy networks and acting less for some common good than for particular interests or in accord with particular norms and values. In these new theories the state appears less as a formal unity defined by a constitution, laws, or rules, than as a complex pattern of networks.

Some theories of governance, notably rational choice theory and much interpretive theory, stand as overt challenges to developmental historicism and even the modernist empiricism that began to emerge in the first half of the twentieth century. Other theories of governance, notably the new institutionalism, are better conceived as attempts to revise the old view of the state in order to allow for behavioral techniques and topics. Historical institutionalists have adopted thin forms of the behavioral use of correlations; they are thus prone to treating states as monolithic entities so that they can search for correlations between a type of state and some other variable. Sociological institutionalists have made way for behavioral topics in that they have begun to rethink the state in terms of diverse organizations characterized by different norms.

The new theories of governance have rethought the state not as a formal unity but as a complex pattern of networks. From this perspective, they differ in their respective approaches to network theory. A rational choice approach to policy networks can be found in the work of Renate Mayntz, Scharpf, and their colleagues at the Max-Planck Institut fur Gesellschaftsforschung.[31] Scharpf's account of policy networks relies on

---

[31] Scharpf, ed., *Games in Hierarchies and Networks*. Also see R. Mayntz and B. Marin, eds., *Policy Networks: Empirical Evidence and Theoretical Considerations* (Frankfurt: Campus, 1991); and, for a useful overview, T. Börzel, "Organizing Babylon: On the Different Conceptions of Policy Networks," *Public Administration* 76 (1998): 253–73.

an actor-centered institutionalism. Networks are institutional settings in which public and private actors interact. They consist of rules that structure the opportunities for actors to realize their preferences. Actors adopt strategies so as to maximize their satisfaction and their resources within the context of such rules. It is arguable that this rational choice approach differs from the power dependence one mainly in the extent to which it uses formal game theory to analyze and explain rule-governed networks.

Several institutionalists adopt a power dependence approach to policy networks.[32] They argue that policy networks consist of resource-dependent organizations. Each of these organizations depends on the others for resources. They have to exchange resources if they are to achieve their goals. Each organization in the network deploys its resources, whether these be financial, political, or informational, to maximize its influence on outcomes. While one might suggest that the relationships between the organizations thus resemble a game rooted in trust and regulated by rules, institutionalists typically explain outcomes and variations between networks by reference not to rational action but to the distribution of resources and the bargaining skills of participants.

So, just as an amorphous institutionalism can combine with other approaches such as regulation theory, so the power dependence approach to network theory can combine not only with rational choice theory but also with Marxist dialectics.[33] The advocates of dialectical approaches to policy networks oppose the methodological individualism associated with rational choice. They argue that network structures and the agents in them have a mutually determining effect on one another. At the micro level, networks are comprised of strategically calculating subjects whose

[32] For the continuing debate between power dependence forms of institutionalism and rational choice perspectives, see K. Dowding, "Model or Metaphor? A Critical Review of the Policy Network Approach," *Political Studies* 43 (1995): 136–58; D. Marsh and M. Smith, "Understanding Policy Networks: Towards a Dialectical Approach," *Political Studies* 48 (2000): 4–21; K. Dowding, "There Must Be an End to the Confusion: Policy Networks, Intellectual Fatigue, and the Need for Political Science Methods Courses in British Universities," *Political Studies* 49 (2001): 89–105; and D. Marsh and M. Smith, "There is More Than One Way to Do Political Science: On Different ways to Study Policy Networks," *Political Studies* 49 (2001): 528–41.

[33] The amorphousness of these dialectical approaches reflects that of institutionalism generally straddling as it does Marxism, organizational theory, and various other strands of midlevel social science, some of which even embrace constructivist or discursive themes. Examples include J. Benson, "Organizational Dialectics," *Administrative Science Quarterly* 22 (1977): 1–22; M. Evans, "Understanding Dialectics in Policy Network Analysis," *Political Studies* 49 (2001): 542–50; C. Hay, "The Tangled Webs We Weave: The Discourse, Strategy, and Practice of Networking," in D. Marsh, ed., *Comparing Policy Network* (Buckingham: Open University Press, 1998), 3–51; Marsh and Smith, "Understanding Policy Networks"; and J. McGuire, "A Dialectical Analysis of Interorganizational Networks," *Journal of Management* 14 (1988): 109–24.

actions shape network characteristics and policy outcomes. However, the beliefs and interests of these actors are products of the macrolevel nature of the relevant networks and their contexts. These macrolevel factors are understood to be ones of power and structure rather than rules of a neutral game.

Interpretive theory shifts our attention to the social construction of policy networks.[34] It eschews the search for generality, correlations, and models found among the other approaches. Policy networks are seen as the contingent products of the actions of diverse individuals, where these individuals may act on very different beliefs and understandings informed by conflicting traditions. At the micro level, interpretive theorists often explore networks in terms of the behavior of a host of everyday makers—citizens and street-level bureaucrats as well as politicians, public officials, and members of interest groups. At an aggregate level, they often explain the behavior of clusters of everyday makers by reference to the discourses, traditions, and dilemmas that inform their webs of belief.

Conclusion

The developmental historicism of the nineteenth century has been replaced by all kinds of new theories of governance. These new theories have had implications for the theory and practice of democratic governance. Most of the rest of this book traces these implications. It draws on interpretive theory to suggest that the new governance arose in part as a result of the spread of new discourses, including some of the theories that have been discussed in this chapter. The next chapter argues that rational choice theory (inspiring neoliberalism) and the new institutionalism (inspiring a reformed social democracy) have had a dramatic impact on the new governance that they purport to analyze. Parts 2 and 3 examine how the state responds to the democratic issues raised by the new governance. The state continues to use the language of representative democracy, and in Britain of the Westminster model, to try to cope with the new theories and new worlds of governance. Equally, the state tries to plug the holes in representative democracy, and in Britain of the Westminster model, by drawing on rational choice theory and the new institutionalism with their varying theories of democracy.

[34] See Bevir and Richards, eds., *Decentring Policy Networks*.

CHAPTER FOUR

New Worlds

THE NEW GOVERNANCE is in large part about the rise of new forms of knowledge or expertise. The last two chapters explored a broader historic shift in knowledge production from developmental historicism to modernist theories of governance based on formal economic and sociological concepts of rationality. Interpretive social science enables us to see how these new forms of social science not only analyze the world but also come to constitute it. So, in this chapter I examine the new worlds that have not only inspired some of the new theories but also been constituted in part by them.

The current interest in governance derives primarily from the belief that reforms of the public sector since the 1980s have created new worlds of governance. The new governance refers here to the apparent spread of markets and networks following these reforms. It points to the ways in which the informal authority of markets and networks increasingly constitutes, supplements, and supplants the formal authority of government.

Recent public sector reform arose in large part from the conviction among academics and policy makers that the bureaucratic, Keynesian, welfare state had become unsustainable. Critics of the state argued that it was being squeezed from above by globalization and from below by the increasing diversity and complexity of civil society. The state could no longer cope with an increasingly complicated, fast-changing world. Perhaps the large, centrally controlled bureaucracies of the postwar era were once apt, or perhaps they have always been problematic. Either way, the critics agreed that the world was changing quickly, and the state, unable to get out of its own way, could not keep up with the pace. The state was too big, and too many demands were being placed on it. Worse still, it was so weighed down by its own bureaucratic bulk that it could not even adapt to the new era. It was, in a word, overloaded.

The perceived crisis of the state led to attempts to reform the public sector. These reforms have generally come in two successive waves. The first wave of reforms drew on neoliberalism and rational choice theory, and in Britain it is associated with Thatcherism. The relevant reforms aimed to make the public sector more like the private one, and even to take certain functions entirely out of the public sector. The second wave of reforms was partly a response to the apparent failings of the first. It often drew on institutionalism and related forms of social science, and in Britain it is associated with New Labour. The reforms emphasized networks and partnerships, giving the state a more managerial or directive role in relation to nonstate organizations.

Neoliberals often imply that their reforms are the single best option for all states at all times.[1] The same might be said more recently about some advocates of partnerships and networks. Moreover, studies of both waves of reform can imply, albeit unwittingly, that change has been ubiquitous. It is worth emphasizing at the outset, therefore, the variety and limits of both waves of reform.

Public sector reform varies from state to state. The neoliberal reforms are associated primarily with Britain and the United States but also with Australia and New Zealand. While many other Western states introduced similar reforms, they did so only selectively, and when they did introduce a particular reform, its content and implementation were often modified in accord with the traditions of the relevant state.[2] Typically, developing and transitional states adopted similar reforms only under pressure from corporations, other states, and international organizations.

Public sector reform also varies inside any given state across policy sectors and policy tasks.[3] For example, even in Britain and the United States, there have been perilously few attempts to introduce performance-related pay or outsourcing into those higher levels of the administration that are responsible for providing policy advice.

The varied extent of public sector reform should make us wary of overstating the transformation of governance. No doubt there have been extensive and important reforms. However, bureaucratic hierarchies still perform most government functions in most states and in most local, regional, and international bodies.[4]

I will return to the question of the extent of the transformation later in this chapter when I decenter the governance narrative. To begin, however, this chapter discusses the two waves of public sector reform. Even today

---

[1] E.g., C. Hood, "A Public Management for All Seasons," *Public Administration* 69 (1991): 3–19.

[2] See Bevir, Rhodes, and Weller, eds., *Traditions of Governance*; and C. Pollitt and G. Bouckaert, *Public Management Reform: A Comparative Analysis* (Oxford: Oxford University Press, 2000).

[3] See G. Boyne et al., *Evaluating Public Management Reform: Principles and Practice* (Buckingham: Open University Press, 2003).

[4] Compare C. Hill and L. Lynn, "Is Hierarchical Governance in Decline? Evidence from Empirical Research," *Journal of Public Administration Research and Theory* 15 (2005): 173–96.

these reforms remain as controversial as ever. Policy makers and commentators continue to debate the merits of various programs of reform. Some argue that the crisis of the state was not as dire as supposed. Some argue that the effects of the reforms are negligible. Others argue that the reforms have actually made matters worse. Furthermore, all these debates about the reforms and their effects are of worldwide importance, for even if the original impetus for public sector reform came from neoliberals and others in developed states, the ideas behind the reforms have had a dramatic impact on aid policies. Donors have made aid dependent on public sector reforms being enacted in recipient states. Donors have prescribed to developing states' reforms based on the ideas and values of developed states. Yet, some commentators not only debate the merits of the reforms in general, they argue that they are particularly ill suited to the circumstances of developing states.[5]

First-Wave Reforms

The first wave of public sector reforms sought to remove some state functions entirely, open others to competition, and introduce private management techniques to the public sector. The reforms consisted mainly of overlapping emphases on new public management, marketization, and privatization. They were pioneered by neoliberal regimes such as the Thatcher governments in Britain and the Reagan administrations in the United States.[6] Later the reforms spread through much of Europe— though France, Germany, and Spain are often seen as remaining largely untouched by the movement—and to developing and transitional states. In developed states, much of the impetus toward NPM originated in fiscal crises. Talk of the overloaded state arose as oil crises cut state revenues and as the expansion of welfare services made state expenditure an increasing proportion of gross national product. In developing and transitional states, the impetus for NPM lay more in external pressures, most notably those associated with structural adjustment programs.

[5] For a warning by someone broadly supportive of the ideas behind the reforms, see A. Schick, "Why Most Developing Countries Should Not Try New Zealand's Reforms," *World Bank Research Observer* 13 (1998): 123–31.

[6] For a more complex account of the rise of neoliberalism that still ultimately emphasizes intellectuals, policy wonks, and politicians in Britain and the United States, see D. Harvey, *A Brief History of Neoliberalism* (Oxford: Oxford University Press, 2005), esp. chaps. 2 and 3. On public sector reform, see D. Savoie, *Thatcher, Reagan, Mulroney: In Search of a New Bureaucracy* (Pittsburgh: Pittsburgh University Press, 1995); and on NPM in particular, also see G. Gruening, "Origin and Theoretical Basis of the New Public Management," *International Public Management Review* 4 (2001): 1–25.

Sources

The first wave of reforms drew on public dissatisfaction with bureaucracy, and also on neoliberalism and rational choice theory, both of which explained and legitimated this dissatisfaction. Neoliberals compared the state's top-down, hierarchical mode of organization with the decentralized, competitive structure of the market. They argued that the market was superior. They concluded that when possible markets or quasi-markets should replace the bureaucratic paradigm of public administration. A quest for efficiency led them to call on the state to transfer organizations and activities to the private sector. Organizations could be transferred by privatization, that is, the transfer of state assets to the private sector through flotations or management buyouts. Activities could be transferred by means of contracting out: the state could pay a private sector organization to undertake tasks on its behalf.

It is perfectly rational to believe in the efficiency of market mechanisms and to deny that private sector organizations embody good management practices, but this was not the position of neoliberals. Most neoliberals were more than ready to combine their faith in markets with a faith that the discipline of the market must somehow validate the management practices of the private sector. They redefined public officials as managers or service providers, and they redefined citizens as consumers or service users. The result was a startling array of trends and fads intended to make providers more responsive to their customers.

Formal analyses based on rational choice sometimes lurk behind the neoliberal reforms of the public sector. Some social scientists suggest that there is an inherent tension between the demand that public agencies be efficient, which requires them to be strong and decisive, and the demand that they be accountable, which requires them to be subordinated and rule-bound.[7] If public agencies are to be efficient, they need the latitude to act on their own, but if they are to be accountable, they must be kept on a tight leash.

At a more general level, the tension between efficiency and accountability appears in the problem of delegating decision making from a principal to an agent. Economists first developed principal-agent theory to analyze this problem of delegated discretion as it appears in the private sector.[8]

[7] E.g., F. Fukuyama, *State-Building: Governance and World Order in the 21st Century* (Ithaca: Cornell University Press, 2004), 1–4.

[8] Many of the issues of corporate governance arise from the separation of control and ownership, and insofar as this separation is more prominent in Britain and the United States than elsewhere, the literature on corporate governance is rooted in British and American capitalism. A pioneering study of this separation was A. Berle and G. Means, *The Modern Corporation and Private Property* (New York: Macmillan, 1993). Over-

Typically economists allowed that the transaction costs of administering a large organization require that principals (normally the shareholders) delegate decision making to agents (normally the professional managers in corporations). Yet the microlevel assumptions of neoclassical economics and rational choice theory imply that organizations are just collections of individuals, each of whom pursues his or her own benefit rather than those of the organization as whole. Thus, the delegation of decision making is risky: the agents may act on their own interests, which may not be those of the principals. Economists tried to minimize this risk by devising incentives and market mechanisms that align the interests of the agents with those of the principals.

The first wave of public sector reforms arose in part from the application of the principal-agent problem to public administration. In the public sector, the principals are the voters and their elected representatives while the agents are public officials.[9] Just as the basic problem of private sector corporations was to ensure that the managers acted on behalf of the shareholders, so the basic problem of public administration appeared to be to ensure that public officials work on behalf of citizens. Neoliberals sought to reform the public sector by extending to it the incentives and market mechanisms that economists had devised to bring the interests of agents into alignment with those of their principals.

So, in the last quarter of the twentieth century, popular and neoliberal narratives combined with more formal analyses to produce a paradigm shift. The new paradigm denounced bureaucracy and public officials and championed markets and entrepreneurs. It turned away from what was now derided as big government, bloated bureaucracy, and uniform solutions, and toward a private sector that was now lauded as competitive, efficient, and flexible. This paradigm shift was also one away from in-

---

views of the economic literature on principal-agent theory include K. Eisenhardt, "Agency Theory: An Assessment and Review," Academy of Management Review 14 (1989): 57–74; and J. Stiglitz, "Principal and Agent," in J. Eatwell, M. Milgate, and P. Newman, eds., The New Palgrave: Allocation, Information, and Markets (London: Macmillan, 1989), 241–53. For an emphasis on recent developments and future prospects, see Sappington, "Incentives in Principal-Agent Relationships."

[9] Much of the literature focuses on the relationship of Congress to the bureaucracy in the United States. See, for example, R. Kiewiet and M. McCubbins, The Logic of Delegation: Congressional Parties and the Appropriations Process (Chicago: University of Chicago Press, 1991). For studies of the issues as they apply to internal bureaucratic structures and to elections and representations, see respectively, G. Miller, Managerial Dilemmas: The Political Economy of Hierarchy (Cambridge: Cambridge University Press, 1992); and J. Fearon, "Electoral Accountability and the Control of Politicians: Selecting Good Types versus Sanctioning Poor Performance," in A. Przeworski, S. Stokes, and B. Manin, eds., Democracy, Accountability, and Representation (New York: Cambridge University Press, 1999), 55–97.

stitutional definitions of good government, which emphasized clear-cut divisions of responsibility set in a context of hierarchical relationships, toward new definitions of efficient processes defined in terms of service delivery and outputs with an attendant emphasis on transparency, user-friendliness, and incentive structures.

Content

The neoliberal reforms had two main strands: marketization and NPM.

Marketization. The most extreme form of marketization is privatization, the transfer of assets from the state to the private sector.[10] Thereafter the state takes little or no responsibility for providing the relevant goods or services to citizens, businesses, or other state agencies. The practice of privatization first arose in Britain. Later it spread elsewhere, notably the formerly communist countries of the Soviet bloc where it was promoted by neoliberal advisers sent over from Britain and especially the United States. Some state-owned industries were floated on stock exchanges. Others were sold to their employees through, for example, management buyouts. Yet others were sold to individual companies or consortiums. Industries subject to dramatic privatizations included telecommunications, railways, electricity, gas, water, and waste services. Smaller privatizations often involved local governments as well as central states; they covered assets such as hotels, parking facilities, and convention centers.

Where privatization was deemed inappropriate, neoliberals advocated other forms of marketization. These other forms remain far more common than privatization. Typically they introduce incentive structures into public-service provision by means of quasi-markets and consumer choice. Marketization aims to make public services more efficient and more accountable to consumers by giving the latter greater choice of service provider. Prominent examples of marketization include contracting out, internal markets, management contracts, and market testing.

- Contracting out (also known as outsourcing) involves the state contracting a private organization on a competitive basis to provide a service. The private organization may be for-profit or nonprofit—it is sometimes a company hastily formed by those who previously had provided the service as public sector employees.

[10] Privatization is even used to refer to marketization in J. Donahue, *The Privatization Decision: Public Ends, Private Means* (New York: Basic Books, 1989). On privatization in my sense of the term see, W. Megginson and J. Netter, "From State to Market: A Survey of Empirical Studies of Privatization," *Journal of Economic Literature* 39 (2001): 321–89.

- Internal markets arise when government agencies are able to purchase support services from several in-house providers or outside suppliers who in turn operate as independent business units who are thus in competition with one another.
- Management contracts involve the operation of a facility—such as an airport or convention center—being handed over to a private company in accord with specific contractual arrangements.
- Market testing (also known as managed competition) occurs when the arrangements governing the provision of a service are decided by means of bidding in comparison with private sector competitors.

Marketization transfers the delivery of services to autonomous or semiautonomous agencies. Advocates of marketization make several arguments in favor of these agencies. They argue that service providers can now concentrate on the efficient delivery of quality services without having to evaluate alternative policies. They argue that the policy makers can be more focused and adventurous since they need not worry about the existing service providers. And they argue that when the state has a hands-off relationship with a service provider, it has more opportunities to introduce performance incentives.

New public management.   Outsourcing acted as one route by which private sector norms spread through the public sector; for even when the professed justification of partnerships is that both the private and public sector benefit from them, the reality is that public sector actors are meant to act more like private sector ones, not vice versa. NPM may be defined as a series of deliberate attempts to reform public sector management in accord with private sector techniques.[11] NPM encourages public sector organizations to think of themselves as more like private sector organizations, and to adopt managerial and budgetary practices from private sector organizations. It aims to shift attention from procedures and formal processes to measures of outputs.

When neoliberals promote measures of outputs, they are often inspired by the role of profits in the private sector. They suggest that the graded, quantifiable nature of profit makes it an excellent yardstick against which to measure performance and so guide future decisions. Of course, critics argue that the aims of the public sector are not amenable to quantification and measurement. Yet, advocates of NPM devise forms of measure-

[11] For practitioners' perspectives, see M. Holmes and D. Shand, "Management Reform: Some Practitioner Perspectives on the Past Ten Years," *Governance* 8 (1995): 551–78; and J. Kamensky, "Role of the 'Reinventing Government' Movement in Federal Management Reform," *Public Administration Review* 56 (1996): 247–55.

ment that they think apply to the public sector—measurements that can be used to set and monitor performance targets for public officials. They thus support the use in the public sector of "best practices" from the private sector with respect to financial management, human resources, and decision making.

NPM consists largely of attempts to foster styles of public management that are oriented toward performance measures and so value for money and closeness to the customer—all of which are typically tied to budgetary reforms. As such, NPM responds to a general concern with achieving effective management in the public sector. But there is no substantial agreement on what constitutes effective management. On the contrary, the innocent observer discovers a bewildering number of concepts of good management, each of which has its own acronym. Management by results (MBR) relies on past results as indicators of future results. Management by objectives (MBO) emphasizes the role of clearly stated objectives for individual managers. Total quality management (TQM) is a more participatory approach that emphasizes an awareness of quality in all organizational processes. Most of these management practices make at least some use of performance measures to audit inputs and outputs and then to relate them to financial budgets. Yet performance measurements also vary widely; there is disagreement about the goals of performance as well as how to measure results properly.

Generally NPM refers not only to new managerial practices and performance measures but also to aspects of marketization. Relevant characteristics of NPM include fragmentation, an output orientation, increased competition, and customerization. While these characteristics often arise from marketization, they also bring private sector norms and practices into the public sector. Fragmentation involves separating policy decisions from the implementation of policies. It provides managers with the freedom to manage. Public sector managers are to be set free from the constraints of bureaucratic rules and regulations so that they can be entrepreneurial and adventurous. The orientation toward outputs involves attempts to identify relationships between resources and outputs, and also efforts to use resources more efficiently to ensure quality outputs. Competition arises from the creation of internal markets within an organization or between organizations. These internal markets are meant to subject the public sector to the competitive pressures associated with the private sector, thereby eliminating or at least reducing inefficiencies. Finally, customerization consists of a greater responsiveness to the demands of service users. Advocates of NPM often suggest that public officials have been too focused on bureaucratic relationships and rules. Competitive pressures and an output orientation are meant to ensure that public sector managers use their newfound managerial freedom to respond to their customers.

It is arguable that two different ideas inspire NPM.[12] One is to give managers more discretion by freeing them from bureaucratic constraints. The other is to direct managers to certain concerns and decisions by subjecting them to the discipline of the market. According to those who want to let managers manage, public officials are good people made to work in bad systems. The shortcomings of the state derive from its bureaucratic structure rather than the inadequacies or self-interestedness of public officials. Public officials possess the skills, knowledge, and experience they need. It is the rigidity of their institutional settings that constrains them, requiring public officials to defer to norms and procedures rather than use their own discretion to respond to circumstances. Hence the call to let managers manage. The state should reduce the constraints of regulation so as to give public officials the freedom to use their discretion to identify and pursue social goods.

According to those who want to make managers manage, public officials are all too likely to pursue their self-interest unless the right set of incentives brings these interests into line with those of the general public. In this view, public sector agencies are often monopolies or quasi-monopolies insulated from competitive pressures, and the absence of competitive pressures means that the self-interest of public officials does not include the efficient delivery of services. Public officials have few incentives to improve performance or even to give much attention to the efficient use of their budgets. Hence the call to make managers manage. The state should introduce competitive pressures so as to compel managers to deliver better services at lower costs. It should introduce the kinds of incentives that markets provide and thus give officials an interest in cost effectiveness. In particular, the state should tie pay to performance and specify objectives for agencies and particular managers even as it gives these managers greater latitude over how they choose to improve their performance and meet their objectives.

Evaluation

The success of the neoliberal reforms is unclear and remains the source of considerable debate.[13] The most positive evaluations imply that the

[12] Compare D. Kettl, "The Global Revolution in Public Management: Driving Themes, Missing Links," *Journal of Policy Analysis and Management* 16 (1997): 446–62; and L. Terry, "Administrative Leadership, Neo-Managerialism, and the Public Management Movement," *Public Administration Review* 58 (1998): 194–20.

[13] Consider, for example, the diverse views found in K. McLaughlin, S. Osborne, and E. Ferlie, eds., *New Public Management: Current Trends and Future Prospects* (London:

reforms will bring (or even have brought) the benefits that they were meant to, including a more dynamic, efficient, and entrepreneurial public sector providing better services for less money. Yet, few people now believe that the reforms proved to be the panacea that they were supposed to be. Studies suggest that NPM generates at best about a 3 percent annual saving on running costs, a modest amount, especially in light of the fact that running costs are typically a relatively small component of total program costs. Even neoliberals often acknowledge that most savings derive from privatization, not reforms in public sector organizations. The success of both marketization and NPM also appears to have varied considerably with contextual factors. For example, many developing and transitional states often found the reforms counterproductive since they lacked a stable framework built on historical experience of credible policies, predictable resources, and a public service ethic.[14] It is interesting to reflect that in this respect privatization and NPM appear to have required the existence of aspects of just the kind of public service bureaucracy that they tried to supplant.

Negative evaluations of the neoliberal reforms tend to emphasize their role in creating or exacerbating problems such as fragmentation of service delivery, lack of central control over the policy process, weak and obscure lines of accountability, and loss of an ethic of public service.

One complaint is that public sector reform aggravated institutional fragmentation. Services are often delivered now by a combination of local government, special-purpose bodies, the voluntary sector, and the private sector. Critics point to an absence of links between organizations. In their view, outsourcing fails to establish proper sustained relationships between state actors and their private sector partners. The worry is that departments of state and their associated agencies are becoming almost wholly unconnected elements. There are no proper mechanisms for ensuring policy coordination.

A similar complaint addresses the decline of the ability of the state to steer other organizations. Public sector reform undermined the strategic

---

Routledge, 2002); and, for more firmly comparative perspectives, B. Peters and J. Pierre, eds., *Politicians, Bureaucrats, and Administrative Reform* (London: Routledge, 2001). New Zealand stands out, at least among English-speaking states, in having commissioned and published an official, independent evaluation. See A. Schick, *The Spirit of Reform: Managing the New Zealand State Sector in a Time of Change*, a report prepared for the State Services Commission and the Treasury (Wellington: State Services Commission, 1996).

[14] Compare the mea culpa of B. Black, K. Reinier, and A. Tarassova, "Russian Privatization and Corporate Governance: What Went Wrong?," *Ekonomski Anali* 44 (2000): 29–117. Also see J. Nellis, *Time to Rethink Privatization in Transition Economies?*, International Finance Corporation Discussion Paper no. 38; and the less formal strictures of Fukuyama, *State-Building*.

capacity of the center. Critics argue that many agencies now work in a policy vacuum. The role of the central state has been restricted to crisis management. When the center does try to exercise some kind of control, it is all too likely to find that it has rubber levers—pulling the lever does not lead to anything happening at the other end.

Many commentators are less concerned with issues of capacity or effectiveness than with the way the reforms measure up against civic values. One complaint is that the reforms hand aspects of public policy over to agencies and private sector organizations that are at best only minimally accountable to elected politicians and so to the public. Critics argue that public sector managers are now accountable to performance measures but not to senior administrators and their political masters. At the very least, there has been a shift in the nature of accountability: public sector managers are perhaps more responsive to the particular citizens who use their services and less to the politicians who represent the public as a whole.

A similar complaint is that the attempts to make public sector managers behave like private ones undermines the ethic of public service. Some commentators argue that the public sector needs to be insulated from competitive pressure precisely so that public officials can concentrate on long-term public goods when making decisions. The reforms encourage them to concentrate instead on short-term, measurable outcomes. Worse still, the result could be that problems of inequity and corruption become more widespread than at present. Too great an emphasis on efficiency ignores the fact that whereas private sector managers pursue profit, public officials have to make decisions about complicated trade-offs between competing values of which profit or efficiency is only one.

Second-Wave Reforms

Discussions of the new governance often highlight NPM. But public sector reform is a continuous process. Indeed the managerial reforms have often given way to a second wave of reforms that are focused on institutional arrangements (especially networks and partnerships) and administrative values (including public service and social inclusion). This second wave of reform includes a number of overlapping trends that are brought together under labels such as "joined-up governance," "one-stop government," "service integration," "whole-of-government," and *Aktivierender Staat*" (activating state). Some commentators even describe this second wave in contrast to NPM as a "governance approach" or "new governance."

Sources

Several reasons lay behind the changing nature of public sector reform. One is the shifting tide of intellectual and political fortunes. The fortunes of neoliberalism and rational choice have ebbed, while those of reformist social democrats and network theory have flowed. The rise of New Labour in Britain is one obvious example of this tide. A second reason is a growing sensitivity to a new set of problems, including terrorism, the environment, asylum seekers, aging populations, and the digital divide. Many of these problems have more to do with collective goods such as security and equity than they do with efficiency. They have led people to turn back to the state.

Arguably the main reason for the changing content of public sector reform lies in the unintended consequences of the earlier managerial reforms.[15] Observers emphasized that NPM had led to a fragmentation of the public sector: because public services were delivered by networks composed of a number of different organizations, there was a new need to coordinate and manage networks. Social scientists inspired by institutionalism and other alternatives to rational choice theory were often highly critical of the first wave of public sector reforms. The critics argued that the reforms had exacerbated problems of coordination and steering. They promoted networks and partnerships as tools with which the state could help to establish joined-up government and manage other organizations in the policy process.

While the second wave of reforms was an attempt to solve problems associated with marketization and NPM, it did not attempt to turn back the clock. The new networks and partnerships were not meant to recreate the kind of hierarchic bureaucratic structures against which the neoliberals had railed. On the contrary, advocates of the second wave of public sector reforms typically saw networks and partnerships as ways of solving both the problems created by the first wave of reforms and the problems those earlier reforms had been intended to address. In this sense, networks and partnerships might be described as attempts to preserve the legacy of the earlier reforms while building state capacity and oversight. Some commentators even argued that although the first wave of reforms was supposed to create markets, it had actually led to a massive proliferation of networks. Typically they then suggested that these networks were superior to markets, but that the state badly needed to devise and enact new strategies for managing them.

[15] For a recent appeal to the unintended consequences of the reforms as a basis for advancing science and expertise, rather than rethinking the roles of expertise and democracy, see C. Hood and G. Peters, "The Middle Aging of New Public Management: Into the Age of Paradox?," Journal of Public Administration Research and Theory 14 (2004): 267–82.

Advocates of networks distinguish them from both the markets that were so praised by neoliberals and the hierarchies that they associate with the bureaucracies that predated the first wave of reforms.[16] Sometimes they acknowledge that hierarchies may make it easier to tackle many problems: hierarchies can divide problems into smaller, more manageable tasks, each of which can be performed by a specialized unit or individual. However, they then add, this approach to problems works only if the problems can be split up into smaller tasks. Today, they conclude, policy makers increasingly confront "wicked problems" that are not amenable to division and specialization, and to solve these problems requires networks.

Like so many ideas informing the second wave of reforms, the concept of a "wicked problem" arose as part of an amorphous midrange social science that linked institutionalism, organization theory, and functionalism. Reformist governments then picked up and adopted these amorphous theories to counter the ideas and policies of rational choice and neoliberalism.[17] Wicked problems are generally defined in terms such as these: a problem of more or less unique nature; the lack of any definitive formulation of such a problem; the existence of multiple explanations for it; the absence of a test to decide the value of any response to it; all responses to it being better or worse rather than true or false; and each response to it has important consequences such that there is no real chance to learn by trial and error. Typically these features strongly imply that wicked problems are interrelated. For example, a particular wicked problem might be explained in terms of its relationship to others, or any response to it might impact others. Classic examples of wicked problems include pressing issues of governance such as security, environment, and urban blight. Yet other contemporary policy issues—housing, economic development, and welfare—also appear too complex to be divided into neat parts that might then be handed over to distinct bureaucratic units.

The growing popularity of partnerships is a response to the perceived effects of the first wave of public sector reforms. The neoliberal

---

[16] These distinctions have spread from sociological and organizational theory to public administration. See, respectively, W. Powell, "Neither Market nor Hierarchy: Network Forms of Organization," *Research in Organizational Behaviour* 12 (1990): 295–336; and L. O'Toole, "Treating Networks Seriously: Practical and Research-Based Agendas in Public Administration," *Public Administration Review* 57 (1997): 45–52.

[17] See, originally, H. Rittel and M. Webber, "Dilemmas in a General Theory of Planning," *Policy Sciences* 4 (1973): 155–69; more recently, J. Conklin, *Dialogue Mapping: Building Shared Understanding of Wicked Problems* (Chichester: Wiley, 2006); for governance and policy, G. Paquet, *Governance through Social Learning* (Ottawa: University of Ottawa Press, 1999); and for government policy Australian Public Service Commission, *Tackling Wicked Problems: A Public Policy Perspective*, 2007.

reforms created networks, but they did not provide public sector managers with the capacity or the skills to manage these networks and address wicked problems. The state confronts a growing number of cross-jurisdictional challenges and a declining ability to respond to them. The drive toward joined-up government and partnerships attempts to address this situation.[18] As the Australian government writes, wicked problems "require broader, more collaborative and innovative approaches," for they "highlight the fundamental importance of . . . working across organisational boundaries both within and outside the APS [Australian Public Service]."[19]

In more general terms, whereas privatization and even outsourcing involved the retreat of the state from a particular activity, partnerships are meant to allow the state to work alongside private sector firms while retaining oversight of them. These partnerships arose in particular when problems lay beyond the reach of any single agency and thus could be dealt with only if agencies banded together in mutually beneficial ways. Again, the first wave of reforms fragmented the state: they broke up the hierarchies of the welfare state, dividing them into smaller units and moving some functions entirely outside the public sector. The diverse actors created by this process then tried to regroup in various ways so as to address shared problems. They searched for shared agendas and new links with one another. Community groups, private firms, and new governmental agencies all had to be integrated into a coherent policy process. The result was the rise of all kinds of networks and partnerships based on common agendas.

Content

The second wave of reforms consists largely of attempts to foster joined-up networks and public-private partnerships.

Joined-up networks. The main thrust of the second wave of reforms has been to improve coordination across agencies. Joined-up governance promotes horizontal and vertical coordination between the organizations involved in an aspect of public policy. Although the boundary between policymaking and policy implementation is blurred, joined-up approaches have a different look in each case. Joined-up policymaking characteristically seeks to bring together all agencies involved in address-

---

[18] Compare V. Lowndes and C. Skelcher, "The Dynamics of Multi-Organisational Partnerships: An Analysis of Changing Modes of Governance," *Public Administration* 76 (1998): 313–33.

[19] Australian Public Service Commission, *Tackling Wicked Problems*, iii.

ing a wicked problem such as juvenile crime or rural poverty. Joined-up policy implementation characteristically seeks to coordinate the activities of agencies involved in delivering services in order to simplify them for citizens: an example is one-stop shops at which the unemployed can access their benefits, training, and job information. In both cases, joined-up governance draws on the idea that networks can coordinate the actions of a range of actors and organizations. Advocates of the reforms suggest that in many circumstances networks will offer a superior mode of coordination to both hierarchies and markets. In this view, networks combine an enabling or facilitative leadership with greater flexibility, creativity, inclusiveness, and commitment. Joined-up governance is thus as much about fostering networks as managing them.

Partnerships. Partnerships can be between public, private, and voluntary bodies, as well as between different levels of government or different state agencies. In many states, the emphasis of partnerships has shifted from competitive tendering and outsourcing to the public sector building and maintaining long-term relationships based on trust as well as contracts with suppliers, users, and other stakeholders. Public-private partnerships are the most prominent part of this shift. They are meant to promote a shared commitment and degree of cooperation that surpasses the specifications of a formal contract.

Not surprisingly, partnerships have been subject to much criticism. On the one hand, some critics accuse partnerships of being barely disguised forms of NPM and outsourcing, and thus of obscuring accountability relationships and weakening public oversight of decision-making processes. On the other hand, neoliberal advocates of the first wave of reforms complain that long-term partnerships erode proper competition among potential service providers.

Despite these criticisms, partnerships continue to flourish.[20] No doubt they flourish in part because they ease the burden of capital investment on the public sector and they reduce risks of development for the private sector. Yet, their advocates argue that they also flourish because they are highly effective: they combine the best features of markets, including flexibility and efficiency, with those of hierarchies, including stability and the ability to concentrate on long-term issues. Partnerships are thus said to overcome the problems now associated with NPM and outsourcing. Their advocates claim that they offer the benefits of stable long-term relationships and genuine cooperation in contrast to the short-term focus

---

[20] For a discussion of the continuing appeal of partnerships in the face of these criticisms, see T. Bovaird, "Public-Private Partnerships: From Contested Concept to Prevalent Practice," *International Review of Administrative Sciences* 70 (2004): 199–215.

on immediate profits that is often associated with contracting out. Some commentators argue that the private sector is marred by an endemic short-termism: competition and the need to make an immediate profit lead companies to neglect long-term investment and stability. This argument suggests that there are some advantages to the public sector being comparatively sheltered from competition. State agencies can concentrate on building collaborative relationships that will provide the long-term advantages associated with stability, trust, and collaboration. Partnerships offer relationships in which success is seen in shared terms.

Evaluation

As attempts to foster "joined-up governance" and "whole of government" approaches to address "wicked problems" are barely a decade old, it is perhaps a bit early to comment specifically on the consequences of this second wave of reforms. Even if one allows that states have long been concerned to manage networks and secure coordination across agencies and departments, the conscious adoption of new theories (and perhaps a new agenda) of networks and partnerships is only just beginning to take effect. Criticisms of the consequences of the second wave reforms are thus often couched as skepticism toward their probable impact.

Some skeptics argue that little has changed, or at least that the only changes have been rhetorical. They point to the fact that states have long been concerned to manage policy networks and to secure coordination across agencies and departments. They imply that the state does not face new problems in the way so many reformers suggest. They argue to the contrary that the main problems of today are ones that have long affected organized political life—the need to balance efficiency, fairness, and democracy, and the need to communicate and coordinate with diverse organizations. The state is still doing much the same things as it always has done. Reformers just describe those things in new ways.

Another group of skeptics argues that the public sector is too complex for actors to be able to predict let alone control outcomes. They suggest that this complexity means that all reforms are shots in the dark. All reforms and all modes of governance generate unintended consequences that then undermine those reforms. All governance fails, they insist. Many of these skeptics then urge humility in the face of complexity.[21] Even if organizational and management theories appear to provide novel insights and lay out new directions for reform, we should not delude ourselves that they are a panacea for all ills.

[21] E.g., Jessop, "Governance and Meta-governance."

Yet another group of skeptics argues that the special nature of the public sector renders inappropriate all attempts to tie it to goals, management techniques, and partners from the private sector. Whereas the private sector has clear measures of efficiency and profitability, there are no appropriate measures for the outputs expected from the public sector. It is important to distinguish here between measurements of outputs and outcomes. Output measurements look only at the organization in question and its specific production. Outcome measurements look at how the organization interacts with its social and institutional environment. Typically citizens want outcomes, not outputs, from the state. Yet, outcomes are much harder to measure, and they often depend on factors outside the control of state actors in a way that means measures of them are not always good indicators of an actor's performance.

A final group of skeptics argues that public-private partnerships are likely to be of more benefit to private actors than public ones. In their view, state actors are rarely able to negotiate favorable terms with private sector ones since state actors generally lack the experience, competitive instincts, and flexibility of private companies. According to these skeptics, partnerships benefit all the participants only if there is an equal distribution of power among them. In public-private partnerships, the ethos and resources of the private firm and the current squeeze on the public sector preclude such equality.

The Governance Narrative

The two waves of public sector reform created new worlds of governance. To some extent the new theories of governance have thus made new worlds in their own images, for rational choice theory was one inspiration for the first wave of reforms and the new institutionalism was one inspiration for the second wave. Equally, the rise of the new worlds of governance contributed to the development of new theories of the state. The new theories and new worlds coalesce in a governance narrative. The governance narrative is especially controversial when applied to Britain, where it stands in such sharp contrast to the older Westminster model. Perhaps the new governance appears more shocking to those stuck with an image of a unitary state and parliamentary sovereignty than to those well used to federal and plural polities. Nonetheless, the governance narrative is new to us all. It describes a shift from a hierarchic state to governance in and by networks. It tells of the rise of a differentiated polity characterized by a core executive operating in and through a proliferating number of policy networks.

Differentiated Polity

A differentiated polity consists of various interdependent governments, departments, and agencies. Governance occurs through a maze of institutions and a complex pattern of decentralized functions. There is limited political integration and administrative standardization. Indeed, governance is fragmented among organizations that cover different territories and deliver different functions. It occurs in and through networks composed of departments, agencies, and other social and political actors. The relevant organizations are interdependent, since each relies on cooperative exchanges with the others to secure its agenda. The networks themselves are often self-organizing, and they have at least some autonomy from the center.

The differentiated polity stands in sharp contrast to a unitary state. A unitary state is characterized by the presence of an identifiable polity that has clear boundaries within which law is formed by a sovereign will. In contrast, a differentiated polity has fuzzy boundaries within which power and authority flow downward, upward, and outward. The new governance arose in part as these flows of power increased as a result of globalization and contracting out.

The contrast between a differentiated polity and a unitary state is especially important for the Anglo-governance school.[22] The Westminster model foregrounds parliamentary sovereignty, cabinet government, executive authority, and a neutral civil service. The Anglo-governance school counters this view with one of a differentiated polity. In their view, central government is just one of several public, voluntary, and private actors involved in the policy process. Even if the center has a preeminent place in networks, it rarely can dictate and control policy. Rather, the center attempts to steer and regulate networks by means of financial controls, negotiations, and audits. This account of a differentiated polity draws attention to gaps between the Westminster model and the actual practice of British governance. It highlights, for example, the importance of links between the EU and subnational authorities in the administration of structural funds.

Concepts such as "networked polity" or "disaggregated state" closely resemble that of the differentiated polity. These other concepts are generally used less to describe gaps in the Westminster model than to point to emerging patterns of European and global governance. They refer to territories that few people ever imagined to be governed by a unitary state. The EU resembles a networked polity in that it relies on a complex

---

[22] For detailed discussion, see Bevir and Rhodes, *Interpreting British Governance*, chaps. 2 and 3.

web of committees and societal associations to advise, manage, and regulate varied aspects of governance.[23] Similarly, global governance seems to resemble a disaggregated state in that it relies on various transgovernmental networks.[24] States and non-state actors collaborate in diverse networks to address shared concerns. While some of these global networks are composed of states and constituted by legal treaties, others are informal networks composed, for example, of national regulators and the main private organizations they regulate. Transnational groups and corporations often generate private governance regimes consisting of the rules, norms, and principles that then guide their actions. Global governance consists in part of attempts to regulate and coordinate such private governance regimes.

Governance at the national, regional, and global levels can be described as differentiated, networked, or disaggregated. Together, these descriptions offer a vivid alternative to the idea of sovereign states located in a largely anarchical international society. They evoke a world composed of networks: individuals and groups organize themselves into multiple, overlapping, and interdependent networks to address common problems. States and international organizations are just groups within these diverse networks.

Core Executive

A core executive is a network of institutions and informal practices that attempts to coordinate government policy. Theories of governance often draw our attention to the diverse organizations that are involved in the formulation and implementation of public policy. These organizations often have divergent motivations, visions, resources, and time-horizons. The core executive consists of institutions that negotiate with these organizations and arbitrate between them so as to integrate government policies. It itself is, however, understood as a fragmented network rather than a unitary agent.

The Anglo-governance school deploys the concept of the core executive to describe central government in a differentiated polity.[25] The contrast is again with the Westminster model. The Westminster model in-

[23] See C. Ansell, "The Networked Polity: Regional Development in Western Europe," *Governance* 13 (2000): 303–33.

[24] Compare A-M. Slaughter, *A New World Order* (Princeton: Princeton University Press, 2004).

[25] E.g., Bevir and Rhodes, *Interpreting British Governance*, 56–58; and, for more detail, R. Rhodes and P. Dunleavy, eds., *Prime Minister, Cabinet, and Core Executive* (London: Macmillan, 1995); and M. Smith, *The Core Executive in Britain* (Basingstoke: Palgrave, 1999).

cludes a strong executive composed of the prime minister and cabinet. The core executive points to a more fragmented view of an executive that is composed of various interdependent departments and agencies and is characterized by weakness as much as strength.

Core executives have been studied in states other than Britain, especially states that have cabinet government.[26] Public sector reforms, such as contracting out, typically result in patterns of policymaking and service delivery that rely on multiple governments, departments, and agencies. As a result, many executives have become more fragmented and more concerned with issues of coordination. The key features of the core executive thus appear to have wide applicability.

Policy Networks

The differentiated polity consists of a core executive operating in and through policy networks. These policy networks consist of governmental and societal actors whose interactions with one another give rise to policies. Typically these actors are linked through informal practices as well as formal institutions, or even instead of such institutions. They are often interdependent: as we have seen, they can secure the outcomes for which they hope only by collaborating with one another. Policy networks vary widely, however. Many typologies place policy communities at one extreme.[27] Policy communities have a limited number of participant groups to the deliberate exclusion of others. The participants share broad values, beliefs, and preferences. They meet frequently, interacting closely on any topic related to the policy area. Moreover, they all have significant resources or power, so their interactions consist of institutionalized forms of negotiation and bargaining. Policy communities are usually organized hierarchically so that the leaders of the participant groups can secure the acquiescence of the members in whatever policies are agreed upon. At the other extreme of many typologies we find issue networks. Issue networks have far more participants. The participants disagree with one another so conflict, not consensus, is the norm. They also have unequal levels of power and widely varying degrees of access, so their interactions are often primarily consultative.

[26] Comparative studies include J. Hayward and V. Wright, *Governing from the Centre: Core Executive Coordination in France* (Oxford: Oxford University Press, 2002); B. Peters, R. Rhodes, and V. Wright, eds., *Administering the Summit: Administration of the Core Executive in Developed Countries* (Basingstoke: Macmillan, 2000); and P. Weller, H. Bakvis, and R. Rhodes, eds., *The Hollow Crown: Countervailing Trends in Core Executives* (Basingstoke: Macmillan, 1997).

[27] E.g., Rhodes, *Understanding Governance*, 29–45.

Concepts such as policy network, policy community, and issue network all refer to government links with other state and societal actors. Other related concepts include epistemic communities, iron triangles, and policy subsystems. All these concepts emphasize how networks decide which issues will be included and excluded from the policy agenda, shape the behavior of actors, privilege certain interests, and even substitute private forms of government for public accountability.

The new governance is often described as rule by and through networks. Indeed, governance has become the most widely accepted term for describing the patterns of rule that arise from the interactions of multiple organizations in networks. The state has become increasingly dependent on other actors. Perhaps it may succeed only through negotiations with other actors in networks.

INTERPRETING GOVERNANCE

According to Mike Marinetto, the Anglo-governance school needs "to undergo an intellectual crisis wrought by the growing weight of criticism."[28] It is very probable that this governance narrative needs rethinking. Far too many accounts of the new governance draw on rational choice theory, and especially the institutionalism that inspired the public sector reforms they seek to narrate. Rational choice theory and institutionalism are, moreover, far too inclined to reify either agency or institutions, as if they were fixed by an objective rationality or objective rules and norms. I propose, therefore, that we rethink governance in terms that draw on an alternative interpretive theory. Let us decenter the governance narrative.

Decentered Theory

To decenter is to focus on the social construction of an institution through the ability of individuals to create and act on meanings.[29] Decentered theory thus unpacks institutions in terms of the disparate and contingent beliefs and actions of individuals. It prompts a conceptual shift away from institutions and organizations, which are often conceived as if they have a content fixed by social norms or causal mechanisms, and toward practices, which in sharp contrast are conceived as the contingent and contestable products of situated agency.

---

[28] M. Marinetto, "Governing Beyond the Centre: A Critique of the Anglo-Governance School," *Political Studies* 51 (2003): 605.

[29] See Bevir, "A Decentered Theory of Governance."

Decentered theory suggests that patterns of rule are the contingent products of diverse actions and political struggles. These actions and struggles are products of the reasoning, beliefs, and desires of the people involved. They occur against the background of traditions and as they confront dilemmas. Decentered theory here challenges the idea that inexorable, impersonal forces are driving a shift from government to governance. It suggests, to the contrary, that numerous actors construct governance differently as they operate against the background of diverse traditions. Decentered theory showcases diverse patterns of governance that are themselves composed of multiple individuals acting on changing webs of belief rooted in disparate traditions. Patterns of governance are both contested and contingent. This view of governance challenges the craving for generality that characterizes most other versions of the governance narrative. Typically it privileges textual and ethnographic analyses of meanings and actions together with particular historical explanations of those meanings and actions.

Decentering Governance

If we decenter the governance narrative, we redefine the differentiated polity, the core executive, and to some extent even the concept of a policy network. In each case, we shift attention from somewhat reified institutions to meaningful practices. In doing so, we suggest that the governance narrative is as much an abstract theory of all patterns of rule as it is an account of a specifically new pattern of rule that emerged in the late twentieth century.

It is often unclear whether the differentiated polity represents a fundamental change in patterns of rule or an abstract concept that seeks to rectify simplistic concepts of the state. We might distinguish here between two accounts of the differentiated polity based on their respective analyses of differentiation. On one hand, the older versions of the governance narrative typically understood differentiation as a process based on functional differences. This concept of differentiation inspires accounts of governance as a complex set of institutions defined by their various social roles. The differentiated polity appears to be a fairly recent outcome of processes of specialization in the state: institutions and the links between them have multiplied in order to serve increasingly specialized purposes. On the other hand, decentered theory implies that differentiation might refer to the different interpretations, beliefs, or meanings that animate practices. This concept of differentiation inspires accounts of patterns of governance as arising out of contingent and competing actions informed by distinct webs of belief. In this view, the differentiated polity is not just a description of recent changes in the world; it is an abstract account of how we should think about all patterns of rule.

The concept of the core executive, likewise, might be theorized in terms of meanings and practices rather than functions. Originally, the core executive was defined functionally in terms of the need to secure coordination. The process of fragmentation was understood as dividing the state into more and more institutions, each of which performed a discrete function. Decentered theory suggests, in contrast, that core executives consist of a number of practices with fuzzy boundaries, and that these practices are made up of contingent and contested meanings and actions. The actors within them interpret them and shape them in different ways in large part because they attach different meanings to them.

Decentered theory suggests that the differentiated polity and policy networks are as much an abstract account of all patterns of rule as they are a specific account of the new governance. The allegedly special characteristics of networks appear, it might be said, in hierarchies and markets. The rules and commands of a bureaucracy do not have a fixed form; rather, they are constantly interpreted and made afresh through the creative activity of individuals. Similarly, the operation of markets depends on the contingent beliefs and interactions of interdependent producers and consumers who rely on trust and diplomacy as well as economic rationality to make their decisions. Once we stop reifying hierarchies and markets, we find that many allegedly unique features of governance through networks are ubiquitous. Power and administrative rationality are always dispersed among diverse practices, technologies, and networks.

Finally, as we saw in the last chapter, decentered theory shifts our attention from typologies of networks to their social construction. It eschews the search for generality, correlations, and models that drive the existing typologies. Policy networks are seen, instead, as the contingent products of the actions of diverse individuals, where these individuals might act on very different beliefs and understandings informed by conflicting traditions. At the micro level, we might explore networks in terms of the behavior of a host of everyday makers—citizens and junior public servants as well as politicians, senior bureaucrats, and members of interest groups. At an aggregate level, we might explain the behavior of clusters of everyday makers by reference to the traditions and dilemmas that inform their webs of belief.

Theorizing Change

Interpretive theory leads us to decenter the governance narrative. The result offers the Anglo-governance school something like the "critical response" for which Marinetto and others are calling. It redefines concepts such as differentiated polity in a more fruitful way, thereby opening up new avenues of inquiry such as ethnographic studies of civil servants. It also offers a similarly fruitful response to the main criticisms of the governance narrative. It provides answers to both the general question of how to explain change in policy networks and the more specific question of how to think about recent changes in the state.

Explaining change. Critics such as Keith Dowding complain that the concept of a policy network is a metaphor, not an explanatory theory, and as a result cannot explain change in networks.[30] Policy network analysis stresses how networks limit participation, decide what issues will appear on policy agendas, shape the behavior of actors, and privilege certain interests. In all these respects, policy network analysis emphasizes stability and continuity. Even when studies of policy networks examine change, they typically appeal to exogenous social factors.[31] They suggest that change is independent of the policy network and the actors in it. They ignore the ability of situated agents in networks to shape and construct their world, choosing how to respond to all kinds of circumstances.

Decentered theory places situated agency at the heart of network governance. It focuses on the diverse practices of governance—practices that are composed of multiple individuals acting on changing webs of beliefs rooted in overlapping traditions. These beliefs and actions change as people respond to dilemmas such as those between their inherited traditions and their experiences of the world. Thus, as we have seen, patterns of governance arise out of diverse actions and political struggles informed by the beliefs of agents as these arise in the context of traditions and dilemmas. Clearly there can be no suggestion that decentered theory neglects either the role of ideas or the games people play. Change in networks arises because people change their patterns of action in response to various dilemmas.

Changing governance. Some versions of the governance narrative suggest that the new governance has hollowed out the state. The concept of a hollow state evokes a decline in the power of the state. The state is often thought of as a sovereign authority over a geographical area; it has the power to accomplish much of its agenda. Yet, much of the governance literature suggests that the authority and power of the state have waned: the state has become increasingly fragmented and is less able to impose its will upon its territory. Several processes have contributed to the hollowing out of the state. Some of the state's functions have moved

---

[30] Dowding, "Model or Metaphor?" Also see J. Richardson, "Government, Interest Groups, and Policy Change," *Political Studies* 48 (2000): 1006–25.

[31] E.g., D. Marsh and R. Rhodes, eds., *Policy Networks in British Government* (Oxford: Clarendon Press, 1992).

up to international and regional organizations such as the EU. While nation states remain important institutions, the growth of regional blocs,
international law, and economic globalization combine to limit their autonomy. Some of the state's functions have moved down to local levels
of government and special-purpose bodies. Devolution moves control of
activities away from the center. Finally, some of the state's functions have
moved out as a result of the increased use of markets and networks to
deliver public services. Even when the state retains a dominant role in
networks, it still must enter negotiated relationships with organizations
in civil society if it is effectively to implement policies.

The concept of the hollow state has met with several criticisms. It has
been argued that because the state voluntarily gave up functions, they do
not count as losses. But one might reply that the concept seeks to describe
the effects of actions irrespective of the motives for them. It has also
been suggested that the state remains powerful since it retains regulatory
control over many of the functions it appears to have lost. This criticism
raises further questions about the new governance. How many of the
lost functions are covered by regulatory bodies? Is the state able to steer
regulatory bodies effectively? Have regulatory bodies been "captured" by
those they are supposed to oversee?

Decentered theory provides a fruitful way of tackling these and related
questions. It rethinks the differentiated polity as an abstract account of
all patterns of rule, and in doing so it opens the way to a more nuanced
account of recent changes in the state. If the features of the state that are
supposed to have arisen as a kind of hollowing out are more or less ubiquitous features of all patterns of rule, surely we should be thinking of a
transformation rather than a weakening of the state. The transformation
associated with the new governance is, in other words, less a hollowing
out of the state than a complex and variegated shift in a pattern of rule.
When new techniques of governance have arisen, they have generally
mingled and competed with the persistence of older techniques.[32] When
the state has sought to withdraw and leave the field to other actors, these
other actors still typically operate in "the shadow" of the state since, for
example, it still does much to define the context in which they negotiate
with one another.[33] Typically, then, even when there has been a change
in the role of the state, this change is one we might characterize less as a
hollowing out and more as a shift in its activity from something like gov-

[32] Compare A. Jordan, R. Wurzel, and A. Zito, "The Rise of 'New' Policy Instruments
in Comparative Perspective: Has Governance Eclipsed Government?," *Political Studies* 53
(2005): 477–96.
[33] Compare F. Scharpf, "Games Real Actors Could Play: Positive and Negative Coordination in Embedded Negotiations," *Journal of Theoretical Politics* 6 (1994): esp. 38.

ernance to something more like metagovernance. The state increasingly concentrates its activity on the broader settings and institutional mechanisms necessary to the formulation and implementation of public policy. Finally, the concept of metagovernance provides just one way of making sense of the idea that the new governance might increase state control over parts of civil society.[34] In some settings, the rise of metagovernance and regulation might constitute a more effective, and certainly more extensive, pattern of control than that which it has replaced.

CONCLUSION

I have tried, like others before me, to shift attention from older concepts of government to newer ones of governance. The term "governance" contrasts with the persistence of concepts of the state as largely monolithic with a strong center that dictates policy. The term "governance" stands in contrast, in particular, to the persistence of the Westminster model of a unitary state with a strong executive.

In correcting dominant images, there exists the danger of appearing to lean too far in the opposite direction. I do not mean to deny that the state can act decisively: obviously the center coordinates and implements policies as it intends some of the time. Nor do I mean to deny the existence in Britain of conventions such as those of cabinet government and parliamentary sovereignty. What I mean to challenge is the long, lingering persistence of concepts of the state as a monolithic, commanding actor. In the case of Britain, I mean to challenge the suggestion that the conventions of cabinet government and parliamentary sovereignty provide an adequate guide to the ways in which public policies are actually formulated and implemented.

The new theories and worlds of governance are of course not especially novel in the challenge they pose to concepts of a unified and commanding state, or, for that matter, to the Westminster model. To the contrary, such challenges date back at least to pluralist ideas of the early and mid-twentieth century. Yet, the concept of the state as monolithic and commanding is constantly brought back into political analysis, if only to enable political scientists to continue to posit different types of state as simplistic variables in their correlations. To some extent, therefore, the

---

[34] Compare J. Newman, "Introduction," in J. Newman, ed., *Remaking Governance* (Bristol: Policy Press, 2005), 1–15; J. Pierre and J. Peters, *Governance, Politics, and the State* (Basingstoke: Macmillan, 2000), esp. chap. 5; and A. Taylor, "Hollowing Out or Filling In? Task Forces and the Management of Cross-cutting Issues in British Government," *British Journal of Politics and International Relations* 2 (2000): 46–71.

new theories and worlds of governance are part of the long, drawn-out twentieth-century struggle against statist theories. Studies of governance stand opposed to the attempts by some historical institutionalists to bring back a largely formal concept of the state. They revisit the more fragmented accounts of the state associated with pluralism, corporatism, and oligopoly.

In revisiting fragmented accounts of the state, the new theories and worlds of governance pose dilemmas for the theory and practice of democracy. How can citizens hold a fragmented state accountable? How can citizens participate in a fragmented state so as to direct policy? How can those fragments of the state that are democratic oversee and direct those that are less open to citizen participation? These and related questions have been posed not only by social scientists but also by governments and international organizations themselves. The next chapter will explore the answers associated with the leading theories of governance. Later chapters examine how governments have drawn on some of these theories to devise constitutional and administrative reforms aimed at enhancing the democratic credentials of the new governance.

PART II

Constitutionalism

CHAPTER FIVE

Democratic Governance

As THE NEW GOVERNANCE emerged from the new theories by which people made sense of problems confronting the state, it began to pose questions of accountability and democracy. Neoliberals argue that "good governance" depends on marketization to promote efficiency and combat corruption. In addition, they sometimes extend the definition of "good governance" to include various democratic principles and practices, thereby raising the question of what content to give democracy. Some neoliberals remain unreflectively wedded to a loosely conceived concept of representative democracy. Others draw on rational choice theory to rethink democracy itself. They often suggest that principles such as freedom and choice are served better by market mechanisms than by voting. Sometimes they even suggest that undemocratic, nonmajoritarian institutions are the only way to prevent rational individuals acting in ways that have collectively irrational consequences. The first wave of reforms thus attempted to roll back the state by means of contracting out and even privatization.

Whatever content neoliberals give to democracy, they generally argue that the new public management is an example of "good governance." In contrast, their critics highlight a tension between NPM and democratic ideals. In the critics' view, when the state contracts out services, it loses the ability to oversee and control public sector activities, which confuses lines of accountability.

The second wave of reforms also appears to have been driven primarily by ideas of promoting efficiency. Its advocates did not disavow marketization, but they did put a greater emphasis on networks, partnerships, and joined-up governance. Once again, however, some critics argue that the reforms undermine democracy. In their view, the reforms are creating a system of governance that is too complex for proper, meaningful accountability. Concerns about "democratic deficits" are widespread. Even policy actors whose main concern is efficiency are troubled by thoughts that falling rates of participation and civic engagement point to a decline in legitimacy that ultimately will undermine the effectiveness of public policy.

Representative democracy has historically been associated with elected officials making policies, which public servants then implement. Public servants are answerable to the elected politicians who, in turn, are accountable to the voting public. However, the new theories and worlds of governance question and disrupt these lines of accountability. In the new governance, policies are being implemented and even created by private sector and voluntary sector actors. There are often few lines of accountability tying these actors back to elected officials, and those few are too long to be effective. In addition, the complex webs of actors involved can make it almost impossible for the principle to hold any one agent responsible for a particular policy. Similar problems arise for democracy at the international level. States have created regulatory institutions to oversee areas of domestic policy, and the officials from these institutions meet more and more often to set up international norms, agreements, and policies governing domains such as the economy and the environment.

There is no consensus on how to reconcile representative democracy with the new governance. To some extent the different proposals reflect the different theories of governance. Rational choice theorists sometimes suggest that markets are just as effective as democratic institutions at ensuring popular control over outcomes. Institutionalists are more likely to concern themselves with the formal and informal lines of accountability needed to sustain representative and responsible government. These institutional issues merge gradually into a larger concern to promote diverse forums for dialogue—a concern that is even more characteristic of interpretive theorists.

Before turning to these democratic issues, this chapter begins by examining "good governance." The concept of good governance arose as international agencies added political conditions to their lending criteria on the grounds that the effectiveness of aid varied according to the governance structures of recipient states. Good governance was from the start associated with liberal institutions and values, including the rule of law, an independent judiciary, checks on executive power, proper accountability, and sometimes pluralism, human rights, and a robust civil society. Several international agencies also tied good governance explicitly to NPM—the increased use of markets, competition, and entrepreneurial management in the public sector.

While the concept of good governance includes democratic concerns, it is still used mainly in the context of aid to developing states. Similar concerns (civic capacity, legitimacy, accountability) appear in discussions of developed states, but the overarching vocabulary there is one of governance and democracy. I am intentionally locating discussion of good governance alongside that of democracy in developed states in order to challenge the implicit idea that the problems of establishing good governance are specific to developing states.

GOOD GOVERNANCE

Concerns about democratic governance first arose in discussions of economic development.[1] Economists came to believe that the effectiveness of market reforms depends on the existence of appropriate political institutions. In some ways, then, the quality of governance initially became a hot topic not because of normative, democratic concerns but because it impinged on economic efficiency, notably the effectiveness of aid to developing countries. International agencies such as the International Monetary Fund and the World Bank increasingly made good governance one of the criteria on which they based aid and loans. Other donors followed suit.

The concept of good governance was thus defined in terms of institutional barriers to corruption and the requirements of a functioning market economy. Good governance required a legitimate state with a democratic mandate, an efficient and open administration, and competitive markets in the public and private sectors. Various international agencies specify the characteristics of good governance so conceived. They want checks on executive power such as an effective legislature with territorial (and perhaps ethno-cultural) representation. Likewise, they stress the rule of law, with an independent judiciary, laws based on impartiality and equity, and an honest police. They require a competent public service characterized by clear lines of accountability and by transparent and responsive decision making. They want the state to promote consensus, mediating among the various interests in societies. And they emphasize the importance of a strong civil society characterized by freedom of association, freedom of speech, and respect for civil and political rights. Some international organizations, such as the World Bank, also associate good governance with the new public management; they encourage developing states to reform their public sectors by privatizing state-owned enterprises, promoting competitive markets, reducing staffing, strengthening budgetary discipline, and making use of nongovernmental organizations. Other international organizations, such as the United Nations,

---

[1] For a brief history, see M. Doombos, "'Good Governance': The Rise and Decline of a Policy Metaphor," *Journal of Development Studies* 37 (2001): 93–108.

place greater emphasis on social goals, such as inclusiveness, justice, and environmental protection.

The vague content of good governance fuels debates about its definition and utility. One way of approaching these debates is to distinguish between dominant policy discourses and critical perspectives on them. The dominant policy discourses are intended to guide donors in their aid policies and thereby prompt reform in states that receive aid. These policy discourses pay less attention to normative democratic concerns than they do to the relations between the state and the market, and especially the kinds of institutional arrangements that determine the effectiveness of economic aid to developing countries. They typically draw on neo-classical economics, neoliberalism, and rational choice theory. Critical perspectives on these policy discourses often appeal to broader accounts of the ways in which power and authority structure different contexts. They focus in particular on the different relations the state has with civil society. These critical perspectives loosely map onto the more abstract theories of coordination and power offered by institutionalists, Marxists, and interpretivists.

Policy Discourses

Many definitions of good governance, such as that of the World Bank, clearly arose against the background of a liberal faith in representative democracy and a free market economy.[2] To some, good governance simply means democratic and competitive elections and the lines of accountability that are thus established. To others, it involves pluralism, respect for human rights, the rule of law, and market principles. The World Bank itself initially used the concept to refer narrowly to institutional and managerial issues of public sector reform. The bank's own Articles of Agreement technically forbid it to consider noneconomic issues when making lending decisions: it is meant to promote sound economic policy and development irrespective of political considerations. Yet the bank's concern with good governance exhibits a trend away from institutional and managerial issues toward more political concerns of legitimacy, participation, a free press, and human rights. In the bank's 1989 report, *Sub-Saharan Africa: From Crisis to Sustainable Growth*, a "crisis of governance" was identified as a key barrier to economic development.[3]

---

[2] D. Williams and T. Young, "Governance, the World Bank, and Liberal Theory," *Political Studies* 42 (1994): 84–100.

[3] World Bank, *Sub-Saharan Africa: From Crisis to Sustainable Growth* (Washington, DC: World Bank, 1989).

The World Bank has come to use the term good governance to cover concerns with technical areas and civil society. The technical concerns include legal frameworks for development (consistent laws, an independent judiciary, and the place in codified law of concepts such as fairness, justice, and liberty) and also capacity building (better policy analysis, stricter budgetary discipline, and public service reforms). The concerns with civil society include legitimacy, transparency, accountability, and participation, all of which are seen as ways of strengthening civil society in order to reduce the power of the state, attack corruption, and ensure the efficient allocation of public resources. The same ends also inform the bank's concern with promoting competition, strong local government, and decentralized administration. In short, although the World Bank does not actually promote liberal democracy outright, it advocates liberal values as the way to efficiency. The World Bank promotes an efficient liberal economy based on free markets through both a liberal state enforcing property rights and contractual obligations and a liberal civil society sustaining and restraining such a state.

Critical Perspectives

Challenges to the policy discourse of good governance typically concentrate on one or more of the following: its vagueness, its neoliberal bias, or its ethnocentrism.

Vagueness. Some critics complain that good governance is too vague a concept to have policy relevance. Merilee Grindle argues, for example, that the good governance agenda has become too long and ill-defined.[4] She complains that the policy discourse on good governance has created a growing list of expectations with little guidance on which recommendations are essential and which are not, which should come first and which should come later, what can be achieved in the short term and what can be achieved only in the long term, and what is feasible and what is not.

Critics of the vagueness of the policy discourse often want to shift the emphasis from a list of conditions for aid to more specific guidelines. They want policy actors to answer questions about the relative importance, temporal ordering, and feasibility of the different recommendations. They want policy actors to address the trade-offs between different goals, to assess the relative importance of various goals, to concentrate on what actually works, and to develop plans specifically for different states.

[4] M. Grindle, "Good Enough Governance: Poverty Reduction and Reform in Developing Countries," *Governance* 17 (2004): 525–48.

Grindle argues that if policy actors began to specify the most important components of good governance, they might develop a more workable agenda. They might shift from a concern with good governance to one with "good enough governance." Good enough governance would focus on a few key priorities and minimally acceptable levels of state performance.

Neoliberal bias. Other critics complain that concepts of good governance entail a bias toward markets.[5] Good governance can be explicitly associated with the promotion of market reforms in the public sector of developing states. More subtly, the content of good governance may embody a concern to promote societies in which the market economy dominates. Institutions like the World Bank explicitly tie the political reforms they associate with good governance to the preconditions for a successful market economy. Yet, the critics argue, an overwhelming commitment to the market economy is just one viable economic theory—one that could be challenged from a Keynesian perspective let alone nationalist economics or state planning. Good governance appears, in this view, to be tainted by its unjustified, or at least highly contentious, dependence on the particular economic theories that became dominant in the Western world—or, more specifically still, the Anglophone world—of the 1980s.

Ethnocentrism. Yet other critics argue that good governance is an ethnocentric concept. These critics complain that the conditions of good governance are assumed to have universal value or appeal whereas they actually rely on the particular Western social and cultural perspective of aid donors. In this view, the global spread of particular standards and practices of good governance is not a result of their intrinsic universality; it is a reflection of the ability of aid donors to push their preferred agenda on to aid recipients. Critics such as Martin Doornbos suggest that ethnocentrism haunts any system that allows donors to specify either conditions for aid or criteria for selecting aid partners.[6] In this view, conditionality and selectivity are always more likely to foster rationalizations of the desires of donor countries than genuine attempts to build responsible democracies in the developing world. Doornbos's own al-

[5] E.g., M. Lombardi and S. Sahota, "International Financial Institutions and the Politics of Structural Adjustment: The African Experience," in S. Nagel, ed., *Handbook of Global Economic Policy* (New York: Marcel Dekker, 2000), 65–92.

[6] Doombos, "'Good Governance.'" Also see Williams and Young, "Governance, the World Bank, and Liberal Theory."

ternative is to reverse the standard situation in which donors develop programs, preferences, and priorities to which recipients then have to try to conform. He proposes that donors think and act less as if they were "in command" and more as if they were "on demand." The "demanding" countries would develop their own programs for reconstruction, and the "supplying" countries then would donate whatever they believed constituted a reasonable contribution to those programs.

PUBLIC SERVICE

Good governance has developed from a concept primarily concerned with management in the public sector to one that addresses concerns about civil society and democratic procedures. A similar trajectory appears in debates in the developed world about the relationship of the new governance to democratic values. These debates arguably began with neoliberal and rational choice critiques of the very concept of public interest. Yet, before long, there arose entirely different worries about NPM undermining the ethics of the public sector. Perhaps the first wave of reform had created a more efficient, market-driven, and entrepreneurial state, or perhaps it had not. Either way, critics of NPM began to worry that the ethics of the private sector and the marketplace might not always be so well suited to the public sector. They argued that the purpose of the public sector is not only to work as effectively and cheaply as possible, but also to embody and promote our social values. Should the quest for profits override impartiality? Were the invigorating effects of civic entrepreneurs worth the loss of strict oversight and clear lines of accountability?

The first wave of public sector reform promoted competition among public agencies and private firms in the context of rules and regulations laid down by the government. The underlying theory derived from economic theories of the market. Proponents of the reforms claimed, more particularly, that marketization empowers customers to make choices while compelling service providers to be more responsive to these choices. In addition, the first wave of reforms promoted the values and techniques of business administration. The underlying theory derived from neoliberalism and rational choice theory. Because rational choice theorists attempt to reduce action to self-interest, they often leave relatively little theoretical space for ideas such as public spirit and public service. The neoliberal theories supporting these reforms replaced the concept of a citizen with that of a consumer. The reforms were supposed to craft a more customer-driven public sector. Agencies were to become more responsive to the short-term interests of the customers of public services.

Marketization and NPM appear to assume, as do many neoliberals, that the public interest is equivalent to an aggregation of individual self-interests formulated privately outside of participation in a civic discourse. Critics of the reforms often argue that this underlying assumption, and so the reforms themselves, represents a denial of citizenship. In their view, the reduction of the public interest to a mere aggregation of individual interests leaves no theoretical space for the public and social nature of our common life. It neglects democratic values, public spirit, and civic discourse. These critics, such as Linda DeLeon and Robert Denhardt, conceive of the public interest as a product of social interaction.[7] It is, they tell us, through participation, cooperation, and democratic debate that citizens enlarge their perspective, thereby reaching a better understanding of the common good. Social interactions lead to a genuine public interest that is more than the sum of our prior individual interests.

If we agree that the first wave of reforms undermines citizenship and civic participation, we might wonder whether the public sector actually remains properly public. Critics such as Shamsul Haque believe that the first wave of reforms diminished the "publicness" of public services.[8] In this view, the reforms eroded the public–private distinction, lessened the role of the public sector, narrowed the composition of recipients, damaged lines of accountability, and undermined trust in government. Haque argues that this erosion of "publicness" has far-reaching implications for public service. In his view, the spread of commercial values and business practices threatens public service ideals such as equality, public interest, human dignity, and social justice; it also threatens an ideal of accountability in which public scrutiny of public services occurs by way of democratic practices such as parliamentary debates, legislative committees, and administrative tribunals. Indeed Haque worries that NPM and marketization embody a profound distrust of public service, and, worse still, that this distrust spills over into the general population. Haque is careful to explain the nature of this worry. On one hand, public distrust of state institutions is an important part of democratic governance: it is right that citizens scrutinize the state, express dissent, and act to promote change. On the other, the spilling out of neoliberal ideas leads not only to a distrust of the state but also to a decline in the public's belief in the importance and effectiveness of their even engaging in such scrutiny, dis-

---

[7] L. DeLeon and R. Denhardt, "The Political Theory of Reinvention," *Public Administration Review* 60 (2000): 89–97.

[8] M. Haque, "The Diminishing Publicness of Public Service under the Current Mode of Governance," *Public Administration Review* 61 (2001): 65–82.

TABLE 5.1
The New Public Service

	Bureaucracy	NPM	NPS
Theoretical basis	Old institutionalism	Neoclassical economics	Sociological institutionalism and democratic theory
Public interest	Defined politically and expressed in law	Aggregation of individual preferences	Product of dialogues in networks
Citizens	Constituents (electoral citizens)	Consumers	Citizens (in policy networks)
Role of the state	Rowing	Steering	Facilitating
Organizational structure	Bureaucracy with top-down authority	Small core contracting out tasks to independent bodies	Collaborative links between public and private bodies
Mechanisms	Administration and law	Markets and incentive structures	Diplomatic negotiation
Discretion	Limited: administrative rules	High: managers are free to manage to meet entrepreneurial goals	Moderate: flexibility within networks
Accountability	Hierarchical	Market-driven	Multifaceted

sent, and action. Hence there is a decline not only in the "publicness" of public service but also the democratic activity of the population.

Worries about the effects of the first wave of reforms led to various attempts to revitalize an ethic of public service. Calls for a new public service typically advocate a shift from market relations between public officials and citizens to collaborative ones in networks. So, for example, table 5.1 adapts the Denhardts' summary of their account of a new public service.[9]

The call for a new public service often relies on defending notions of citizenship that stand in contrast to more market-based identities such as clients or consumers. For example, Eran Vigoda distinguishes between responsiveness to citizens as clients and collaboration with citizens as partners.[10] He argues that NPM tries to solve problems in governance by promoting responsiveness to clients. Proponents of NPM want to improve the delivery of public services by making them more responsive to the desires of citizens conceived as consumers. Yet, Vigoda continues, when

[9] R. Denhardt and J. Denhardt, "The New Public Service: Serving Rather than Steering," *Public Administration Review* 60 (2000): 554.

[10] E. Vigoda, "From Responsiveness to Collaboration: Governance, Citizens, and the Next Generation of Public Administration," *Public Administration Review* 62 (2002): 527–40.

responsiveness is defined in relation to consumers, it stands in opposition to collaborative work with citizens. An overemphasis on responsiveness leads to neglect of the possibility of active participation by citizens in the processes of governance.

According to Vigoda, the bureaucratic welfare state was neither responsive nor collaborative: it concentrated power in public agencies, it insulated the public sector from interactions with the public, and it preserved state power, especially the control of the state over decisions and resources. The first wave of public sector reforms attempted to break up this centralized bureaucracy in order to promote responsiveness. But reforms such as marketization and NPM neglect the significance of collaboration and, as a result, make citizens ever more cynical about the state. Vigoda concludes, therefore, that we need to move from an excessive emphasis on responsiveness to greater recognition of the importance of collaboration. In short, he argues for something very like the second wave of public sector reforms. As they often do, themes from communitarianism, institutionalism, and interactionism lurk behind calls for partnership and collaboration as possible routes to increased legitimacy and increased effectiveness.

REPRESENTATIVE GOVERNMENT

It is perhaps ironic that international agencies and Western donors began to emphasize good governance just as the proliferation of markets and networks posed questions about their own democratic credentials. The new governance sits oddly beside the ideal of representative and responsible government in accord with the will of the majority. It involves private and voluntary sector actors in policy processes even though these actors are rarely democratically accountable in as straightforward a way as are public officials.

Whether or not the first wave of reforms lead to more efficient and responsive public services, they certainly pose problems of transparency and legitimacy. Private sector actors are not democratically elected. Typically they are not directly accountable to elected representatives. Thus, an increase in their role in the public sector raises questions of accountability. There are many responses to the tension between governance and democracy, varying from the suggestion that we might benefit from less democracy, through proposals to make networks and markets more accountable to elected officials, and on to calls for a radical transformation of democratic practices. Again, some social scientists have sought to justify the democratic deficits associated with the rise of unelected actors, others have tried to rethink the concept of accountability so that it might fit better with the realities of the new governance, and yet others have at-

TABLE 5.2
Rethinking Democracy

	Rational choice	*Institutionalism*
Basis of democracy	Representation	Representation
Common good	Aggregate of individual interests	New public service
Citizenship	Consumerist	Communitarian
Rethinking democracy	Nonmajoritarian institutions	Social inclusion
Rethinking accountability	Performance accountability	Horizontal or network accountability
Examples		
1. Public sector	1. Hood	1. Denhardt and Denhardt
2. Democracy	2. Majone	2. Putnam

tempted to imagine new institutional patterns that might make the new governance fit better with older concepts of accountability and democracy. Table 5.2 provides a schematic overview of some of the democratic ideas associated with the new theories of governance.

Nonmajoritarian Theories

The suggestion that we might benefit from less democracy generally comes from rational choice theorists. Their argument contrasts democracy, which allows citizens to express their preference by voting only once every few years and only by a simple "yes" or "no" for a whole slate of policies, with the market, which allows consumers to express their preferences continuously, across a range of intensities, and for individual items. In addition, rational choice theorists worry that democracy entails certain political transaction costs that lead to incessant increases in public expenditure. They argue, for example, that the cost of many items of expenditure are thinly distributed across a large population, so individual voters have little reason to oppose them; but the benefits are often concentrated in a small proportion of the population that thus clamors for the increased expenditure. Thus, rational choice theorists such as Giandomenico Majone advocate nonmajoritarian institutions as ways of protecting crucial policy areas, such as banking and budgeting, from democracy.[11]

---

[11] G. Majone, "Nonmajoritarian Institutions and the Limits of Democratic Governance: A Political Transaction-Cost Approach," *Journal of Institutional and Theoretical Economics* 157 (2001): 57–78.

It is perhaps worth saying explicitly that "nonmajoritarian" is little more than a euphemism for "undemocratic." There are concepts of democracy that place relatively little emphasis on majority decision making; for example, the radical democratic theories discussed later often place greater emphasis on participation and dialogue even when they grant a considerable role to majority decision making. However, Majone and other neoliberals are not interested in promoting radical democracy but rather want to insulate a range of institutions from democratic processes.

To point out that Majone is arguing against democracy is to clarify, not invalidate, his argument. There are well-known reasons why we might want to protect a range of goods, including human rights, from democratic decision making. Few of us would want a majority of the population to be able to decide that everyone of a particular race should be exterminated. The danger of the word "nonmajoritarian," however, is that it often may hide the fact that the argument being made is actually about restricting democracy.

A positive theory of nonmajoritarian institutions differs from arguments for the constitutional protection of human rights in that it appeals not to moral or political values but to social scientific theories about rationality and efficiency. Majone's argument relies on fairly technical analyses of political transaction costs and a credibility gap associated with a time-inconsistency problem. He uses these analyses to suggest that a delegation of powers to independent nonmajoritarian institutions reduces the political transaction costs that politicians incur because they lack a reliable "technology of commitment."

Majone relies on fairly technical analyses instead of appeals to moral values to create a positive theory. Positive theories purport to be scientific, empirical theories, and their advocates often define them in contrast to normative, ethical ones. He wants to explain why nonmajoritarian institutions arise, not to argue that they are good. However, like many rational choice theorists, he believes that we can explain social phenomena by modeling them on assumptions about human rationality, and in this case his claim that nonmajoritarian institutions are rational comes so close to the claim that society would do well to adopt them at least under appropriate circumstances that the distinction between positive and normative theories becomes a very fine one indeed—so fine, it disappears.

Just as Majone wants to show how nonmajoritarian institutions can be explained on assumptions of rationality, so he briefly offers a positive rational-choice theory of democracy or majority decision making.[12] In

---

[12] There are, of course, various positive (rational choice) theories of democracy. Majone's seems rather beside the point in that it shows why and when democracy is rational if it exists. Surely, even from a rational choice perspective, the trick is to show why and when

his view, majority rule is a rational strategy of decision making because unanimity is simply impossible to reach. Yet, if the costs become too high, the rationality of majoritarianism ceases to apply, and nonmajoritarian institutions become rational. The fairly technical parts of Majone's argument are those that define the relevant costs and the circumstances under which they are manifest. One relevant cost (a political transaction cost) is attached to the political processes of reaching an agreement and then enforcing it. Another cost (the time-inconsistency problem) arises because elected politicians lack credibility when they try to commit themselves to long-term objectives—they lack credibility because their interests are bound up with short-term concerns such as winning the next election. According to Majone, the creation and maintenance of nonmajoritarian institutions is a rational response to political transaction costs and the time-inconsistency problem. Politicians (or political principals) defer control over certain policy areas—most importantly central banking—to nonmajoritarian institutions (or agents) to avoid transaction costs and lend credibility to their long-term commitments.

It might be argued against Majone that to show that nonmajoritarian institutions are rational is not to prove their legitimacy, let alone accountability. Majone responds to this argument by challenging assumed concepts of legitimacy. He defends a fiduciary principle according to which specific policy competences or even elements of national sovereignty can be legitimately transferred to independent institutions that depend on the confidence of the public for their legitimacy. In this view, nonmajoritarian institutions have a kind of substantive legitimacy because of the results they achieve and the resulting confidence the public places in them. Their accountability thus consists in their being at least tacitly responsible for the results they achieve.

Accountable Institutions

Many institutionalists are uncomfortable with the growth of nonmajoritarian, undemocratic government. Often they associate the growing role of such organizations with growing public distrust of politics and especially the state.[13] Institutionalists have responded to the democratic issues raised by the new worlds of governance by trying to rethink the nature of democratic legitimacy. Historically politicians and public officials were

---

it can be rational for people to create democracy; that is, (1) why and when rational citizens will overthrow authoritarian states to establish democracy, and (2) why and when rational elites will let go their grip on power by introducing democracy. For one recent attempt to get at the latter issue, see D. Acemoglu and J. Robinson, *Economic Origins of Dictatorship and Democracy* (New York: Cambridge University Press, 2005).

[13] See Haque, "Diminishing"; Vigoda, "Responsiveness."

held responsible for the way they did things as well as the results they achieved—for means as well as ends. The concept of legitimacy privileged representation and accountability, with the actions of unelected agents being controlled, evaluated, and sanctioned by elected officials who, in turn, are answerable to citizens at the polling booth. Today many institutionalists propose expanding this concept of democratic legitimacy to emphasize a responsiveness associated with efficacy, legal accountability, or social inclusion. They suggest the following:

- That we link the legitimacy of organizations and their decisions to *effectiveness* in providing public goods.[14]
- That we ascribe legitimacy to organizations that are created and regulated by democratic states no matter how long and obscure the lines of delegation.[15] In this view, democratic legitimacy persists whenever elected assemblies set up independent organizations in accord with rules that are enforced by independent bodies such as the courts. Legitimacy persists because the independent organizations are *legally accountable*, and because a democratic government passed the relevant laws.
- That the legitimacy of institutions and decisions might rest on their being fair and *inclusive*.[16] Proponents of this view often emphasize the importance of a strong civil society in securing a form of accountability based on public scrutiny. Voluntary groups, the media, and active citizens monitor institutions and decisions to ensure that they are fair and inclusive and so to give or deny organizations the credibility required to participate effectively in policymaking processes.

[14] Performance accountability arose in part as a quest for public sector alternatives to profitability. In the United States, it resulted in the Governance Performance and Accountability Act (1994). Similar ideas and practices are, of course, widespread. There is still, however, much debate about the nature and even the possibility of suitable measures of performance. See, for contrasting perspectives, P. Kettner and L. Martin, "Performance, Accountability, and the Purchase of Service Contracting," *Administration in Social Work* 17 (1993): 61–79; and M. Dubnick, "Accountability and the Promise of Performance: In Search of the Mechanisms," *Public Performance and Management Review* 28 (2005): 376–417.

[15] I will consider examples referring to states and regional organizations below, but it is worth noting that the logic of the argument also applies to global networks and organizations. See Slaughter, *A New World Order*; and A. Moravcsik, "Is There a 'Democratic Deficit' in World Politics? A Framework for Analysis," *Government and Opposition* 39 (2004): 336–63.

[16] Even this idea is now beginning to appear in the policy discourse of international institutions such as the World Bank. See World Bank, *Social Accountability in the Public Sector: A Conceptual Discussion and Learning Module* (Washington, DC: World Bank, 2005).

Clearly the amorphous nature of institutionalism reappears in these diverse ways of rethinking legitimacy. In particular, rational choice institutionalists often emphasize effective performance in a way that resembles other rational choice arguments in favor of nonmajoritarian institutions—and as such I will not go over the material again here. Instead I will look first at institutionalist attempts to redefine legal accountability with reference to the example of the European Union, and second, in a later section, at institutionalist accounts of legitimacy that rely on social inclusion.

When institutionalists emphasize new patterns of legal accountability and inclusion, they characteristically rethink accountability to fit the horizontal relationships that abound in networks. Mark Considine argues, for example, that we need to retain a concern with responsiveness but alter the way in which we think about how to provide it.[17] Accountability involves a legal obligation to be responsive to the voices and interests of those affected by public policies. Such responsiveness depends on those affected having information relevant to evaluating the policies. Thus, the relevant information—such as the expenditure of public funds or the exercise of public authority—must be given to legislators and the public. Likewise, responsiveness depends on those affected having the power to compel public servants to act appropriately. Thus, legislators (and so the citizens who elect them) have to be able to compel public officials to comply.

Institutionalists such as Considine believe that the new governance requires new ways of securing the conditions of responsiveness. Historically, the dominant lines of authority and accountability were vertical ones. Yet, marketization and NPM more or less deliberately undermined these historic lines of accountability as part of a quest for a more efficient public sector. Considine argues here that the first wave of public sector reform left public officials confronting the tension between remaining in the old bureaucratic lines of accountability and moving outside of them in order to forge collaborative and contractual relationships with voluntary and private sector actors. The rise of contracting out and partnerships made it increasingly difficult to hold service providers accountable. For institutionalists such as Considine, the moral of the story appears to be less a need to rethink contracting out than to rethink our historic concept of accountability to fit the new worlds of governance. Older one-dimensional forms of accountability, with their emphasis on following rules and being honest with superiors, are no longer appropriate. Instead institutionalists advocate a greater emphasis on navigational competence,

[17] M. Considine, "The End of the Line? Accountable Governance in the Age of Networks, Partnerships, and Joined-up Services," *Governance* 15 (2002): 21–40.

that is, the proper use of authority ranging freely across the multidimensional terrain of the new governance.

The institutionalist attempt to develop a horizontal concept of accountability also informs more overtly legal studies. Lawyers too examine tensions between old patterns of accountability and the new relationships of contracting out and partnership. For example, Martha Minow tries to allow for the benefits she associates with the new governance—notably flexibility and efficiency—while responding to the threat that it may erode our access to information about services, our capacity to review agencies, and our ability to control them.[18] She too fears that the rise of private actors as deliverers of public services may undermine the legitimacy of state action, and that the greater role played by private interests and financial profit may undermine trust in the state.

For Minow, the problem is to combine the flexibility and efficiency of the new governance with appropriate public standards and governmental oversight. Excessively rigid laws and regulations may lead the new private service providers to act like state organizations, thereby undermining the gains they bring in innovation and efficiency. Equally, however, ineffective legal standards and scrutiny may lead to excessive profiteering and eventually a decline in trust of the state. Minow argues that the solution lies in a new framework that respects public values, places people (not results) at its center, and remains publicly open about the source of its norms, its authority, and powers of enforcement. She hopes such a framework will enable the state to retain the option to exit relationships with private actors, the ability to voice disagreement with private actors and their actions, and the capacity to remain in partnership with a private actor so as to give it a vote of confidence.

DEBATING THE EUROPEAN UNION

Concerns about the accountability of private actors in the new governance often overlap with broader debates about the democratic deficits associated with certain types of governmental structures. The European Union figures especially prominently in these broader debates. It is an example of a governmental structure in which there is a vast array of committees and officials who are at best only very indirectly accountable to citizens. The officials are barely accountable to the EU parliament. Rather, they are meant to be responsive to the member states. But the member states are treated here as their governments, not their citizens.

[18] M. Minow, "Public and Private Partnerships: Accounting for the New Religion," *Harvard Law Review* 116 (2003): 1229–70.

Thus, EU officials are largely insulated from the citizens of the member states. The resulting debate over the democratic legitimacy of the EU pits procedural accountability against new concepts of legitimacy that place more emphasis on performance. Let us look briefly at an illustrative example of each side in the debate.

Christopher Lord and David Beetham want to hold the EU to historic concepts of accountability and legitimacy. They argue that the EU should meet the same criteria of legitimacy required of liberal democratic states.[19] They reject arguments about the special character of the EU as a nonstate actor. In particular, they challenge the idea that the EU can acquire legitimacy through a kind of postparliamentary politics. Until the 1990s commentators suggested that the EU derived its legitimacy indirectly by way of its member states; they deferred concerns about the EU itself until its institutions had gained experience and proved their ability. Yet, Lord and Beetham argue, the stakes have now changed. Today the EU is more or less on a par with states in terms of the kinds of decisions it makes and the authority with which it does so. Thus, the EU should be held to the same standards of legitimacy as are liberal democratic states. Lord and Beetham specify three dimensions of legitimacy for liberal democratic states: performance, democracy, and identity. Performance (or results) consists of the state meeting the needs and values of its citizens. Democracy consists of the exercise of public control based on political equality. The sense of a shared identity among a state's citizens explains citizens' loyalty and obedience. This shared identity is the most important of the three criteria since its absence would cast doubt on the legitimacy of the state no matter how well the state managed the other two criteria. Lord and Beetham suggest that the EU must itself now meet these three criteria of legitimacy. They conclude that it performs efficiently but needs to do much more both to democratize its institutions and to promote a common identity among its citizens.

Andrew Moravcsik assesses the legitimacy of the EU in a manner that places greater emphasis on performance.[20] He holds the EU to criteria of legitimacy that apply to liberal democratic states, but his criteria of legitimacy differ from those of Lord and Beetham. Moravcsik argues against judging the EU by our ideal democratic standards. For him, the important question is not whether or not the EU is the kind of democratic state we want; it is, rather, whether the EU is more or less as democratic as other states we are happy to describe as democratic. He dismisses many

---

[19] C. Lord and D. Beetham, "Legitimizing the EU: Is There a 'Post-Parliamentary Basis' for Its Legitimation?," *Journal of Common Market Studies* 39 (2001): 443–62.

[20] A. Moravcsik, "In Defence of the 'Democratic Deficit': Reassessing Legitimacy in the European Union," *Journal of Common Market Studies* 40 (2002): 603–24.

democratic issues as misguided in their reliance on "utopian" concepts of democracy. If we replace such utopian concepts with reasonable criteria, he adds, we will conclude that the EU does not have a democratic deficit. For Moravcsik, these realistic criteria derive in part from recognition of the rise of the new governance: we should hold the EU to standards set by states when they delegate powers to nonmajoritarian institutions such as central banks, constitutional courts, regulatory agencies, criminal prosecutors, and insulated executive negotiators. Critics of Moravcsik may note the irony of his appeal to the democratic shortcomings of the new governance to defend similar shortcomings in the EU. Nonetheless, Moravcsik himself insists that when judged by his criteria, the EU is democratically legitimate. EU policymaking is transparent, effective, and responsive to the demands of citizens, and EU actors are held in check by constitutional checks and balances, a separation of powers, fiscal limits, indirect democratic controls, and an increasingly powerful parliament. Moravcsik even challenges the suggestion that the EU should seek to become more democratic. He argues that the division of labor between the EU and its member states is such that the EU specializes in those aspects of governance which, far from requiring more political participation, actually need to be insulated from political pressures for the very reasons scholars like Majone offer in favor of nonmajoritarian institutions.

SOCIAL INCLUSION

Institutionalists typically respond to the legitimacy issues associated with the new governance not only by evoking horizontal patterns of legal accountability but also by expanding concepts of social inclusion. Their appeals to social inclusion are also attempts to address the legitimacy worries that arise from declining rates of political participation. As we have seen, many commentators have explained the trend of citizens withdrawing from politics by reference to public sector reform. Their view is that popular skepticism and dissatisfaction with the state reflects the spillover of neoliberal ideas, the complexity of the new governance, or the appearance of profit motives in the public sector. Today there is evidence of just such a retreat from political engagement: even the percentage of the population who vote has been in decline in many developed states. Perhaps falling rates of participation do reflect problems with the new governance. Perhaps there are other reasons for the decline of civic engagement—larger cultural and social trends, for example. Or perhaps worries about a decline in civic engagement have themselves produced such a decline or at least made processes visible that otherwise would have been of little import. In any case, the concern with declining rates of participation has spread rapidly to politicians and public officials. It now inspires those aspects of the second wave of public sector reforms that seek to build up civic capacity and engage citizens. Several commentators quickly advocated partnerships as a way of involving citizens, voluntary associations, and other actors in democratic processes so as to increase trust and civic capacity. The attempts to boast civic capacity thus brought an inclusive civil society based on social capital and partnerships to the fore of debates about good, democratic governance.

Social Capital

Social capital refers to the features of organizations that are meant to be conducive to coordination and cooperation. It includes networks, voluntary associations, norms, and social trust. Robert Putnam famously argues that the direct engagement of Americans with government has declined steadily and sharply for a generation or more.[21] This decline occurred despite the rising levels of education, where previously the level of an individual's education was often considered the best indicator of his or her level of political activity. For Putnam, the slow demise of a robust civil society explains the decline in public service and political participation. He appeals to empirical evidence to support the claim that networks of civic engagement powerfully influence the quality of public life and the performance of social and political institutions. Communities that foster social connections, political participation, and civic engagement are more likely to sustain positive programs in areas such as education, poverty, unemployment, health, and the prevention of crime and drug abuse. Vibrant social networks also enhance economic development. Putnam's message is clear: increase social capital.

Increasing social capital has become a policy aim of governments such as the EU. The EU White Paper on governance of 2001 expresses the worry that Europeans remain disappointed with and uninterested in European political institutions.[22] Many people are affected by the EU's policies without feeling connected to its institutions. The question thus arises of how to bridge the gap between the transnational institutions and the citizens who are governed by them but feel excluded from them. How can the EU acquire greater democratic legitimacy in the eyes of its citizens? Historically the EU has tried to bridge the gap either by liberal constitutionalism and the granting of rights, or by strengthening the basis of the EU in the constitutions and institutions of its member states.[23] The White

[21] Putnam, *Bowling Alone*.

[22] See Commission of the European Communities, *European Governance: A White Paper* (Brussels: COM, 2001), 428.

[23] Compare W. Wallace and J. Smith, "Democracy or Technocracy? European Integration and the Problem of Popular Consent," *West European Politics* 18 (1995): 137–57.

Paper suggests that the gap might be better bridged through an appropriate civil society.

Institutionalists and governments, including Putnam and the EU, promote a robust civil society as the route to democratic legitimacy. Yet, their critics complain that they actually elide important debates about the nature of a robust civil society. For example, Kenneth Armstrong argues that the EU's vision of civil society actually suffers from the very democratic deficits that afflict its transnational governance.[24] Ironically, the White Paper's vision of a civil society reproduces the very democratic problems that beset the EU and that it tries to address. The White Paper institutionalizes the diversity of voices found among civil society actors, and it embodies an ethnic nationalism that is based on the supposed need for shared values, norms, and history.

Critics of the EU White Paper often promote more open and diverse concepts of civil society. Like Armstrong, they advocate a civil society that encourages a diversity of voices, and they contrast this vision of a multiform, multidimensional, and multilevel civil society with the Europeanized, automized, and governmentalized society envisaged in the White Paper. For a start, the critics envisage a multiform or pluralistic civil society that covers diverse types of participation from the civic engagement of individual citizens through contracts and partnerships with private and voluntary organizations and on to the formal involvement of various groups in the policy process. In contrast, the White Paper looks for authoritative actors in civil society who organize at the European level and then provide a single coherent voice. In addition, the critics envisage a multidimensional civil society in which actors might play diverse roles from deliberation through consultation and advising and on to the delivery of public services. The White Paper looks instead to a civil society in which transnational institutions develop their political roles independently of the direct control of their constituency. Finally, the critics envisage a multilevel civil society that includes actors from the subnational, national, and transnational levels, while the White Paper governmentalizes civil society by handing over to nonstate actors more and more of the tasks that historically have been undertaken by the state.

Partnerships

Many governments, including the EU, have turned to local partnerships as a means of addressing social exclusion. There has been a widespread shift from concepts of poverty that concentrate on material depriva-

[24] K. Armstrong, "Rediscovering Civil Society: The European Union and the White Paper on Governance," *European Law Journal* 8 (2002): 102–32.

tion to ones that focus on social exclusion. Poverty is often now defined in terms of social capital, notably an inability to exercise one's social and political rights as a citizen. Poverty is, in this view, a consequence of social exclusion, including inadequate education, poor health conditions, homelessness, loss of family support, unemployment, and a lack of voice. The second wave of public sector reform includes attempts to address such social exclusion through partnerships. The new local partnerships differ not only from corporatist partnerships but also from the partnerships associated with NPM. Indeed, they are a response to the perceived failings of marketization and NPM. They are a response to concerns about democratic deficits and declining levels of citizen participation as well as part of the broad trend consciously to promote network governance.

Many commentators are skeptical about the effectiveness of network governance and especially local partnerships. They doubt that local partnerships actually live up to the rhetoric of cohesion, trust, and integration. To assess the effectiveness of the new partnerships, social scientists have examined their capacity, inclusiveness, accountability, and performance. In the case of the EU, Mike Geddes concludes that although the new partnerships involve more nongovernmental actors in policymaking processes, by no means all (or even most) of the key actors in shaping the future of a locality are among those involved in the partnerships.[25] Typically the new partnerships are undermined by problems of complexity and coordination, and their limited capacities and capabilities. The partnerships often fail, in other words, precisely because they operate in the context of the new governance and the decline of state capacity brought on by neoliberalism and globalization.

We might try to mitigate such skepticism by distinguishing between partnerships according to whether they are built from above or from below.[26] Some research suggests that partnerships are more likely to promote the inclusion of excluded and disadvantaged groups if they are built from below. This research echoes our earlier contrast between two visions of civil society. On the one hand, local partnerships may be based on a kind of corporatist model: the state may initiate partnerships in order to secure representation of the relevant stakeholders. These partnerships tend to revolve around the interests of local economic, political, and administrative elites. Typically they try to tackle exclusion by reintegrating a marginalized locality (as represented by its elites) into

---

[25] M. Geddes, "Tackling Social Exclusion in the European Union? The Limits to the New Orthodoxy of Local Partnership," *International Journal of Urban and Regional Research* 24 (2000): 782–800.
[26] Ibid.

the capitalist economy. On the other hand, local partnerships may be built by the citizens themselves. These partnerships are less focused on mainstream investments in business, training, and industrial property. They are more likely to attend to the informal or social economy, including credit unions, voluntary associations, and local systems of exchange. These latter partnerships come far closer to capturing a multiform, multidimensional, and multilevel civil society. Yet policy makers generally neglect them, leaving them inadequately resourced in part because they do not mold themselves to fit requirements for state funding, and in part because the rhetoric and policy of local partnerships assume the possibility of an inclusive society in a way that precludes engagement with questions about the role of local elites in processes of exclusion.

RADICAL DEMOCRACY

Discomfort with the democratic credentials of the new governance can lead citizens to search for new avenues of civic participation, or at least to try to enhance the existing avenues of participation. Indeed, I have already pointed to a contrast between, on the one hand, the liberal, constitutional, and elitist ideas driving much government policy, and, on the other, plural, participatory, and bottom-up alternatives. Typically these alternatives draw on traditions of radical democratic theory in addition to, or even in place of, the liberal tradition with its focus on representative and responsible government. No doubt a more pluralist and participatory democracy could stand as a response to the same worries over falling rates of social capital and civic engagement that helped to inspire the second wave of public sector reform—advocates of radical democracy have certainly been known to appeal to arguments from efficiency. Nonetheless, proponents of more pluralist and participatory styles of democratic governance justify their position in more normative, ethical terms. They argue that greater pluralism and participation will promote inclusion, empowerment, social justice, liberty, and equality.

For much of the twentieth century, social democrats (and other radicals) placed more emphasis on social justice than democracy. Social democrats tried to capture existing liberal democratic states and then use them to promote social welfare and social justice. Recently, however, there has been a resurgence of interest in democratic theory. Perhaps this interest in radical democratic ideas is in part a negative reaction to a loss of faith in the viability of concerted action to promote social justice. Perhaps it is in part a reaction to the rise of values associated with recognition (as opposed to redistribution) as class identities seem to have become less central at least in relation to those of gender and ethnicity.[27] Whatever the source of the resurgence of interest in democratic theory, it raises the question of how (if at all) democracy is to be combined with a commitment to social justice or, for that matter, other substantive values we might hold.

Empowered Participation

Archon Fung and Erik Olin Wright bring together radical democracy and social justice when they argue that the challenge facing the "Left" today is to develop democratic strategies that advance its historic values.[28] They want to fuse a historic commitment to equality, social justice, and liberty with a renewed emphasis on popular control over collective decisions. They call their proposed fusion empowered deliberative democracy. They argue that it takes participation, deliberation, and empowerment as seriously as it is prudent and feasible to do.

Empowered deliberative democracy builds on three key principles. The first is a focus on specific, tangible problems. Fung and Wright suggest that this focus on tangible issues may bring results to neglected sectors of society. The focus on concrete problems such as municipal budgets, public safety and health, and the training of workers may foster cooperation at the local level and so raise confidence in the efficacy of state action. The second principle behind empowered deliberative democracy is the involvement of individual citizens alongside public officials. Fung and Wright suggest that the participation of ordinary citizens provides a way of moderating the viewpoints of trained experts to allow for local knowledge and experience in the search for solutions to local grievances. Citizen involvement reduces the role taken by inefficient and sluggish bureaucracies. Finally, the third principle behind empowered deliberative democracy is a reliance on deliberative procedures. Ordinary citizens are to agree solutions to tangible problems in dialogue with one another. Fung and Wright envisage citizens listening to each other and, after due consideration, reaching a shared decision. In their view, consensus and collective action depend on such deliberation. They suggest that continuous joint planning, problem solving, and strategizing offers a way of moving beyond self-interest toward decisions based on collective reasoning.

Fung and Wright attempt to go beyond an account of the principles of empowered deliberative democracy to describe some of its specific insti-

---

[27] For the socialist debate over redistribution and recognition, see N. Fraser and A. Honneth, *Redistribution or Recognition? A Political-Philosophical Exchange*, trans. J. Golb and C. Wilke (London: Verso, 2003).

[28] A. Fung and E. Wright, "Deepening Democracy: Innovations in Empowered Participatory Governance," *Politics & Society* 29 (2001): 5–41.

tutional features. One feature is the devolution of the authority to make public decisions to empowered local units. Local units are to have the political and administrative powers needed to generate and implement policies, and to be held accountable for these policies. Fung and White suggest that such devolution helps to move decision making away from technocratic experts toward ordinary citizens. Another institutional feature of their vision is the creation of networks based on links among empowered local units and between these units and more centralized authorities. These networks are necessary, Fung and White tell us, to facilitate the distribution of resources, to solve the problems that local units cannot address, to deal with incompetent decisions, and to diffuse innovation and knowledge across local units. These networks also help to forge lines of communication and accountability between the local units and superordinate organizations. The final institutional feature of empowered deliberative democracy is the creation of state institutions to guide the empowered local units toward collective action. Yet, while state institutions may thus coordinate decentralization, they themselves are to be remade in the image of a mobilized, deliberative, democratic, and grassroots form of organization. Clearly Fung and Wright hope that their proposals will manage to institutionalize a kind of radical, participatory, and even oppositional ethos.

Systems Perspectives

It is important to recognize that many governments have adopted an agenda close to that of empowered deliberative democracy in an attempt to promote social capital and democratic legitimacy. The second wave of public sector reform tries to institutionalize some of the ideas and institutional features advocated by Fung and Wright—dialogue, participation, consensus, empowerment, and, of course, social inclusion. Typically, however, these reforms are not attempts to promote a radical, participatory, and oppositional ethos among citizens. On the contrary, they are more akin to technocratic responses to worries about the effectiveness and perceived legitimacy of existing political institutions. They are, to put the matter simply, more about systems governance than radical politics.[29]

The EU White Paper on Governance is, yet again, a good example of systems governance. Although the White Paper promotes networks, participation, and inclusion, its viewpoint remains that of the political

---

[29] I have written in more detail about this distinction in M. Bevir, "Democratic Governance: Systems and Radical Perspectives," *Public Administration Review* 66 (2006): 426–36.

system. The concern of the White Paper is how to make public policies more effective and legitimate. Networks, participation, and inclusion are promoted as means to these specific ends, not as part of a radical democratic project. The White Paper opens by suggesting that "political leaders" today need to find effective policy solutions to major problems and overcome popular distrust of governing institutions. Later, when the White Paper first mentions democracy and the need to link institutions to citizens, it does so specifically because "this is the starting condition for more effective and relevant policies." Later still the White Paper explains the principle of participation by saying little more than "the quality, relevance and effectiveness of EU policies depend on ensuring wide participation throughout the policy chain—from conception to implementation." The impetus behind system governance is not, it seems, a radical democratic commitment; rather, it is the belief that "policies can no longer be effective unless they are prepared, implemented and enforced in a more inclusive way."[30]

System governance derives principally from the institutionalist arguments that networks are more efficient than hierarchies and that dialogue and consensus can build political legitimacy and so effectiveness. It is a top-down and elitist project. It seeks to institutionalize values such as dialogue, participation, and inclusion in large part because experts say that doing so will lead to more efficient and effective governance. Experts, often new institutionalists or communitarians, have turned the values of radical democrats into technocratic solutions to the ills of the public sector and civil society.

Much is to be gained from distinguishing system governance from radical democracy. System governance leads to elite programs of dialogue and inclusion in an attempt to make policies more effective and legitimate, and its primary commitment is still to such effectiveness and legitimacy. In contrast, radical democrats want participation to go along with a primary commitment to deliberation and ethical conduct. To radical democrats, system governance typically resembles incorporation and consultation rather than pluralism and dialogue. Whereas system governance encourages the incorporation of diverse interests in state institutions, radical democrats might perhaps assign elements of governance to associations other than the state, and whereas system governance implies that the goal of consultation is a consensus that is allegedly necessary for an integrated society, radical democrats might perhaps regard disagreement as a prerequisite of the deliberation they rely on to forge compromises.

---

[30] Commission of the European Communities, *European Governance*, 3 and 10.

The Problem of Ethnocentrism

If we are to forge a radical democracy either in a multicultural society or at a transnational level, we will need to confront the ethnocentric assumptions embedded in many radical accounts of power and democracy, perhaps including those of Fung and Wright. At the very least, we should reconsider the legitimacy of operating with concepts of power and social relations that remain saturated with the historical legacy of colonialism. Even a radical democratic politics cannot escape power. Thus, the question should be: how can we create forms of power that are compatible with democracy and yet challenge ethnocentric assumptions?

As a start we might follow John Slater in identifying four interconnected features of an adequate answer to this question.[31] First, a politics of democratization must take into account the history of encounters between the West and the non-West. It is only by considering the colonial nature of power and its geopolitical effects that we can move beyond perspectives that frame the West as universally relevant. Second, and nevertheless, neither colonial legacies nor the nonuniversal nature of the West should lead us to ignore concepts or approaches just because they originated there. Once we admit that democracy may mean different things in different contexts, we might engage in dialogues in an attempt to relate these different meanings to one another and thereby foster greater cross-cultural understanding. Third, democratic reform, especially in the third world, requires radical changes in the way we understand Western and non-Western concepts of democracy and citizenship. Finally, if we really are to move beyond our ethnocentric assumptions, we must pay more attention to transnational territoriality, that is, to spaces and interactions that fall outside the clear domains of sovereign states.

CONCLUSION

The new worlds of governance pose clear issues of accountability and democracy. Different theories of governance encourage different responses to these issues. Rational choice theorists are more likely than others to reject the idea of the common good or to define it as a mere aggregation of individual interests, to think of citizens as consumers expressing their individual preferences, to rethink accountability in terms of performance, and to defend nonmajoritarian institutions as solutions to various collec-

---

[31] D. Slater, "Other Domains of Democratic Theory: Space, Power, and the Politics of Democratization," *Environment and Planning D: Society and Space* 20 (2002): 255–76.

tive irrationalities. Institutionalism is more amorphous. Rational choice institutionalists often echo the ideas just listed. In contrast, many other institutionalists are more likely to defend concepts of the public good, to promote an ethic of public service, to define citizenship in relation to norms and communities, and to rethink accountability and legitimacy in terms of the horizontal ties between networks and social inclusion. For all their differences, rational choice theorists and institutionalists generally share a continuing attachment to the idea of a representative democracy. Some radical democrats are more suspicious of this idea. They rarely want to discard representation entirely. But they do suggest that the rise of new worlds of governance provides further reasons to develop more participatory and pluralist forms of democracy.

Different theories of democracy are not just academic visions. To the contrary, like the new theories of governance, they are beliefs that have inspired political actors to remake the world in ways that have created the very worlds of governance to which they refer. This interaction between theories and worlds is crucial for many of the arguments in this book. We have already seen how rational choice theory and institutionalism, respectively, lay behind parts of the first and second waves of public sector reform. Now, in the next two chapters, I will argue that states have generally responded to the democratic issues raised by the new governance in terms again set by rational choice theory and especially institutionalism. Programs of constitutional and judicial reform rely on representative democracy combined with a faith in these forms of expertise.

CHAPTER SIX

Constitutional Reform

How DOES THE previous chapter on democratic governance help us to make sense of programs of constitutional reform? We could compare the reforms with different concepts of democracy. Perhaps we thereby might judge how well the reforms do or do not fit with whichever concept of democracy we find most compelling. We could give the reforms marks out of ten. But it is arguable that the marks we gave would say more about our own visions of democracy than about the reforms themselves. An alternative approach becomes possible once we allow that concepts of democracy are embedded in traditions that then inspire political practices. Particular theories of democratic governance inspire programs of constitutional reform. Thus, we may understand the reforms better if we identify the historical traditions that have inspired them.

This book is informed by a concern with the impact of social theory on the world. Social scientists are generally far too inclined to conceive of their theories as accounts of a largely independent world. They bring theory and world together only in restricted ways. They treat the world as independent evidence by which to test and evaluate their theories, especially their empirical theories. And they treat their normative theories as ideals by which to judge the moral worth of actions and practices in the world. So, for example, in the case of governance, social scientists typically treat rational choice and institutionalism as accounts of prior changes in the world, and they typically treat normative theories of public service ethics and democracy as ideals by which to evaluate and advocate various reforms. In sharp contrast, I favor a more interpretive approach in which the social world arises from people acting on various beliefs, perhaps including theories from the social sciences. Given that our theories help to make our world, properly to explain the social world, social scientists must recover the beliefs and theories that inspire the relevant actions and practices. Fully to explain the new worlds of governance, social scientists must grasp the role played by rational choice theory and institutionalism in constructing it. Fully to explain programs of constitutional reform, we must appeal to the democratic theories that they embody.

More specifically, this chapter will argue that contemporary programs of constitutional reforms are often inspired by institutionalism and a representative concept of democracy. Institutionalist accounts of the new governance have led to recognition of markets and networks and the problems they pose for democratic accountability and political legitimacy. But attempts to respond to these problems remain constrained by a representative idea of democracy. This chapter illustrates this argument with a detailed study of the constitutional reforms of the New Labour governments in Britain. My argument is that New Labour's reforms have been constrained by a focus on representative democracy, and more particularly, by a lingering adherence to the Westminster model.

SOCIALISM AND DEMOCRACY

Particular traditions of democratic thought have inspired New Labour. A skeptic might remind us that politicians are rarely political theorists. It is true no doubt that Tony Blair and Donald Dewar did not spend much time reading their Locke and Rousseau—although when Labour was in opposition Gordon Brown was said to spend part of the parliamentary summer recess studying weighty tomes of economic theory in the libraries of Boston. Still, even the most unreflective politician acquires conscious and tacit beliefs through processes of socialization, and these beliefs include ideas on the nature of democracy. The politicians, civil servants, and advisers responsible for New Labour's constitutional reforms operated with conscious or tacit concepts of democracy.

One way to make sense of New Labour's constitutional reforms is to show how they draw on concepts of democracy that are themselves characteristic of the traditions of thought and practice that have inspired New Labour. From this perspective, the reforms draw on a representative concept of democracy that has been characteristic of the liberal and Fabian traditions of socialism that have dominated the Labour Party for most of its history. The party remains wedded to a representative theory of democracy tied to the Westminster model rather than more radical socialist theories. It might not surprise people to learn that New Labour relied on Liberal and Fabian traditions of socialism. But it is well worth pointing out that New Labour thereby neglected participatory and pluralist alternatives.

The Westminster Model

The Westminster model lurks in the background of most of the British case studies in this book—the studies of constitutional reform and judicial reform, and arguably those of public sector reform and police reform. Even today the Westminster model is the dominant if threatened image of British government.

There are numerous definitions of the Westminster model, but they generally include the following elements:[1]

- A unitary state based on a strong adherence to constitutional conventions
- Parliamentary supremacy taking precedence over popular sovereignty
- A strong system of cabinet government
- A two-party system based on single-member constituencies
- Accountability through elections and majority party control of the executive
- Elaborate conventions for the conduct of parliamentary business
- An institutionalized opposition

Clearly the Westminster model presupposes representative democracy. Indeed it leaves little room for other forms of democracy insofar as these would challenge its privileging of an elected parliament.

Historically, the Westminster model has also been loosely associated with a range of rather vague substantive and methodological ideas about politics and how to understand it. These vague ideas include a focus on rules and institutions, the use of legal-historical methods, and a personalized view of power. In particular, the Westminster model has often, though by no means invariably, gone along with a historiography that comes perilously close to telling a story of the progressive development of British government. This historiography emphasizes gradualism and the capacity of British institutions to evolve and cope with crises. It feeds into a tendency to celebrate the practical wisdom of the British constitution.

Throughout the twentieth century political scientists became increasingly skeptical of the adequacy of the Westminster model. Arguably, the earliest challenges came with the rise of behavioral topics such as policy networks. Political scientists began to portray parliamentary sovereignty as little more than a formal veneer beneath which policy is really made by a central executive that is fragmented across various policy networks. Skepticism about the Westminster model was further exasperated as British institutions appeared to founder on recurrent crises. The skep-

---

[1] E.g., D. Verney, "Westminster Model," in V. Bogdanor, ed., *The Blackwell Encyclopaedia of Political Science* (Oxford: Blackwell, 1991), 637. Also see P. Dunleavy, "The Westminster Model and the Distinctiveness of British Politics," in P. Dunleavy et al., eds., *Developments in British Politics*, 8th series (Basingstoke: Palgrave Macmillan, 2006); and A. Gamble, "Theories of British Politics," *Political Studies* 38 (1990): 404–20; and, for the Westminster model in the context of the new governance, D. Richards and M. Smith, "The Tensions of Political Control and Administrative Autonomy: From NPM to a Reconstituted Westminster Model," in T. Christensen and P. Laegreid, eds., *Autonomy and Regulation: Coping with Agencies in the Modern State* (Cheltenham: Edward Elgar, 2006), 181–201.

tics bemoaned government overload, adversary politics, elective dictator-ship, pluralistic stagnation, loosening party discipline, and the erosion of parliamentary control of the executive.[2] They called for constitutional reconstruction. Indeed, the literature on constitutional reform grew ever larger from the 1960s to the early 1990s as numerous political scientists cataloged the growing divergence between constitutional theory and po-litical practice.[3]

Yet the Westminster model survives in spite of the many cracks. It sur-vives above all as an image to which politicians and public officials orient themselves. Many political actors in Britain still use the language of the Westminster model to describe their world. The adherence of political actors to the Westminster model means that it is to some extent a self-fulfilling prophecy. Of course the mere fact of people believing something does not make it so. Equally, however, if all relevant actors behave in accord with a set of conventions, such as those governing parliamentary procedure, then those conventions will indeed operate. What is more, when actors believe in the normative value of the Westminster model, they might promote reforms that keep something like it in place. This chapter and the next argue that tacit adherence to the Westminster model has severely restricted the imaginative scope of constitutional reform in Britain.

Competing Socialisms

The Labour Party has been divided on democratic issues from the mo-ment of its inception as the Labour Representation Committee in 1900.[4] The main division is between a liberal representative concept that fits with the Westminster model and participatory and pluralist alternatives that overturn the Westminster model.

[2] Examples include, respectively, King, "Overload"; S. Finer, ed., *Adversary Politics and Electoral Reform* (London: Anthony Wigram, 1975); Lord Hailsham, *The Dilemma of Democracy* (London: Collins, 1978); S. Beer, *Britain Against Itself* (London: Faber, 1982); A. Birch "The Theory and Practice of Modern British Democracy," in J. Jowell and D. Oliver, eds., *The Changing Constitution* (Oxford: Clarendon Press, 1989), 87–111; and B. Crick and A. Hanson, eds., *The Commons in Transition* (London: Fontana, 1979).

[3] See, from the beginning and end of this era, B. Crick, *The Reform of Parliament: The Crisis of Government* (London: Weidenfeld and Nicolson, 1964); and A. Barnett, C. Ellis, and P. Hirst, eds., *Debating the Constitution: New Perspectives on Constitutional Reform* (Cambridge: Polity, 1993).

[4] Compare L. Barrow and I. Bullock, *Democratic Ideas and the British Labour Move-ment 1880–1914* (Cambridge: Cambridge University Press, 1996). For more general studies of the various strands that make up British socialism, see S. Pierson, *Marxism and the Ori-gins of British Socialism* (Ithaca: Cornell University Press, 1973); and S. Pierson, *British So-cialism: The Journey from Fantasy to Politics* (Cambridge: Harvard University Press, 1979).

A liberal representative concept of democracy aims to protect citizens from the state, and to make sure that the state pursues policies in the interests of its citizens. Sovereignty resides with the people, but it is exercised on their behalf by a small number of elected representatives. The executive branch of government is accountable to a legislative assembly composed of representatives. The legislative assembly is then accountable to the citizens through regular elections. Typically, a constitution limits state power and secures civil rights.

A participatory and pluralist concept of democracy aims more at self-rule and emancipation. Citizens should have as much control as possible over their own daily lives. Sovereignty may be dispersed among the several institutions that shape people's daily activities, and it may be exercised by the direct participation of the members of each institution. Participation should be extended from decision making to the processes of implementation. Measures may be needed to ensure that all people have the resources they need for effective participation.

Early socialist debates over representative and participatory concepts of democracy reflected different visions of the role of the state in a socialist society. The Fabians and some Marxists upheld representative democracy. They argued that the state had to take on new functions and play a more active role in civil society: the state had to take control of the unearned increment and use it for social purposes. The Fabians advocated an extension of liberal democracy, notably the right to vote, in order to ensure that this increasingly active state remained trustworthy.

Ethical socialists and syndicalists were more attracted to participatory democracy. They argued that civil society needed to be purged of the abuses they associated with competitive individualism and capitalism. They called for the democratization of civil society. The ethical socialists wanted civil society to embody a democratic fellowship. The syndicalists wanted to establish democracy in the associations that made up civil society.

One of the main debates among the early socialists thus concerned the relative roles to be played in a socialist society by a democratic state and democratic associations in civil society. To simplify, we might say that the view that came to dominate the Labour Party fused ethical socialism with Fabian economics to emphasize the role of the state, but that this view was always challenged by socialists influenced by syndicalist themes in Marxism or by nongovernmental themes in ethical socialism.

Labour and Democracy

One particular view of democracy came to dominate the Labour Party during the first three decades of the twentieth century. At that time, the leading figures in the party—Keir Hardie, Philip Snowden, and Ramsay

MacDonald—condemned capitalism in much the same way as had the ethical socialists. In their view, the competitive market brought out people's base instincts instead of their moral ones: capitalism turned people into selfish and acquisitive beings. The leading Labour politicians turned to the Fabians for an economic analysis of capitalism that buttressed their moral views. They accepted a Fabian analysis of interest as analogous to land rent: just as the landlord gets an unearned payment from the value of land, so capitalists do from improvements in productive methods and social location that owe nothing to their efforts or abilities. They also accepted the Fabian denunciation of the uncoordinated nature of the market: whereas capitalism relied on a haphazard and chaotic clash of individual interests, socialism would eliminate waste by organizing economic life on a scientific basis.

The Labour Party's reliance on Fabian economics led it to emphasize various forms of state intervention at the expense of attempts to democratize civil society. For a start, the existence of an unearned increment present in all economies suggested that the state should be in charge of collecting this surplus and using it for the benefit of the community. The Labour Party's mock budget of 1907 advocated taxation so as to collect unearned increments of wealth and then use them for "communal benefit."[5] Labour politicians advocated several measures to deal with the social surplus in the economy. To secure the surplus, they called for taxation, legislative restrictions on property, and eventually public ownership of the means of production. To deploy the surplus for communal benefit, they called mainly for increased state provision of social welfare. They also advocated various degrees of public ownership of the means of production in order to end the anarchic nature of capitalist production.

When socialists appealed to the state to correct the failings of capitalism, they often raised fears of too powerful a state. Labour politicians allayed this fear by stressing the ethical nature of a truly democratic state. As MacDonald explained, "the democratic State is an organization of the people, democratic government is self-government, democratic law is an expression of the will of the people who have to obey the law."[6] Labour politicians defined democracy in terms taken again from Fabians and ethical socialists. They equated democracy with representative institutions and a spirit of fellowship. They rarely showed enthusiasm for other forms of popular control.

By the end of the First World War, the Labour Party had accepted social democratic ideas that committed it to an extended role for the state.

[5] P. Snowdon, "The Socialist Budget 1907," in J. Hardie, ed., *From Serfdom to Socialism* (Hassocks: Harvester, 1974), 7.

[6] R. MacDonald, *Socialism and Society* (London: Independent Labour Party, 1905), 70.

This commitment gained additional strength from the many liberals who found their way into the Labour Party as it became the leading alternative to the Conservatives. These liberals too challenged the idea that the market constituted a harmonious, self-regulating system.[7] They had begun to look to the state to right the failings of the market. They agreed with the Fabians on the need for representative institutions to ensure that the state could be trusted to play this expanded role.

Submerged Alternatives

The dominant outlook in the Labour Party drew on Fabian economics. Opposition to this outlook drew on syndicalist forms of Marxism and nongovernmental forms of ethical socialism. The leading syndicalists— notably Tom Mann and James Connolly—were Marxists. They argued that the ills of capitalism could be overcome only through a transformation in industry. The state was to play no (or almost no) role. Their Marxist economics did not demand a greater role for the state. They envisaged a harmonious civil society in which capitalism had been replaced by a system based on worker-owned industrial units. They also argued that any leadership became a self-serving bureaucracy, so leaders had to be subject to strong democratic control. Even worker-owned industrial units would need to institutionalize popular control through a range of measures. The syndicalists and other Marxists thus opposed the Labour Party's restricted view of democracy as representative government. They proposed an extension of popular control through devices such as the initiative and referendum.

Ethical socialists often expressed a romantic medievalism. They wanted a world of craftsmen united in guilds. These guilds would embody an ideal of fellowship. A. J. Penty espoused this medievalism in his *The Restoration of the Gild System*, which inspired the other begetters of guild socialism, A. R. Orage and S. G. Hobson.[8] The early guild socialists drew on themes from ethical socialism. They identified fellowship as the spirit of democracy. They wanted individuals to exercise full control over their own daily activities in a cooperative and decentralized society. They thus advocated transferring the control of industry from financiers to craftsman. Ethical socialists also believed that the cure for capitalism lay in this moral ideal of fellowship, and they suggested that the political realm was irrelevant—perhaps even detrimental—to fellowship. In their view, the moral economy did not require state intervention, and anyway state-owned industries might replicate the commercial ethic of private

---

[7] See M. Freeden, *Liberalism Divided* (Oxford: Clarendon Press, 1986).

[8] A. Penty, *The Restoration of the Gild System* (London: Swan Sonnenschein, 1906).

companies. Thus, they concluded that social democrats should focus not on parliamentary politics but on promoting an ideal of fellowship. The guild socialists did not define democracy as representative government. They defined it to include local control of institutions in civil society, and they wanted these institutions to be largely autonomous from the state.

Later, as a liberal socialism reinforced the dominant Fabian emphasis on a representative concept of democracy, so other groups in the Labour Party continued to draw on themes from syndicalism and nongovernmental socialism. The latter challenged the party's statism and restricted concept of democracy. During and after the First World War, for instance, pluralists such as G.D.H. Cole and Harold Laski fused guild socialism with syndicalism, and also aspects of Fabian thought, in an attempt to revitalize democratic voices in the party. Cole wrote, "a representative system on a geographical basis is certainly not the last word of democracy."[9] Elsewhere he fleshed out an alternative vision of a democratic society that provided "the greatest possible opportunity for individual and collective self-expression to all its members" by means of "the extension of positive self-government through all its parts."[10]

NEW LABOUR AND THE CONSTITUTION

Surely we should not be surprised that New Labour followed the dominant liberal and Fabian traditions in the party? Several commentators have traced New Labour's constitutional reforms to movements such as Charter 88 and the particular dilemmas posed for Labour by the long period of Conservative dominance from 1979 to 1997.[11] I would only add that New Labour reacted to these dilemmas and drew on these movements in a way that reflected its debt to the dominant traditions in the party. Accordingly, it is correct to say that the Labour Party's debt to liberal constitutionalism meant that historically it paid little attention to constitutional reform; but it is wrong to imply either that the liberal nature of the current reforms means they represent a break with Labour's past or that the Labour Party historically has not included dissenting voices calling for more radical constitutional reform.[12]

[9] G. Cole, "Conflicting Social Obligations," *Proceedings of the Aristotelian Society* 15 (1914–15): 159.

[10] G. Cole, *Guild Socialism Restated* (London: Leonard Parsons, 1920), 9.

[11] On Charter 88 and New Labour, see M. Evans, *Charter 88: A Successful Challenge to the British Political Tradition?* (Aldershot: Dartmouth, 1995); and M. Evans, *Constitution-making and the Labour Party* (Basingstoke: Palgrave Macmillan, 2003).

[12] For the argument that Labour has rarely shown much interest in constitutional reform, see B. Jones and M. Keating, *Labour and the British State* (Oxford: Oxford University

New Labour's adherence to representative democracy and even the Westminster model is of a part with the dominant voices in the party's history. We might even suggest that Blair, Brown, and Peter Mandelson—three of the main architects of New Labour—were respectively the exemplars of the ethical socialist, Fabian or social democratic, and liberal traditions in the party.[13] Blair emphasized the value of community, related community to his Christian faith, and placed a heavy emphasis on moral exhortation. Brown appears more concerned to relate New Labour's ideas and policies to values such as equality. Mandelson was the most committed to the liberal themes of choice and the market.

It is perhaps because New Labour followed the dominant liberal and Fabian traditions in the party that it remained tied to representative democracy and arguably the Westminster model. Its major constitutional reforms exhibit little interest in extending participation beyond legislative assemblies. There is little concern to advance democratic pluralism in the associations that make up civil society. Nobody should underestimate the extent of New Labour's constitutional reforms; they may well come to be seen as a decisive moment in British political history.[14] Nonetheless, the extent and drama of the reforms do not alter the fact that they concentrate almost exclusively on representative assemblies, elections, and, as we will see in the next chapter, human rights.

New Labour's reliance on a liberal representative concept of democracy was clear from the start. The Labour Party began informal talks regarding constitutional reform with the Liberal Democrats in the mid-1990s while still in opposition to a Conservative government. The talks led to an agreement to work together after the election. The agreement reflected the Labour Party's growing willingness to pursue a liberal vision of multilevel territorial governments, electoral experiments, and human rights, to the exclusion of alternative socialist concepts of democracy. The agreement covered the following: reform of the House of Lords, devolution in Wales and Scotland, a referendum on proportional representation, and a bill of rights.

Representative assemblies and elections remained the overwhelming focus of New Labour's constitutional innovations. Table 6.1 provides

---

Press, 1985). For the argument that the reforms thus come from a nineteenth-century liberalism alien to the Labour Party, see V. Bogdanor, "Constitutional Reform," in A. Seldon, ed., *The Blair Effect: The Blair Government 1997–2001* (London: Little Brown, 2001), 139–56.

[13] There are now biographies of most of the leading actors in the New Labour drama. These include D. MacIntyre, *Mandelson: The Biography* (London: Harper Collins, 1999); J. Rentoul, *Tony Blair* (London: Little Brown, 1995); and P. Routledge, *Gordon Brown: The Biography* (London: Simon and Schuster, 1998).

[14] For a historical perspective, see V. Bogdanor, ed., *The British Constitution in the Twentieth Century* (Oxford: Oxford University Press, 2003).

a list of the main statutes and their objectives under the Blair govern-ments.[15] The overall results have been categorized under the headings of devolution, parliament, local government, and electoral reform.

Devolution

Devolution is the most visible of New Labour's reforms. It has done much to break up the unitary state of the Westminster model. However, it remains constrained by old concepts of nations, territorial integrity, and geographic representation.

Scotland. The Scotland Act of 1998 created a Scottish Parliament at Edinburgh with legislative powers over a wide range of domestic af-fairs. It established a list of reserved powers to be kept by Westminster, while devolving all remaining powers to the Holyrood Parliament in Ed-inburgh. The Barnett formula provides for the Scottish administration being more or less entirely funded by a block grant from Whitehall. Yet the Holyrood Parliament was also given the power to raise three pence per pound in income tax. While that tax-raising power might appear to cover only a negligible amount, it is nonetheless more than that given to the other devolved parliaments.

After its formation the Holyrood Parliament began to pursue some policies that differed from those of New Labour at Westminster. Notable examples include more generous support for university students and free residential care for the elderly. Despite the occasional differences in social policy, however, the relationship between Edinburgh and London was harmonious and stable. The two governments built a cooperative work-ing relationship. Some observers argued that this rapport might become strained if the Labour Party lost its dominance at either level, leaving a non-Labour government in London at odds with a Labour administra-tion in Scotland, or a Labour government in London at odds with a pre-dominantly non-Labour administration in Scotland. But the latter is now the case, and the working relationship still appears solid enough.

The Holyrood Parliament itself has contemplated reviewing the state of Scottish devolution. The former first minister Jack McConnell raised the thorny question of whether Westminster should give further powers to Edinburgh.[16] He wanted to review the possibility of Holyrood control-

---

[15] In addition to looking at the statutes listed, readers might consult the resources pro-vided by the Constitution Unit, School of Public Policy, University College, London (http://www.ucl.ac.uk/constitution-unit). The unit's publications, available through its website, in-clude a quarterly newsletter (*Monitor*) and a record (*Constitutional Update*) that provides an authoritative overview based on the newsletter.

[16] *Sunday Times*, July 24, 2005.

TABLE 6.1
Constitutional Statutes under New Labour

Year	Statute	Policy objective
1997	Referendum (Scotland and Wales) Act 1997	To authorize prelegislative referendums in Scotland and Wales
1998	Scotland Act 1998	To establish Scottish Parliament
	Government of Wales Act 1998	To establish Welsh Assembly
	Human Rights Act 1998	To incorporate ECHR into UK law
	European Communities (Amendment) Act 1998	To incorporate Treaty of Amsterdam of October 1997
	Regional Development Agencies Act 1998	To establish regional development agencies and to designate regional chambers
	Bank of England Act 1998	Independence for the Bank of England
	Greater London Authority Referendum Act 1998	To authorize referendum on Greater London Authority
	Data Protection Act 1998	To give effect to EC Data Protection Directive (95/46/EC)
	Registration of Political Parties Act 1998	Provision for legal recognition of political parties
1999	European Parliamentary Elections Act 1999	To change voting system to regional-list proportional representation
	Greater London Authority Act 1999	To establish Greater London Authority
	Access to Justice Act 1999	To establish Legal Service Commission and Reform legal aid, rights of audience, family court reform
	House of Lords Act 1999	To remove all but 92 hereditary peers
2000	Disqualifications Act 2000	To allow members of Irish Parliament to sit in the House of Commons and the devolved assemblies
	Local Government Act 2000	To provide for elected mayors and separate executives
	Freedom of Information Act 2000	To create new statutory right of access to information
	Political Parties, Elections and Referendums Act 2000	To establish Electoral Commission and regulate elections and referendums
	Terrorism Act 2000	To amend and extend existing counter-terrorism legislation

TABLE 6.1 *(continued)*
Constitutional Statutes under New Labour

Year	Statute	Policy objective
	Representation of the People Act 2000	To introduce rolling voter registration and experiments in new voting methods to make voting easier
2001	Election Publications Act 2001	To postpone the operation of requirements introduced by Political Parties, Elections and Referendums Act 2000
	House of Commons (Removal of Clergy Disqualification) Act 2001	To remove the disqualification of members of clergy from membership of the House of Commons
	Elections Act 2001	To defer local government elections to coincide with general election on May 5, 2001
	Anti-Terrorism, Crime and Security Act 2001	Series of antiterrorism measures
2002	European Communities (Amendment) Act 2002	To ratify the Treaty of Nice signed by UK government in February 2001
	Sex Discrimination (Election Candidates) Act 2002	To exclude from the Sex Discrimination Act 1975 certain matters relating to selection of candidates by political parties
2003	Regional Assemblies (Preparation) Act 2003	To authorize referendums on regional assemblies in English regions
	European Parliament (Representation) Act 2003	To reduce number of UK seats in European Parliament from 87 to 78, and enfranchise Gibraltar
	European Union (Accessions) Act 2003	To give effect in UK law to EU enlargement, increasing EU from 15 to 25 member states
	Courts Act 2003	To modernize criminal justice system through unified courts system
2004	European Parliamentary and Local Elections (Pilots) Act 2004	To enable experiments with more flexible methods of voting
	Scottish Parliament (Constituencies) Act 2004	To maintain Scottish Parliament at 129 members
	Civil Contingencies Act 2004	To provide for unified executive control in a state of emergency
2005	Constitutional Reform Act 2005	To abolish office of Lord Chancellor, and establish new Supreme Court and Judicial Appointments Commission

TABLE 6.1 *(continued)*
Constitutional Statutes under New Labour

Year	Statute	Policy objective
	Prevention of Terrorism Act 2005	To introduce control orders to restrict suspected terrorists who cannot be deported
	Inquiries Act 2005	Statutory framework for operation of government inquiries
2006	Equality Act 2006	To establish the Commission for Equality and Human Rights
	Electoral Administration Act 2006	To reform voter registration and tighten voter security
	Government of Wales Act 2006	To increase powers and reform structure of the Assembly and to end dual candidacy in constituencies and top-up list

Source: A. McDonald and R. Hazell, "What Happened Next: Constitutional Change Under New Labour," in A. McDonald, ed., *Reinventing Britain: Constitutional Change under New Labour* (London: Politico's, 2007), pp. 12–14. I am grateful to Andrew McDonald for permission to use this table.

ling firearms, drugs, casinos, abortion, broadcasting, and immigration. But he barely mentioned altering the current system used to finance the government of Scotland. Indeed, the devolved administration has thus far shown little interest in modifying the Barnett formula or exercising its power to raise taxes.

In May 2007 the Scottish National Party won the Scottish Parliament election. The Nationalist Alex Salmond became first minister, and the Holyrood Parliament fell into the hands of a different party from that which ruled at Westminster. It remains to be seen if this will damage the formerly cooperative relationship between the two governments. The new Scottish government quickly published a glossy consultation document on independence entitled *Choosing Scotland's Future*.[17] The document also considers other constitutional options. It advocates the transfer of additional powers from Westminster to Holyrood in areas such as economic and fiscal policy, employment and trade union law, social security and pensions, broadcasting, antiterrorism and firearms law, and energy and climate change policy.

[17] *Choosing Scotland's Future: A National Conversation Independence and Responsibility in the Modern World* (Edinburgh: Scottish Executive, 2007).

Wales. Crafting devolution for Wales proved more awkward than for Scotland. The 1997 referendum for devolution was passed by only a narrow margin. Voter turnout in elections for the Welsh Assembly has repeatedly proved disappointing. Labour's first two candidates for leadership in the Welsh Assembly were unsuccessful. The Welsh Labour Party opposes the electoral top-up system. The constitution and powers of the Welsh Assembly have been criticized as modest and even impracticable.

The Government of Wales Act (1998) created a directly elected National Assembly. The powers of the Assembly encompass secondary legislation, such as orders and statutory instruments. Westminster retains primary legislation. The setup is more or less the reverse of that for Scotland: some powers are explicitly given to Wales, and any that are not mentioned are reserved to Westminster. The Welsh Assembly has no power to raise revenue.

Like the Holyrood Parliament, the Welsh Assembly has already reviewed the devolution arrangements. In 2002 First Minister Rhodri Morgan established an all-party commission chaired by Lord Richard to examine both the electoral system for the Welsh Assembly and the powers of the Assembly. The Richard Commission reported in March 2004.[18] It recommended major changes. The proposed changes included a new constitution that would establish a formal separation of powers between the legislative and executive branches of Welsh government. The report also recommended that primary legislative powers be given to the Assembly. It suggested that the number of members in the Assembly should increase from sixty to eighty, and that they be elected by a system based on a single transferable vote (STV).

Westminster responded to the Richard Commission in June 2005. It approved the new constitution of the Assembly. It also proposed a three-stage program for the devolution of greater powers to the Assembly, beginning with framework legislation, moving through the grant of legislative authority by Order in Council, and ending with the granting of primary powers if that were approved by a referendum. Westminster ruled against STV in favor of an additional member system in which candidates cannot appear for both individual constituencies and the top-up list. The House of Lords was against this ban on dual candidacy, but it ultimately conceded to the House of Commons. The Government of Wales Act (2006) introduced the new arrangements.

On May 3, 2007, the third election to the Welsh Assembly failed to give any party an outright majority. Plaid Cymru, the Welsh Nationalists, formed a minority government. The need to implement the Government

---

[18] *Report of the Richard Commission on the Powers and Electoral Arrangements of the National Assembly for Wales* (Cardiff: National Assembly for Wales, 2004).

of Wales Act (2006) made an agreement between Plaid Cymru and opposition parties especially important. A prolonged period of negotiations led in early July 2007 to the formation of a coalition between Welsh Labour and Plaid Cymru.

Northern Ireland. The Northern Ireland Act of 1998 established a partnership form of devolution. The act consisted of a multiparty agreement between the parties in Northern Ireland as well as an agreement between the governments of Britain and Northern Ireland. It created a directly elected Assembly with legislative powers whose members are elected by STV. The act required that the executive contain representatives from the nationalist and the unionist communities. Similarly, the Assembly had to operate in a consociational, not majoritarian, fashion, requiring some resolutions to earn "cross-community support" if they were to pass. These provisions were intended to foster cooperation between the two communities. In practice, cooperation proved elusive. The Assembly was repeatedly suspended, and its suspension in 2002 led to five years of direct rule from Westminster.

Direct rule eventually came to an end. Devolution was finally restored on May 8, 2007. The first minister of the new devolved government is the Rev. Ian Paisley, leader of the Democratic Unionist Party. The deputy first minister is Martin McGuinness of Sinn Féin. The first minister and the deputy have equal standing and equal powers in the new administration. The main priorities for the draft Programme for Government were agreed with relative ease. They include high-quality public services; a competitive, outward-looking economy; the rebuilding of infrastructure; measures to tackle poverty, intolerance, and racism; and improvements in education and health.

English regions. New Labour initially toyed with the idea of devolution to English regions. But a referendum on an assembly for the North East failed, and thereafter the government dropped the issue. Primary and secondary legislation for the whole of England is still in the hands of Westminster. After Brown replaced Blair as prime minister on June 27, 2007, he did slightly restructure the administrative arrangements for the English regions. The government then created two new departments in Whitehall—a Department for Innovation, Universities, and Skills (DIUS) and a Department of Business, Enterprise, and Regulatory Reform (DBERR). The DBERR will now oversee the regional development agencies. It is responsible for monitoring the regional economic performance Public Service Agreement (PSA). Brown also introduced designated junior ministers for each standard region of England. These ministers are meant to give each region a voice. The unelected regional assemblies will be dissolved, and their planning responsibilities will go to Regional Development Agencies.

Parliamentary Reform

While the most visible of New Labour's constitutional reforms has been the creation of new devolved assemblies, other reforms have applied to the historic assembly at Westminster, especially the House of Lords.

The House of Lords. Reforming the House of Lords has proved a difficult task for New Labour. The government ran into constant opposition from the Lords itself. Nonetheless, it did make some headway with the House of Lords Act (1999) and, as we will see in more detail in the next chapter, the Constitutional Reform Act (2005).

Under the House of Lords Act, all but ninety-two of the hereditary peers were removed from the Upper House, leaving a House of Lords dominated by the nigh-on six hundred lifetime peers. Thereafter when one of the ninety-two hereditary peers died, a replacement was to be elected from among an electoral college consisting of all the hereditary peers inside and outside the House.

The House of Lords Act was meant to be the first phase of a wider reform of the Lords. The government began the second phase by forming a royal commission chaired by Lord Wakeham to explore how best to proceed. The Wakeham Commission reported in 2000, proposing an end to the honors system and party patronage, and advocating the introduction of an elected element in addition to the nominated members of the Upper House, although without a consensus as to how large the elected element should be.[19] These recommendations, along with several others, were presented to the House of Commons in 2003. The Commons rejected them all.

In its election manifesto of 2005, the Labour Party advocated a new approach to Lords reform.[20] The approach involved considering the powers of the Lords alongside its composition. The aim was thereby simultaneously to narrow its powers and ensure it had more legitimacy. The government promised a free vote on the composition of the Lords. In these circumstances, however, securing a majority in the House of Commons, much less in the House of Lords, would be no easy feat. Indeed, the Liberal Democrats have expressed their opposition to

[19] *The Royal Commission on the Reform of the House of Lords*, Cm 4534 (2000).
[20] Labour Party, *Britain Forward Not Back* (London: Labour Party, 2005).

codification of the powers of the Upper House. Still, the government trudges on. In May 2006 it established a Joint Committee on Conventions to consider the relationship between the House of Lords and the House of Commons.

The House of Commons. Attempts to reform the House of Commons have been desultory. In 1997 the Labour government established the Independent Commission on the Voting System to consider alternative systems for electing the Commons. Lord Jenkins, a prominent Liberal Democrat from the Lords, chaired the commission. The Jenkins Commission reported in 1998, proposing that Britain adopt an alternative vote system topped-up by list-based proportional representation on a county and city basis.[21] The government then promised a referendum on maintaining the first-past-the-post electoral system. Nothing happened.

Local Government Reform

While the unwritten nature of Britain's constitution blurs the distinction between constitutional and administrative affairs even more than usual, there remains a fairly clear distinction between them. Local government reform can be primarily constitutional or administrative. Unfortunately, although New Labour flirted with democratic innovations, notably elected mayors, its approach to local government concentrated overwhelmingly on administrative measures—best value, comprehensive performance assessment, and local area agreements—that are better left for chapter 9.

A Mayor for London. The Greater London Authority Act (1999) transformed the government of Britain's capital. It created a Greater London Authority (GLA), consisting of both the directly elected mayor and a twenty-five member Assembly. The post of mayor was entirely new. The GLA is responsible for administering Greater London, which covers the thirty-two London boroughs as well as the City of London. The Assembly's role is mainly to scrutinize the actions of the mayor and, if it sees fit, to make amendments to the mayor's annual budget. The powers given to the mayor by the 1999 act were fairly modest and subject to strict oversight by Whitehall. It could be argued that the GLA deals mainly with transport matters.

Electing a mayor for London proved controversial. Ken Livingstone, having failed to get adopted by the Labour Party, instead won as an in-

[21] *The Report of the Independent Commission on the Voting System*, Cm 4090, 2 vols. (1998).

dependent. As mayor, Livingstone's flagship policy has been the imposition of a congestion charge on all vehicles entering Central London. This policy has proved successful and popular. A review of London's government granted the mayor further powers in the areas of housing, planning, skills, culture, and waste management. When Livingstone failed to get reelected in May 2008, he lost not to a Labour loyalist but to a maverick Conservative, Boris Johnson.

Beyond London. The Local Government Act (2000) required local authorities to abandon the old committee system of government. Local authorities had to adopt instead one of three alternatives: a cabinet system, a city manager system, or a directly elected mayor. If they want to adopt the mayoral option, there must first be a successful referendum on the issue. In 2004 the Scottish Parliament passed a Local Governance (Scotland) Act that introduced STV for the election of local councilors.

Electoral Reform

Electoral reform was part of New Labour's agreement with the Liberal Democrats. The Liberals' main aim seems as far off as ever: general elections to the House of Commons still use the first-past-the-post system. However, British citizens now find themselves using several alternative systems in other elections.

Elections to the new devolved assemblies rely on proportional representation. Both Scotland and Wales use an additional member system (AMS), which gives voters two votes—a regional vote as well as a constituency one. Most assessments to date on the operation of these proportional systems are favorable. Voters understand what they are meant to do. They are, however, somewhat less informed about how votes are actually translated into seats. Only a minority grasp that the second (list) vote, rather than the first (constituency) vote, determines the number of seats a party wins. Some mistakenly think that the second vote denotes their second choice rather than acting as a list vote.

The European Parliamentary Elections Act (1999) introduced a regional list form of proportional representation for elections to the European Parliament. It was preceded by the Registration of Political Parties Act (1998), which paved the way for a list system by requiring political parties to register. Later, in 2000, the Political Parties, Elections, and Referendums Act established an Electoral Commission to oversee the new funding arrangements for political parties. The commission also has responsibility for running referendums, and it acts as an independent source of information on electoral processes.

WHAT DOES IT MEAN?

New Labour has made some dramatic reforms to the British Constitution. Of course the constitution changed in part due to British membership of the European Union. Yet the extent of New Labour's reforms goes far beyond what was required. To exhibit New Labour's debt to a representative concept of democracy is not to deny the extent of the reforms. Far from denying the extent of the reforms, I believe that they have already reshaped Britain, and they have opened the door to futures that the government probably neither intended nor would have wanted.[22] Britain has been altered for good, and the processes of change are still very much playing themselves out. Nonetheless, if the extent of New Labour's reforms helps explain the attention devoted to questions they raise, then recognition of New Labour's debt to certain theories of democratic governance might cast new light on these questions. How can we make sense of the content of the reforms? What prospects do the reforms open up for Britain? What is the alternative?

The Content of the Reforms

Let us look first at debates about the content of the reforms.

Were the reforms programmatic? Many observers think that the reforms are insufficiently programmatic.[23] They take Lord Irvine to have admitted as much, and Lord Falconer to have done his best to impose a retrospective consistency upon a hodgepodge of reforms. In their view, for instance, the schemes for territorial governments have diverse sources in the different demands of particular territories. Other observers—most notably the researchers of the Constitution Unit, University College, London—sometimes suggest that New Labour has developed a fairly coherent constitutional agenda. They imply that Lord Irvine almost said as much, and Lord Falconer then made it crystal clear. In their view, for instance, the schemes for territorial government appear as components of an admittedly vague plan for multilevel governance throughout Britain.

---

[22] The idea that the reforms would develop a momentum of their own was suggested very early on by, for example, A. Barnett, *This Time: Our Constitutional Revolution* (London: Vintage, 1997).

[23] The asymmetrical nature of devolution reflected various pragmatic considerations. See A. Henderson, "A Porous and Pragmatic Settlement: Asymmetrical Devolution and Democratic Constraint in Scotland and Wales," in A. McDonald, ed., *Reinventing Britain: Constitutional Change Under New Labour* (London: Politico's, 2007), 151–69.

To some extent the debate between these two views is misleading. Whether or not we find coherence depends primarily on the level of abstraction at which we look for it. But to recognize New Labour's debt to particular concepts of democracy is to cast new light on this debate. Even if New Labour did not set out with a consistent agenda, the major constitutional reforms are loosely coherent in their shared debt to a liberal representative concept of democracy. As we will see in chapter 9, moreover, the wider reforms of the public sector are loosely coherent in their shared debt to institutionalism and communitarianism. Finally, the reforms of the constitution and the public sector loosely fit together in that a liberal representative concept of democracy creates a space for the kind of expertise offered by institutionalists and communitarians.

How do the reforms relate to New Labour's style of governance? Numerous critics label New Labour as made up of "control freaks."[24] Many of them then point to severe tensions between the constitutional reforms and the desire of the center to retain control. There was endless commotion over a Blair "presidency" that seemed to concentrate power at 10 Downing Street and the Cabinet Office.[25] The idea of a Blair presidency of a Bonapartist order fused several issues. It suggested that Blair himself combined the charisma and ease of a rock star with considerable tactical reach. It highlighted the ways in which his government tried to strengthen the control of the prime minister and his staff over policy and its presentation. And it suggested that Blair was the most powerful prime minister in living memory. Few would deny that the changes at Number 10 and the Cabinet Office had a centralizing thrust. The Policy Unit mutated into the Policy Directorate when it merged with the Prime Minister's Private Office. As soon as he was elected, Blair surrounded himself with a network of special advisers. The number of special advisers rose from eight under John Major to twenty-seven under Blair. Total staff employed at Number 10 rose from 107 under Major to 200 under Blair. At first, the new central institutions focused on improving communications, with Alastair Campbell heading the Strategic Communications Unit. Later the emphasis fell on policy advice. Number 10 does not shrink from attempts—often comically inept attempts—to influence outcomes in the national parliaments and in London.

The tension between the constitutional reforms and a centralizing style of governance appears slightly different once we recognize New Labour's debt to particular concepts of democracy. Consider the main constitu-

---

[24] E.g., N. Jones, *The Control Freaks: How New Labour Gets Its Own Way* (London: Politico's, 2001).

[25] Compare Bevir and Rhodes, *Governance Stories*, chap. 6.

tional reforms. Here tension exists between the multiple levels of government created by any programme of devolution, on one hand, and, on the other, a belief in the expertise offered by social science. Likewise, if we look ahead to chapter 9, on the reform of the public sector, we might glimpse a tension between, on one hand, a clear-cut commitment to certain outcomes and, on the other, the expertise of the communitarians and the new institutionalists, according to which the outcomes are best achieved through increased citizen participation and a proliferation of networks. Neither tension is simply one of style. Both tensions reflect the limitations of the traditions on which New Labour has relied. What does government do when it follows the experts but does not reach the predicted outcomes? It pulls on levers in an attempt to exert direct control over outcomes. But the levers are now rubber ones. The attempts to control fail.

How radical were the reforms? A final debate about the content of the reforms is that about how radical they are. Tories and Whigs lament the radical nature of the reforms. They deride New Labour for undertaking an immoderate and wholesale onslaught of the constitution.[26] If there is need for reform—and they often suggest there is not—they would rather it be more gradual and more in accord with the grain of a constitution that has served so well to date. In contrast, other critics reprove New Labour for timidity.[27] Typically they would have the government adopt a codified constitution.

To some extent the contrast between these two sets of critics is again misleading: the respective views reveal more about the critics' own political ideas than about how radical the reforms are. Still, to recognize New Labour's debt to particular theories of democracy is, here too, to cast new light on the debate. The Tories and Whigs protest too much. No doubt the reforms unsettle the idea of Britain as a unitary state, but this idea has always been something of a myth. And, besides, the reforms clearly go with the grain of one of the most well established traditions in British politics—they derive from the liberal representative concept of democracy. This concept of democracy is, of course, perfectly compatible with a codified constitution. Thus, critics who advocate codification are perhaps not far from New Labour. Perhaps it is a little too neat to

[26] Examples include J. Redwood, *The Death of Britain?* (London: Palgrave Macmillan, 1999); and N. Johnson, *Reshaping the British Constitution: Essays in Political Interpretation* (Basingstoke: Palgrave Macmillan, 2004).

[27] Examples include J. Tomaney, "End of the Empire State? New Labour and Devolution in the United Kingdom," *International Journal of Urban and Regional Research* 24 (2000): 672–88; and T. Nairn, *After Britain: New Labour and the Return of Scotland* (London: Granta, 1999).

say that they voice a radical liberalism that believes in abstract principles while New Labour enacts a Whiggish liberalism that looks more to guidelines drawn out from existing practices. Even so, New Labour and its radical critics clearly share background assumptions associated with a liberal representative concept of democracy. The radical imagination could range further afield.

The Prospects for Reform

The radical imagination might look to various sources for inspiration, including New Labour itself, the European Community, and perhaps civil society. Let us look now at the prospects for the reforms.

The European dimension.   One debate about the prospects for reform concerns the continuing impact of the EU. Britain's accession to the European Community in 1972 left it subject to a higher law. Changes in European law may bring about changes in Britain's constitution. Nonetheless, it is unlikely that the EU will be a source of changes that differ significantly from those made by New Labour. To the contrary, the impact of the European Union has typically been through the legalization and judicial review of various human rights. Nor is that all. The European Commission appears to subscribe to many of the communitarian and institutionalist ideas that lurk behind New Labour's reforms of the public sector. As we saw in the last chapter, the commission's White Paper on European Governance of 2001 defines the goal as an opening up of policymaking to make it more inclusive and accountable, where inclusivity and accountability appear to be desirable because they will lead to more effective policies and lend the EU greater legitimacy.[28] We might ask: What will happen if the inclusivity does not lead to the desired increase in effectiveness? Will the Commission, like New Labour, find itself simultaneously devolving power and seeking to specify and control outcomes?

An inner momentum.   Another debate about the prospects for reform concerns their inner momentum. Once power has been devolved, it becomes hard to control not only outcomes but also processes. Perhaps the legislative assemblies and executive agencies created by New Labour will take the reforms in directions that the government neither intended nor would welcome. There have been some highly visible examples. Londoners dared to elect Livingstone. Morgan eventually won through in Wales. There have also been numerous less clear-cut and less well-publicized examples of New Labour losing control. It was arguably dissatisfaction in

[28] Commission of the European Communities, *European Governance.*

Wales itself that did most to instigate the Richard Commission's proposals to move from the original devolution model (in which the National Assembly fused executive and parliamentary aspects) to arrangements closer to the Westminster model—a suggestion the government seems to have accepted. Again, the governments of Scotland and Wales have clearly defined their health care policies in contrast to those promoted by New Labour in England.[29] The prospect of diverse public policies is one of the most exciting to emerge from New Labour's reforms. The new political authorities might forge a pathway to participatory and pluralist alternatives to a liberal representative democracy filled out by the expertise of the social sciences. However, if they are to do so, they will have to break with the dominant traditions in the Labour Party and indeed British politics more generally.

What Is the Alternative?

New Labour's attempts to reform the British state embody a representative theory of democracy together with themes from the new institutionalism. The prospects for a radical alternative look fairly bleak. Nonetheless, participatory and pluralist traditions in the Labour Party continue to inspire hope for an alternative. It is important here, I believe, to distinguish between, on one hand, socialist alternatives based on critique, pluralism, and participation, and, on the other, socialist alternatives that are based on a claimed expert knowledge about the workings of capitalism and globalization.[30] The former would surely involve some kind of suspicion of the latter's claims to expertise and the objectifications on which they depend. It seems to me that socialist alternatives that appeal to scientific knowledge of the inexorable workings of capitalism and globalization are likely to lead to a downplaying of democratic issues in favor of attempts to reassert the state's role and expertise in the provision of welfare. At stake here is the balance of "social justice" and "democratic self-rule" in a "social democratic" tradition that has leaned, in my view, too much toward the former.

Alas, it is today a daunting task to retain faith in participatory and pluralist ideals. We must distinguish them from liberal representative ones while also meeting the obvious objections to them. Tentative suggestions will no more establish clear water between participation and representa-

[29] Compare Bevir and Rhodes, *Governance Stories*, chap. 8.
[30] For an otherwise admirable account of New Labour's constitutional reforms that unfortunately appeals to such expertise, see Evans, *Constitution-making and the Labour Party*.

tion than they will reassure those who worry that pluralism leads to elitism. Maybe we are dealing with fuzzy boundaries, not sharp dichotomies. Certainly participatory and pluralist themes find several echoes in New Labour's reforms, notably in devolution and in its advocacy of partnerships between the public sector and the voluntary and private sectors. Yet, as well as these echoes, we find important contrasts.

Participatory and pluralist democrats might rethink the representative concept of democracy that informs New Labour's constitutional reforms. They might attempt to extend democratic practices to various associations of producers, consumers, and others. Whereas New Labour has adopted a program of constitutional reform composed of devolution to national parliaments and doses of electoral reform, an alternative might establish new forums in which citizens can deliberate, formulate policies, and connect with the state. Whereas New Labour typically relies on indirect representation in the institutions of the state, an alternative might assign aspects of governance to democratic associations other than the state. Whereas New Labour promotes partnerships in which the state plays an active role, regulating and controlling outcomes, an alternative might hand over aspects of government to associations other than the state. Whereas New Labour's partnerships aim to deliver services more effectively with little concern for the inner workings of the organizations with which the state cooperates, an alternative might be committed to extending democratic principles to groups in civil society. This alternative would lead, for instance, to a greater concern with the democratic nature of the Labour Party itself.

Participatory and pluralist democrats also might rethink the institutionalist measures that, as we will see in chapter 9, inspire much of New Labour's reform of the public sector. They might subdue expertise in favor of attempts to form and implement public policies in ways that encourage citizen participation. This alternative too finds echoes in New Labour's reforms, notably the idea that networks should involve relevant stakeholders. But again there are important differences. New Labour appears to be wedded almost exclusively to a representative democracy in which public policy is implemented by a managerial elite that is in turn subject to direction and supervision by a political elite who in turn are accountable to the popular will through elections. However, an alternative might promote deliberation throughout the policymaking process including implementation. Whereas New Labour seems to assume that administration can be a purely neutral or technical matter of implementing the will of the legislature, an alternative might allow for the involvement of citizens throughout the processes by which administrative agencies actively interpret and define the will of the legislature.

CONCLUSION

Britain's largely unwritten constitution makes it especially difficult to draw a sharp distinction between constitutional reform and broad institutional changes, and, more particularly between constitutional and administrative reforms. Devolution and its cohorts are often spoken of as constitutional reforms. But we might suggest that the reforms modify institutional arrangements rather than establishing a wholly different system. Consider a strong analogy: the delegates who met in Philadelphia in 1789 were supposed to initiate broad institutional reforms through amendments to the Articles of Confederation. In actuality, they engaged in constitutional reform, building an entirely new political system more or less from scratch. New Labour's reforms are clearly closer in spirit to the intended institutional amendments than to the dramatic new constitutional creation that actually appeared at Philadelphia. The point of this analogy is not to belittle the changes wrought by New Labour; the changes have clearly been dramatic. Instead, the analogy seeks to muddy unnecessarily sharp distinctions between constitutional, institutional, and administrative reforms.

In all its reforms, New Labour has clung to representative democracy and expertise at the expense of an attempt to build a new political system based on alternative democratic imaginaries. New Labour has attempted to save representative democracy from various challenges by drawing on the very forms of expertise that inspired the challenges. In this chapter we have looked at devolution, parliamentary reform, and electoral reform, all of which remain defined by the historical ideals of representative democracy. In the next chapter, we will explore an area of constitutional reforms—the judiciary—in which New Labour has tried to address failings in representative democracy by shifting decision-making powers from elected assemblies to apparently neutral experts. Later, in chapters 9 and 10, we will explore how New Labour's administrative reforms similarly respond to challenges to the state by drawing on the very forms of expertise that posed those challenges.

CHAPTER SEVEN

Judicial Reform

IMMEDIATELY FOLLOWING the 1997 election, the New Labour government began to pursue a series of radical constitutional reforms with the intention of making British political institutions more effective and more accountable. As a result of these reforms, the judiciary has witnessed more change in the last ten years than in the entire past century. The Human Rights Act (1998) dramatically extended the practice of judicial review. The Constitutional Reform Act (2005) overhauled the Lord Chancellor's Office and the process of judicial appointments and set the scene for the creation of a supreme court.

How are we to interpret judicial reform under New Labour? What are its implications for democracy? One way of answering these questions is to describe New Labour's reforms as part of the broad pattern of juridification that many social scientists have observed taking place in various states as well as transnational and international spaces. But to appeal to this broad pattern of juridification is only to push back our questions. How are we to explain juridification? What are the implications of juridification for democracy?

In this chapter, I approach general questions about juridification through discussion of Britain in comparative contexts. To begin, I outline the conventional view of the role of the judiciary in the Westminster model as presented by A. V. Dicey. Next I suggest that the Westminster model obscured the fact of a dispersed pattern of rule in which the judiciary sometimes played a role very different from that described by Dicey. Juridification is part of the rise of new theories and worlds of governance that highlight and exacerbate the limitations of the Westminster model as an account of British politics. From this perspective, New Labour's judicial reforms appear as attempts to solve problems associated with the new governance, and yet, ironically, the reforms are themselves constrained by an increasingly outdated Westminster model as well as by a belief in expertise.

Table 7.1 provides a summary of the changes from Dicey to New Labour. It also points to an alternative response to the new governance based on a move away from the Westminster model and policy expertise toward a more participatory democracy and dialogic public policy.

TABLE 7.1
From Dicey to New Labour

	Dicey— Westminster model	New Labour— Juridification	An alternative
Democratic theory	Liberal representative	Liberal representative	Participatory
State theory	Formal constitution	Network governance	Plural networks
Public administration	Enacts legislation	Active in policymaking process	Facilitates citizen deliberation
Accountability	Procedural	Performance	Inclusive participation
Law	Above politics	Expert knowledge	Elite discourse
Role of judges and courts	Enforce parliamentary will and rule of law	Enforce human rights and welfare	Promote self-rule in collective practices

THE JUDICIARY IN THE WESTMINSTER MODEL

New Labour's judicial reforms are part of a wider process of juridification. In particular, they are an example of politicians handing more power and decisions to judges and courts in an attempt to address problems of effectiveness and accountability that have arisen as new theories and worlds of governance have eroded confidence in older images of the judiciary, such as that associated with the Westminster model. Often they are attempts to formalize through law what otherwise might be decided by democratic processes.

The Nineteenth-Century Background

Relatively few general accounts of the British constitutional and political system were published before the middle of the nineteenth century. When they came, they rushed in. The year 1867 alone saw the appearance of William Hearn's, *Government of England*, Alpheus Todd's *Parliamentary Government in England*, and Walter Bagehot's *English Constitution*. Erskine May's *Constitutional History of England* had appeared a few years earlier in 1861. During the next two decades, several other classic studies were published, including Edward Freeman's *The Growth of the English Constitution* (1872), Sir William Anson's *The Law and Custom of the Constitution* (1886), and most important for us, Dicey's *Introduction to the Study of the Law of the Constitution* (1885).[1] These classic works

[1] General studies of nineteenth-century political thought include S. Collini, D. Winch, and J. Burrow, *That Noble Science of Politics: A Study in Nineteenth Century Intellectual*

were characteristically written against the background of Whig historiography, and they entrenched the broad outlines of what became the
Westminster model.

The rush of interest in the constitution arose in part out of a concern
with the development of representative and responsible government in
the colonies.[2] Todd's family had emigrated to Canada when he was eight,
and Hearn had moved to Australia in 1854 to take up a professorship
at the University of Melbourne. Nonetheless, the main source of concern
with the constitution was the debates around the Reform Act of 1867.
During the nineteenth century, from early fears of Jacobinism to the late
rise of socialism and the New Unionism, the British state constantly faced
the threat and reality of popular protests demanding an extension of political and social rights. These protests were met by a series of Reform
Acts, such as that of 1867, which slowly extended the franchise to an
ever-larger proportion of adult males. Yet, the Reform Acts, precisely
because they extended the franchise, exacerbated a widespread anxiety
about the entry of the lower classes into government. Even radical liberals were affected by this anxiety, with, for example, J. S. Mill advocating
a system of plural voting as a means to preserve the competence of the
electorate.[3] One component of the anxiety was the idea that the extension
of the franchise would disrupt social stability and constitutional principles. Dicey examined the constitution to dispel this idea. The Westminster
model was to some extent a construction of conservative Whigs responding to anxieties about popular participation.

Dicey on the Constitution

Dicey himself tried to alleviate fears over the spread of democracy by appealing to a constitution in which popular participation was restrained
by parliamentary sovereignty, the rule of law, and informal constitutional
conventions. In doing so, he provided the classic account of the place of
the judiciary in what was to become the Westminster model.

Parliamentary sovereignty. Dicey begins his analysis of the British
legal system by looking at Parliament. He writes, "the sovereignty of Parliament is (from a legal point of view) the dominant characteristic of

History (Cambridge: Cambridge University Press, 1983); and M. Francis and J. Morrow,
A History of English Political Thought in the 19th Century (London: Duckworth, 1994).

[2] On the global and imperial forms of constitutional theory at this time, see D. Bell, *The
Idea of Greater Britain: Empire and the Future of World Order, 1860–1900* (Princeton:
Princeton University Press, 2007).

[3] J. S. Mill, "Considerations on Representative Government," in *Collected Works of John
Stuart Mill*, vol. 19.

our political institutions."[4] Parliamentary sovereignty denotes the power of Parliament (composed of the monarch, the House of Lords, and the House of Commons) to make or unmake any law it chooses, and no other person or institution can overrule its laws. Parliament is the only body with the authority to make laws. Thus, parliamentary sovereignty implies the subordination of the judiciary, which cannot challenge an act of Parliament.

The attempt to subordinate the judiciary might appear to fail in light of the common law. The common law appears to allow judges to make laws by establishing precedents that are then binding upon their successors. Dicey argues, however, that the practice of the common law does not really contradict the supremacy of Parliament since "judicial legislation is … subordinate legislation" to Acts of Parliament.[5] Crucially, for Dicey, there is nothing in the constitution akin to the judicial review provided by the Supreme Court in the United States. To the contrary, Parliament ultimately has supreme authority in every jurisdiction, including the rights of the individual.

At this point parliamentary sovereignty begins to resemble just that kind of despotism which so enraged many eighteenth- and nineteenth-century radicals. Parliament appears to be a leviathan against which individuals have no appeal and from which they can expect no redress. Dicey argues, however, that two limitations circumscribe the actions of even the most despotic ruler. First, no prudent monarch or government would knowingly pursue a morally repugnant law that might incite the people to revolt. Second, even tyrants who have the power to make unilateral decisions are unlikely to take certain actions given the cultural context in which they govern.

Rule of law. If parliamentary sovereignty appears as a counter to popular participation, the rule of law is, for Dicey, something of a counter to parliamentary despotism. Legislators in Parliament are constrained by a commitment to the rule of law. Dicey identifies the rule of law rather narrowly with known rules, equality, and respect for precedent. For a start, Dicey argues that government operates in accord with known rules rather than arbitrary caprice or even discretion. Dicey also argues that Britain, unlike its counterparts, has long boasted a notion of equality before the law, according to which all individuals are treated similarly regardless of class or rank. Finally, Dicey associates the rule of law with the way in which the principles that protect individual liberties have become entrenched over time through the decisions of judges. In his view,

---

[4] A. Dicey, *Introduction to the Study of the Law of the Constitution* (London: Macmillan, 1902), 34.
[5] Ibid., 58.

although some other states rely on enumerated powers and formalized rights, Britain's use of precedent is a more effective way of ensuring individual liberties.

It is difficult to see how Dicey's account of the rule of law can be reconciled with his principle of parliamentary sovereignty. To mention just one issue: if Parliament is bound to follow known rules rather than make and unmake laws on a whim, how can it be free to do as it pleases? Dicey himself argued that far from being in conflict, the two ideas actually reinforced one another: "the sovereignty of Parliament ... favours the supremacy of the law, whilst the predominance of rigid legality throughout our institutions evokes the exercise, and thus increases the authority, of Parliamentary sovereignty."[6] Yet, his argument here is vague, controversial, and arguably implausible. To say that parliamentary sovereignty favors the supremacy of the law is not to say it favors a rule of law based on formal equality and respect for precedent. Likewise, it is far from clear why Parliament requires a strong legal system, rather than, for example, a strong executive branch of government.

Constitutional conventions. The final section of *Introduction to the Study of the Law of the Constitution* is in part an attempt to explain how the rule of law can operate alongside parliamentary sovereignty. Dicey's explanation consists of an appeal to the importance of constitutional conventions. He argues that the legal system consists not only of the procedural enforcement of rules and precedents but also of informal "customs, practices, maxims, or precepts which are not enforced or recognised by the Courts, [and which] make up a body not of laws, but of constitutional or political ethics."[7] The unwritten constitution of Britain holds these conventions and implicit rules as vital to the operation of democracy. Indeed, Dicey elevates the customs and conventions into a "constitutional morality" to which he then appeals in order to limit the powers of a popularly elected Parliament.[8] A sovereign Parliament that adheres to these constitutional precepts will not oppose the supremacy of law and so the individual liberties secured by precedent.

After Dicey

Dicey's constitutional views proved extremely influential among both academics and political actors. Even if Bagehot loomed as large over the imagination of political scientists interested in government, Dicey clearly defined the agenda for legal scholars and others interested in the constitu-

[6] Ibid., 402.
[7] Ibid., 413.
[8] Ibid., 424.

tion and the judiciary.[9] For most of the twentieth century the dominant image of the British political system was of a Westminster model defined in terms of parliamentary sovereignty. The Westminster model suggests that the courts merely interpret acts of Parliament to the best of their abilities. Judges are meant to rule in accord with the intention of the legislature: their decisions are meant to reflect how a given act was designed to function. Judges are not meant to challenge, let alone overturn, legislation as they can in, for example, the United States. Indeed, by combining parliamentary sovereignty with a concept of the rule of law that was based on precedent, Dicey's followers implied that a judge should never actually challenge an existing law, regardless of whether that law arose from a legislative act or from the past decision of a judge. Any attempt by the courts to reexamine the content of law appeared to be an abuse of their power.[10]

Social scientists and legal scholars have been slow to recognize the impact of their work on the world they study. It is thus important to mention the extent to which Dicey and his followers helped to construct the very world about which they wrote. Their constitutional views influenced political and legal actors, thereby helping to bring into being the kind of constitution they argued existed. One prominent example is the comparatively weak development in the twentieth century of administrative laws covering the expanding welfare state. Britain proved slow to devise an administrative law that applied solely to government actions and procedures and not to private corporations or individuals. Many jurists believed that such an administrative law was incompatible with Dicey's account of the role of equality and precedent in the rule of law. British administrative law thus tended to develop through the application of case law based on private law.

For a hundred years Dicey's *Law of the Constitution* was the preeminent work in the field. Of course, Dicey's views were challenged often and vigorously during that time. Sir Ivor Jennings in particular argued that the constitution should be understood in the context of social and economic changes.[11] Yet, despite such challenges, Dicey's authority began to crumble only in the 1970s. Just as Dicey's views reflect the problems of nineteenth-century democratization, so the turn away from his views owes much to the new theories and worlds of governance. New theories,

---

[9] Bagehot did not discuss either parliamentary sovereignty or the rule of law, and he showed no interest in the constitutional role of courts and judges. See W. Bagehot, *The English Constitution* (London: Oxford University Press, 1963).

[10] Compare K. Davis, "The Future of Judge-Made Public Law in England: A Problem of Practical Jurisprudence," *Columbia Law Review* 61 (1961): 202.

[11] I. Jennings, *The Law and the Constitution* (London: University of London Press, 1933).

such as behavioralism and rational choice theory, undermine his assumptions about the behavior of political actors and institutions. New international worlds, notably the rise of the European Union, challenge the practicability of his concept of parliamentary sovereignty. New domestic worlds, including contracting out and regimes of regulation, challenge his concept of the rule of law.

JURIDIFICATION AND GOVERNANCE

The new theories and worlds of governance decisively undermine the Westminster model. A process of juridification challenges Dicey's account of the role of judges and the courts in Britain. New Labour's reforms are simultaneously an extension of this process of juridification and a response to problems associated with it. Yet, before we turn to New Labour, we should briefly explore the way in which the new governance has undermined Diceyan ideas such as those about parliamentary sovereignty and a subordinate judiciary.

Defining Juridification

The word "juridification" is used in several different ways to capture various changes that make law a more powerful and prevalent force in state and society. Law and judges are, it seems, playing more prominent parts in our collective decision making and so in structuring social life. The popularity of the notion of juridification owes much to Jurgen Habermas. For Habermas, and many others, juridification has a narrow meaning.[12] It refers to the tendency of modern states to deploy the law to transform civil society and private life. The state transforms private life into a public matter especially through its extension of the welfare state. However, while this narrow notion of juridification draws attention to some changes in regulatory laws, it risks occluding other ways in which law is increasingly penetrating politics and society. In Britain, for example, the Thatcher governments of the 1980s used legal regulations less to expand welfare than to regulate local government in an attempt to roll back the state.[13] Thatcherism provides an example of juridification occurring alongside an attempt to reduce the role of the state in the market, civil society, and private life.

---

[12] J. Habermas, "Law as Medium and Law as Institution," in G. Teubner, *Dilemmas of Law in the Welfare State* (Berlin: W. de Gruyter, 1986).

[13] See J. Gyford, S. Leach, and C. Game, *The Changing Politics of Local Government* (London: Unwin Hyman, 1989).

A broader concept of juridification might refer to all the ways in which an expanded role for law narrows the scope for democratic processes in civil society and even state institutions themselves. Juridification thus captures not only the expanding range of laws but also the growing reliance on judges and courts to interpret and apply laws. These processes constrain the space for democratic decisions. Even when a representative institution creates a rule on an issue and hands the application of that rule to the courts, it thereby constrains the space for any future democratic decisions on that issue. When the application of the rule is given over to the courts, then citizens (and legislators and public officials) have an incentive to try to get their way on that issue by employing a lawyer rather than by engaging in democratic politics. This broader concept of juridification covers the ways in which law continues to become more powerful even as neoliberal governments and their successors seek to roll back and reform the welfare state.

Lars Blichner and Anders Molander identify five different types of juridification, emphasizing that they need not occur simultaneously.[14] First, "constitutive juridification" is the process by which the norms of a political system are created or changed in order to improve the competencies and role of the legal system. This process refers not only to the expansion of the administrative and welfare state but also, as we will see, to the expansion of judicial review. A second type of juridification can occur when legal regulation is expanded or increasingly differentiated. Third, juridification takes place when social actors, in and outside government, increasingly refer to the law to resolve conflicts. A fourth type of juridification is identified with the judges and the courts playing an increasingly prominent role in lawmaking. In Britain, and the EU more generally, the European Court has facilitated the courts' expansion into lawmaking. Yet, as we will see, this type of juridification sometimes might be less a result of the judiciary grabbing for power than of the government and citizens forcing the judiciary to take on a greater role. Finally, a fifth type of juridification is a vague process in which people increasingly come to define themselves and others in legal terms, such as what it means to be an EU citizen.

Understanding Juridification

Once we expand our concept of juridification to cover the diverse processes identified by Blichner and Molander, we need to relate it not only to the welfare state but, arguably more importantly, to the rise of mar-

[14] L. Blichner and A. Molander, "What Is Juridification?," *Northwestern Journal of International Law and Business* 97 (1996): 354–97.

ketization, contracting out, networks, joined-up governance, and other related developments. How are we to understand and explain juridification so conceived? How can we explain Dicey's increasing irrelevance?

We might begin by relating juridification to the new governance. To relate juridification to more general changes in governance and the state is neither particularly controversial nor particularly original. Lars Trägardh and Michael Carpini write, "the juridification of politics to a considerable extent must be understood in empirical, rather than normative terms; that is, as one expression of the broad secular trend that is currently challenging the political order that we call 'national democracy.'"[15] They then go on to identify the relevant secular trends with both globalization and the rise of a modern individualism, concluding that a globalized market society is hollowing out the state from above and below.

Trägardh and Carpini offer little concrete discussion of the ways in which the new governance leads to juridification. We can get a sense of some of the processes involved, however, if we return to the attempts of the Thatcher governments to regulate local government.[16] As was mentioned above, central government used law to constrain local government as part of its attempt to promote marketization, the new public management, and other aspects of the new governance. In addition, when central government attacked established bureaucratic norms and procedures, it created a climate of uncertainty such that political actors, including central and local governments, turned to the courts to determine their rights and duties.

More generally, the new governance has led to juridification through the following general processes.

- The new theories of governance drew attention to the ways in which the law played a more extensive role than was suggested by previous theories, including those proposed by Dicey.
- The new worlds of governance, including the rise of transnational institutions and contracting out, gave the law a more extensive role than it previously had.
- Politicians, judges, and citizens have been inspired by the new theories to respond to the new worlds in ways that have given the law a yet more extensive role.

[15] L. Trägardh and M. Carpini, "The Juridification of Politics in the United States and Europe: Historical Roots, Contemporary Debates and Future Prospects," in L. Trägardh, ed., *After National Democracy: Rights, Law and Power in America and the New Europe* (Oxford: Hart, 2004), 42.

[16] Compare M. Loughlin, "Law, Ideologies and the Political-Administrative System," *Journal of Law and Society* 16 (1989): 21–41.

Let us illustrate each of these processes with examples from British politics prior to New Labour's rise to power in 1997.

New Theories of Governance

New theories of governance have drawn attention to the ways in which the law plays a more extensive role than that suggested by Dicey and the Westminster model. Gaps in Dicey's theories and the Westminster model became visible in the 1930s as modernist social scientists began to pay more attention to behavioral topics such as policy networks and political parties. It is surely no accident that the most famous early twentieth-century critic of Dicey, Sir Ivor Jennings, was one of the social scientists writing between the wars who focused on the actual behavior of political actors (individuals and institutions) rather than their formal constitutional roles; he foreshadowed contemporary scholars of public administration and governance who evoke a core executive and policy networks in ways that challenge the Westminster model.[17]

Various new theories suggested that the courts always had played an active role in British politics. While early twentieth-century constitutional lawyers focused on topics inherited from Dicey, paying little attention to administrative law, social scientists began to pay more and more attention to public administration and the policy process. Once legal scholars too began to take note of the administrative state, Diceyan opposition to a distinct administrative law seemed implausible, as did the idea that the judiciary remained above politics.[18] Among the roles that the judiciary has long played in British politics are, first, judicial review based on case law and, second, administrative regulation by ombudsmen, tribunals, and inquiries.

Insofar as Diceyan-inspired constitutional lawyers paid attention to administrative law, they concentrated on the case law of judicial review by the courts. As we saw, Dicey's attempt to reconcile parliamentary sovereignty with the rule of law was unconvincing. The courts use case law as the basis for a type of judicial review, and judges review government actions against procedural values such as proportionality and reasonableness. Lord Reid, as a member of the judicial committee of the House of Lords, played a notable role in the development of just such judicial review after the Second World War. More recently, in 1993, when the Home Office proceeded with a deportation despite having assured the

---

[17] I. Jennings, *Cabinet Government* (Cambridge: Cambridge University Press, 1936); and I. Jennings, *Parliament* (Cambridge: Cambridge University Press, 1939).

[18] E.g., I. Harden and N. Lewis, *The Noble Lie: The British Constitution and the Rule of Law* (London: Hutchinson, 1986).

court that it would not do so, the courts even decided that ministers could be in contempt of court.[19]

The influence of Dicey meant that constitutional lawyers were slow to recognize the extent to which law intervened in politics not only by judicial review but also by ombudsmen, tribunals, and inquiries.[20] While many tribunals and inquiries that judges lead are fairly uncontentious investigations into national disasters such as the collapse of crowd barriers at Hillsborough football stadium, even these inquiries can have direct policy and legal implications, such as the requirement that certain stadiums be seating only. What is more, judges also head tribunals and lead investigations that concern the actions of government ministers, parliamentarians, civil servants, and street-level bureaucrats. For example, Harold Macmillan initiated such an inquiry into the Profumo affair. Or, in the Thatcher years, Lord Justice Scarman examined the causes of race riots in Brixton, London.

New Worlds of Governance

New worlds of governance have given the law a more extensive role than it had previously. As we saw in chapter 4, the new worlds of governance did not arise as part of an inexorable process of functionalization, rationalization, or modernization independent of the theories of policy actors. To the contrary, the new worlds of governance can be seen as products of the new theories of governance: neoclassical economics and rational choice theory inspired contracting out and other neoliberal reforms, and institutionalist theories of networks are now inspiring attempts to promote partnerships and joined-up government. In mentioning new worlds of governance, therefore, I want to suggest that new policies, such as contracting out, and new institutions, such as the EU, extended the role of law in political decision making.

Neoliberal reforms of the public sector often transformed administrative relations into legal ones.[21] For example, contracting out replaced the hierarchic relationships of a bureaucracy with a contractual one between purchaser and provider. The rise of such legal relations meant that the courts had to play a greater role in defining where formal powers and liabilities lay in a range of public services.

---

[19] *M v Home Office* [1993] 3 *All ER* 537 (HL).

[20] A fine exception is C. Harlow and R. Rawlings, *Law and Administration* (London: Butterworths, 1997).

[21] Compare P. Vincent-Jones, "The Limits of Near Contractual Governance: Local Authority Internal Trading Under CCT," *Journal of Law and Society* 21 (1994): 214–37.

A far more dramatic impact came about as a result of Britain's involvement with the EU.[22] In 1966 Britain recognized the right of individual petition to the European Court of Human Rights. In 1972 Britain's accession to the European Union allowed for legal appeals also being made to the European Court of Justice (ECJ) in Luxemburg. More generally still, Parliament then accepted European law into the British Constitution. In principle Parliament was (and, as we shall see, by and large still is) free to vote not only to leave the EU but also to reject any part of European law, although equally, of course, other members of the EU would probably see any attempt by Britain to reject significant European laws as a breach of its treaty obligations. Still, over time European law has come in practice to act as something akin to a higher law for Britain. The most dramatic moment in the assertion of the supremacy of European law came with the *Factortame* cases of 1990 and especially 1991.

The *Factortame* decision arose out of a dispute about fishing rights. The Merchant Shipping Act of 1988 effectively barred foreign companies from fishing in British waters in a way that seemed contrary to European law. When a Spanish company, Factortame, appealed, the British courts deferred the issue to the ECJ while saying that they could not strike down an act of Parliament. The ECJ declared that the House of Lords did have the authority to overturn parliamentary legislation so as to uphold European law. In 1991 the British courts decided the case by declaring that when domestic and European law appeared to conflict, the courts should assume that Parliament intended to give precedence to European law.[23] Thus, the courts have come to adjudicate differences between national and supranational legislation.

Responding to Governance

Politicians, judges, and citizens have been inspired by the new theories to respond to the new worlds in ways that have given the law a yet more extensive role. At a very general level, an increased awareness of the role of law has prompted many political actors to intensify their practices of self-scrutiny. For example, the growth of a regime of regulation, and with it a consciousness of regulations, has prompted many local governments and executive agencies to see and manage themselves in increasingly legal terms. Legal consciousness and legal relations have

[22] Among the extensive literature on the impact of the EU, see D. Nicol, *EC Membership and the Judicialization of British Politics* (Oxford: Oxford University Press, 2002); and, for a comparative perspective, A-M. Slaughter, A. Sweet, and J. Weiler, eds., *The European Court and National Courts—Doctrine and Jurisprudence: Legal Change in its Social Context* (Oxford: Hart, 2000).

[23] *R v Secretary of State for Transport, ex p. Factortame Ltd (No. 2)* [1991] 1 AC 603.

thus become more prominent in all kinds of everyday practices of governance.

Politicians have actively given the courts a greater role. The new governance began with some politicians using the courts to challenge older ways of regulating social life. More recently the new governance has left many politicians grasping for new levers of control and worrying about declining levels of participation and trust. The Thatcher governments used the courts as well as industrial tribunals to restructure labor relations. They also created numerous regulatory bodies to oversee privatized industries, independent executive agencies, and the contractual relationships that rose with outsourcing. Later, John Major, as prime minister, turned to judges to address the questions of ethics that arose over the conduct of several members of his government. Lord Justice Scott led an inquiry into the arms for Iraq affair. Lord Nolan conducted a general review of ethical standards in public life. The government responded to the Nolan report by replacing the older practice of self-regulation by the House of Commons with one headed by a new parliamentary commissioner for standards.

Judges can actively grab for a greater role. Sometimes they are inspired by the rise of new patterns of global governance: high court justices from different countries form an increasingly distinctive and self-conscious network, drawing on one another's decisions in a way that gives international norms authority over domestic governments.[24] Sometimes they are inspired by a liberal institutionalism in which the judiciary stands as an independent branch of government defending the rights and welfare of individuals, and perhaps the public interest.[25] The Thatcher years certainly saw several individual judges acting—often to the chagrin of the government—in just this way. More generally, during the late 1970s, the Law Commission advocated a series of procedural reforms to strengthen judicial review, and some of the reforms were passed in the Supreme Court Act (1981). In particular, the act simplified the procedure for invoking a legal remedy in public law disputes. It made judicial review far more accessible and common.

Finally, citizens have occasionally forced the courts to take on a more active role. There are parallels here between developments in Britain and the United States. Some legal scholars argue that the United States has witnessed the rise of a culture of "adversarial legalism": as popular trust

[24] See Slaughter, *A New World Order.*

[25] See, for a British example, the writings of the Court of Appeal judge Sir J. Laws, especially J. Laws, "Law and Democracy," *Public Law* 72 (1995): 73–93; and J. Laws, "The Constitution: Morals and Rights," *Public Law* 73 (1996): 622–35. For a scholar offering an extended defense of a similar position, see T. Allan, *Law, Liberty and Justice: The Legal Foundations of British Constitutionalism* (Oxford: Clarendon Press, 1993).

in politicians has declined, so individuals and interest groups have turned to the courts and litigation to check government action and resolve disputes.[26] To this well-known story I would add only the suggestion that the decline of popular trust in politicians owes something to the spread of a loose set of beliefs about the self-interested nature of political action, beliefs not unlike the informing assumptions of neoclassical economics and rational choice theory.[27] Adversarial legalism thus appears as a broad phenomenon inspired by the spread of concepts of economic rationality and the theories of governance to which these have given rise.

NEW LABOUR'S REFORMS

New Labour's judicial reforms are a further example of politicians promoting juridification in response to the new governance. I do not want to deny that the reforms seek to promote and protect individual rights and welfare in a branch of the state that is largely independent of the executive—a view that I suspect is held by many of those responsible for the reforms. Rather, I want to suggest that this liberal institutionalist view is itself one that people came to hold in response to the new governance.

Look again at table 7.1. The new theories and worlds of governance lead to an emphasis on network governance rather than the formal constitution. There is widespread recognition now that civil servants, street-level bureaucrats, judges, and others do not merely enact legislation but also interpret, make, and redefine public policy. Thus, the new governance gives rise to dilemmas of effectiveness and accountability. How can the government effectively realize its policies when these are subject to redefinition and even resistance all down the policy chain? By what procedures can citizens hold accountable all the diverse actors in the policy process, many of whom are unelected? New Labour has responded to these dilemmas of efficiency and trust by promoting juridification. It has turned to judges as experts who can provide efficient protection of

---

[26] E.g., R. Kagan, *Adversarial Legalism: The American Way of Law* (Cambridge: Harvard University Press, 2001).

[27] It is thus ironic (perhaps tragic) to find political scientists trying to explain adversarial legalism by showing how it is a rational choice for actors in certain institutional contexts. On the one hand, insofar as the rise of new theories of governance means that citizens, judges, and politicians increasingly act on an economic concept of rationality, these explanations are of course right. But, on the other, insofar as these explanations take this concept of rationality for granted, rather than treating it as historically contingent, they manifest the culture that they seek to explain, thereby obscuring the possibility of any profound alternative. See T. Burke, *Lawyers, Lawsuits, and Legal Rights* (Berkeley: University of California Press, 2002).

human rights and welfare. It hopes that the performance of lawyers will create widespread trust in this new pattern of rule, thereby giving the state greater legitimacy.

New Labour has been inspired by the new theories of governance to respond to what seems to be a new world in ways that give law a more extensive role. New Labour's reforms thus embody recognition of the limitations of the Westminster model. Yet, ironically, the reforms also embody a lingering attachment to the Westminster model. New Labour has clung to the vestiges of parliamentary sovereignty, and to an image of representative democracy in which elected politicians make policy on the advice of experts.

The Human Rights Act (1998)

As we saw in the previous chapter, when New Labour came to power in 1997, it was committed to a program of constitutional reform that concentrated on devolution, Parliament, and electoral practices. The reforms also included alterations to the British judiciary. The main judicial reform was the incorporation of the European Convention on Human Rights (ECHR) into British law. This reform was realized through the 1998 Human Rights Act (HRA). Arguably, New Labour justified the HRA primarily in terms of effectiveness. Government spokespeople argued that the reform would create a more efficient system within which citizens could appeal to the ECHR without having to take "the long road to Strasbourg." They also suggested that through the HRA, domestic courts would screen cases before they went to Strasbourg, thereby reducing the long and embarrassing list of cases in which European judges ruled against the British government. Government spokespeople also appealed at times to trust and accountability. They argued that the HRA would increase the level of trust in government by giving citizens the security of knowing that the courts would prevent the state misusing its power.

The Human Rights Act incorporated the European Convention on Human Rights into domestic British law. The ECHR contains a set of standards and absolute rights that no member state can circumvent through its own domestic legislature. Britain readily adopted the convention's charter back in the 1950s. Indeed, the British government of the time played a significant part in preparing and drafting the charter, perhaps not quite foreseeing the extent to which it might be used to oppose later government actions. The HRA challenges Britain's long tradition of common law in favor of an enumeration of vague general principles. It also means that Parliament concedes to the judiciary the power of reviewing legislative acts against a formal written document. Section 3 of the Act explicitly states, "primary legislation and subordinate legislation must be read and given effect in a way which is compatible with the Convention rights."

The HRA continues to be confined by the limits of a Diceyan concept of the judiciary and its relationship to Parliament. By empowering the courts with a new capacity to review domestic legislation, the act effectively welcomes the courts into the policymaking process. But this break with the Westminster model is constrained by an attempt to uphold parliamentary sovereignty. The HRA still leaves the courts only interpreting legislation that has already been passed. It does not technically allow them even to overturn an act of Parliament. To the contrary, according to section 4 of the act, a declaration that legislation is incompatible with the ECHR simply refers that legislation back to Parliament.

The Constitutional Reform Act (2005)

The Human Rights Act might have seemed no more than a reluctant response to international pressure for adherence to the ECHR. But New Labour continued to attempt to reform the judiciary's lack of formal, independent, and transparent procedures. Finally, after years of opposition from the House of Lords, the government passed its Constitutional Reform Act (CRA) in 2005. The CRA introduced dramatic changes to the office of the Lord Chancellor and the judicial appointments process, and it even proposed the creation of a Supreme Court. Once again, the government justified the reforms in large part by appealing to effectiveness and trust. The reforms, especially those to the office of the Lord Chancellor, were intended to make the operations of the judiciary more efficient and more transparent.

The lord chancellor.   No proposed feature of the CRA met nearly as much resistance as the elimination of the Office of the Lord Chancellor. Ultimately the government decided to keep the office while radically limiting its powers. Historically, the lord chancellor has served as an important interbranch actor with responsibility for coordinating the judiciary's actions with the government's agenda. The lord chancellor has had a wide variety of duties as both Speaker of the House of Lords and head of the judiciary. The CRA separates these two roles, giving the duties of the latter to a lord chief justice. The government argued that one person could not adequately serve the interests of both the judiciary and the government, especially after the HRA had increased the independence of the courts. The government also suggested that making the head of the judiciary more independent would address concerns about centralization and a lack of transparency. Thus, the new lord chief justice has become the central figure in upholding the autonomy and independence of the judiciary.

The lord chief justice is now responsible for reporting before Parliament to discuss issues of importance to the judiciary. The lord chief justice also gives "designated directions" on the procedural operations of the judicial system. Additionally, in what may seem like a trivial point of semantics, the CRA includes an addendum making numerous alterations to previous acts that refer to the lord chancellor as a parliamentary equivalent to the speaker of the House of Commons; it replaces these references with "speaker of the House of Lords." Other facets of the lord chancellor's historic duties, like control over judicial appointments, are now shared between the lord chancellor and the lord chief justice through procedural consultation. Finally, in addition to inheriting powers, the lord chief justice has been imbued with new powers meant to address British needs in an age of judicial autonomy from Parliament. The reduced role of the lord chancellor adds to the growing separation of powers among the branches of government.

Judicial appointments. In addition to circumscribing the lord chancellor's statutory powers, the CRA transformed the method of judicial appointments. Although the queen was nominally in charge of appointments, in practice the lord chancellor determined them by advising the monarchy. Here too the lord chancellor has lost ground—this time to a new Judicial Appointments Commission. The appointments process has become more formal and independent. The Judicial Appointments Commission screens potential candidates on the basis of merit. (In an attempt to increase accountability and representation, the commission will include legal scholars, judges, and laypeople.) The role of the lord chancellor is largely restricted to rejecting nominees deemed unfit. The CRA has also modified the process for disciplining judicial actors. The power to remove and suspend jurists is now shared between the lord chancellor and the lord chief justice.

A supreme court? The CRA hints at an even more formal separation of powers in its proposal for a supreme court. Historically the highest court in Britain has been composed of the law lords, all of whom are, by virtue of being law lords, also members of the House of Lords. The proposed supreme court will consist of twelve senior judges who will be selected through consultation between the lord chancellor and the Judicial Appointments Commission and only then recommended to the queen by the prime minister. This same appointment process will apply to the president and deputy president of the proposed supreme court. Once in office, supreme court judges will serve for the duration of their lives unless they are removed through a bicameral decision. The president of the court will decide all its other operating principles and rules after consulting with the lord chancellor. The lord chancellor will have little direct impact on the cases the court hears or the procedures it adopts. The lord chancellor's role appears to be limited to securing proper accommodation for the court (part 3, section 50) and administering its costs (part 3, section 53). The jurisdiction of the court will cover the responsibilities held at present by the law lords together with matters arising from the new forms of judicial review and from devolution—the latter of which are currently covered by the Judicial Committee of the Privy Council.

The Reforms in Practice

New Labour's judicial reforms are a response to the problems the new governance poses for the Westminster model, and yet they also cling to the vestiges of the Westminster model. The result is a tension in the way the government treats law and the courts. On the one hand, the lingering presence of the Westminster model encourages the government to treat the law as separate from politics. The application of the law here involves a neutral expertise. The courts appear as instruments for applying government policy, which now includes an adherence to the ECHR, and for protecting fundamental rights and interests. On the other hand, the emerging presence of the new governance encourages the government to treat judges and the courts as part of the policymaking process. The application of the law is here an open, creative, and political act. The courts appear as sites of political games in which the government and judges alike are players trying to cajole and coerce one another into adopting and promoting particular policies and outcomes.

Recognition of the tension between these two views of law casts doubt on New Labour's hope that its reforms will increase effectiveness and legitimacy. Rather, the political role of law in the new governance already seems to be undermining the hope of effectiveness, in terms of protecting rights as well as implementing policy, and over time this failure of effectiveness might well undermine any legitimacy that the courts currently possess based on their performance.

The new theories of governance suggest that the government's use of law will meet with resistance from all kinds of political actors, including the courts themselves as well as local governments and citizens. The center will lose control of its judicial reforms just as it will of its administrative ones. Indeed, after September 11, 2001, the government increasingly began to grumble about the ways in which its reforms were operating. The most dramatic application of the HRA came in 2004 when the courts declared an antiterror law, which allowed for foreign nationals being detained indefinitely if they could not be deported, to be incompatible with the ECHR.[28] Tony Blair and David Blunkett, then home secretary, complained of judges overturning parliamentary decisions and suggested the HRA might have to be revised. Later, in 2006, when a court decided against the government's efforts to deport some Afghani hijackers, Blair ordered the Home Office and the Department of Constitutional Affairs formally to review the HRA.

It might appear that examples of the courts overruling the government are examples of the success of the HRA in providing for protection of rights and welfare. Yet the state of civil liberties in Britain is in fact bleak. Blair presided over a greater erosion of defendants' rights, freedom of protest, and personal privacy than any other postwar premier.[29] The Terrorism Act (2000) and the Regulation of Investigatory Powers Act (2000) subordinate individual rights to the supposed needs of crime control. This erosion of civil liberties has taken place not only through measures taken against terrorism after September 11 but also as a result of New Labour's attempt to curb antisocial behavior and balance rights with responsibilities. The larger point is, of course, that network governance means the center cannot control the judiciary, but also that the judiciary cannot control the center. Rights and liberties are enacted and protected by a network of actors that includes citizens, social movements, the administration, and the central government and the judiciary.

COMPARATIVE PERSPECTIVES

The British case suggests that juridification is a response to the new theories and worlds of governance, and it appeals to expertise in a manner that shrinks the space for democracy. These suggestions gain further plausibility from comparative examples such as the United States, the European Union, and international politics.

The United States

In British debates, the United States is often evoked as an example of strong, independent courts protecting codified rights through judicial review. The role of the judiciary in American politics reflects arguments for expertise and especially nonmajoritarian institutions as checks on

---

[28] *A and Others* v. *Secretary of State for the Home Department* [2004] *UKHL* 56.

[29] For an early study, see H. Fenwick, *Civil Rights: New Labour, Freedom, and the Human Rights Act* (London: Longman, 2000).

popular democracy.[30] *The Federalist* made this argument clear during the debates on the U.S. Constitution. In *Federalist* No. 10, James Madison advocated a separation of powers in which the judiciary would act as a check and balance to the majoritarian nature of the legislature. Similarly, in *Federalist* No. 78, Alexander Hamilton argued that the judiciary had to be independent and unaccountable to the public so that it might serve as an effective counter to the tyranny of the majority.

Juridification in the United States thus expands the domain of long-established nonmajoritarian institutions. This juridification appears in the growing use of litigation to protect rights, the use of courts to define policy, and the increasing use of administrative law. In each case, actors have turned to the courts partly in response to the new theories and worlds of governance.

Citizens and voluntary organizations have increasingly turned to the courts rather than democratic institutions to claim and protect rights. In the period after World War Two, the clauses on due process and equal protection in the fourteenth amendment to the U.S. Constitution were used to extend the rights identified by the constitution from the federal level to the states. This process of incorporation enabled groups to appeal to the Supreme Court when they could not secure their rights at the state level. Thus, for example, African Americans got the Supreme Court to strike down racial segregation in cases such as *Brown* v. *Board of Education of Topeka*. A similar process enabled women to claim the right to use contraception and have abortions in, respectively, *Griswold* v. *Connecticut* and *Roe* v. *Wade*. Less well-known examples of such juridification include *Gideon* v. *Wainwright*, which secured the right of convicts to publicly funded legal representation.

Politicians have increasingly turned to the courts to define and implement policy.[31] Sometimes they use the courts to sidestep a bureaucracy that they perceive not as neutral but as liable to be taken over by their political enemies. Sometimes they use the courts as an instrument for controlling state and local governments. Sometimes they use the courts to shift the costs of a policy from government taxation to a mandate imposed by the court on private actors.

Finally, political actors have turned to administrative law as a means of plugging gaps in accountability highlighted by the new governance. Suspicion of bureaucratic discretion inspired calls for greater accountability and transparency, inspiring the "giving reasons requirement," which seeks to limit the space for arbitrary or biased administration by

---

[30] J. Madison, A. Hamilton, and J. Jay, *The Federalist Papers*, ed. T. Ball (Cambridge: Cambridge University Press, 2003).

[31] Compare Burke, *Lawyers, Lawsuits, and Legal Rights*.

legally mandating that public officials give reasons for their decisions. This requirement has expanded the scope of judicial review of administrative laws.[32] For example, the Administrative Procedures Act required that rules be accompanied by concise general statement of their basis and purpose, and judicial review then became a way of ensuring that agencies do not stray from these statements. Over time, moreover, stakeholders often increase their involvement, forcing administrative agencies to give more detailed justifications, and so giving the courts even more opportunities for review.

Appeals to the courts to protect rights, define policy, and secure administrative standards entail a sidestepping of alternative democratic processes. Yet, as we saw in the case of Britain, juridification is liable to undermine itself, since the new governance encourages political actors to treat the courts as part of political processes. In the United States, the growing use of litigation to sidestep democracy has contributed to the increasing politicization of judicial nominations and elections.

The European Union

Whereas the United States shows how juridification extends existing nonmajoritarian institutions, the EU provides an example of the creation and then expansion of such institutions. We have already seen how developments in the EU contributed to juridification in Britain. Now we might add that juridification has occurred at the European level. The role of courts in European policymaking has constantly expanded.

- Article 177 of the EEC Treaty of 1958 allowed for the ECJ getting involved in disputes involving a conflict between EU law and national law: when EU law is material to adjudication in national courts, the presiding national judge may (sometimes must) ask the ECJ for a "preliminary ruling" on the correct interpretation of EU law and then apply that ruling in settling the case.
- The doctrine of supremacy: in *Costa*, the ECJ ruled that in any conflict between EC and national laws, EC law has primacy.[33]
- The doctrine of direct effect: in *Van Gend en Loos* and then *Van Duyn*, the ECJ ruled that treaty provisions and directives can grant individuals rights that member states must respect and national courts must uphold.[34]

---

[32] See M. Shapiro, "The Giving Reasons Requirement," in M. Shapiro and A. Sweet, eds., *On Law, Politics and Judicialization* (New York: Oxford University Press, 2002), 228–58.

[33] *Costa v. ENEL*, case 6/64, ECR 585 et seq., ECJ 1964.

[34] *Van Gend en Loos v. Nederlandse Administratie der Belastingen*, case 26/62, ECR 1, ECJ 1963; and *Van Duyn v. Home Office*, case 41/74, ECR 1337, ECJ 1974.

- The doctrine of indirect effect: in *Von Colson*, the ECJ ruled that national judges must interpret national law in conformity with EC law.[35]
- The doctrine of governmental liability: in *Francovich*, the ECJ ruled that national courts can hold member states liable for damages caused to individuals due to a member state failing properly to implement an EC directive.[36]

This process of juridification owes much to theories of governance associated with the economic concept of rationality. For a start, many commentators argue that the ECJ and other nonmajoritarian institutions, including the European Central Bank and even the European Commission itself, arose as responses to collective action problems.[37] They argue, in the case of the ECJ, that EU member states have a collective interest in promoting common laws, but that each state has an individual interest in avoiding the costs of compliance, and the member states responded to this collective action problem by empowering the ECJ as a third party institution capable of monitoring and enforcing compliance. In addition, the constant expansion of the role of the courts is often justified in terms of the type of performance accountability inspired by the concerns associated with principle-agent theory: the ECJ is said to produce better outcomes than would other national or European policy actors. Even when the role of the ECJ is justified in terms of transparent procedures, transparency is generally associated with principles being able to give more explicit agendas to agents if the courts are involved.

Whatever justifications there might be for juridification in the EU, it shrinks the space for democracy. The ECJ is an alternative source of decisions to both the European parliament and national legislatures. Local political decisions are being supplanted by supranational judicial decisions.

---

[35] *Von Colson v. Land Nordrhein-Westfalen*, case 14/83, ECR 1891, ECJ 1984.

[36] *Francovich and Bonifaci v. Italy*, case 6/90 and 9/90, ECR 5357, ECJ 1991.

[37] E.g., A. Sweet, "The European Court and Integration," in Shapiro and Sweet, eds., *On Law, Politics and Judicialization*, 1–45. Here too political scientists often explain juridification using the economic concept of rationality that informs much of it. Ironically, if they do not historicize that concept of rationality, they thus present as natural or inexorable processes that are contestable and contingent, and they also present their own explanations as formally valid rather than as historical narratives. For a pertinent example, see A. Sweet and M. Thatcher, "Theory and Practice of Delegation to Non-Majoritarian Institutions," *West European Politics* 25 (2002): 1–22.

International Politics

Related developments in international law have been ably highlighted by Anne-Marie Slaughter.[38] She traces the emergence of a global legal system that is not a hierarchy topped by a world supreme court resolving disputes between states and ruling on international law, but rather a system of networks based on decentralized and interdependent relationships among judges. These networks are forming both horizontally among national courts and vertically between national courts and supranational courts. Slaughter identifies three varieties of global judicial networks: information networks, harmonization networks, and enforcement networks.

Information networks are characterized by the sharing of information between judges and courts. Judges around the world are turning to each other's case laws, especially in areas relating to human rights. Of course, such exchange itself is not new. Yet, Slaughter argues persuasively that judges are now actively and self-consciously seeking it out. Moreover, new technologies facilitate their doing so. Courts around the world increasingly make their cases available to other judges by, for example, posting them on the Internet. Legal research tools like Lexis-Nexis and Westlaw include decisions from Australia, Britain, Canada, the EU, Hong Kong, Ireland, Mexico, New Zealand, Russia, and Singapore. High court judges meet up more frequently at professional seminars, lectures, and training programs.

Harmonization networks arise as information networks generate a consensus. The most conspicuous harmonization networks are those involved in regulation. Slaughter then extends the concept to cover the emergence of other global consensuses especially over human rights. Judges around the world are using the ECHR, even in states that have not adopted it. The South African Supreme Court referred to cases relating to the ECHR in a case that ruled the death penalty unconstitutional. The Israeli High Court of Justice cited an ECHR decision when it struck down certain interrogation techniques. More generally, as judges look around the world for opinions that provide insights on their own cases, so they may build a global consensus on various legal issues.

Enforcement networks arise as courts come to enforce the consensuses associated with harmonization networks. The emergence of global bankruptcy litigation provides an example. States largely left the matter to the courts, and judges around the world negotiated informal agreements in the absence of formal international treaties. The courts thereby created

[38] Slaughter, *New World Order.*

an international bankruptcy litigation regime based on the Cross-Border Insolvency Cooperation Protocols.

While Slaughter ably highlights juridification in international politics, her explanation of the process sometimes appears too reliant on the sociological concept of rationality. She suggests that the rise of global judicial networks can be explained functionally: globalization and related changes have raised a number of transnational and global problems such that, in the absence of formal international laws and treaties, courts by necessity must construct regimes by themselves. This explanation is fairly correct, as long as the functional demands and pressures are not reified. Judges and other policy actors were certainly reacting to the new worlds of governance, but they were not bound to conceive of these worlds or to react to them as they did. Rather, new theories of governance helped to make policy actors aware of transnational exchanges and issues many of which involve nonstate actors. New theories of governance also encouraged policy actors to treat judicial networks, as opposed to state action and legal hierarchies, as effective and legitimate vehicles for addressing such issues.

A DEMOCRATIC ALTERNATIVE

Judicial review has long been defended as an important constraint on democracy. It is meant to protect individual rights against government intrusion and a tyranny of the majority. Equally, however, democrats (including many British socialists) have long complained that judicial review is a legalistic and even arbitrary form of rule that lacks proper structures of accountability and is, moreover, relatively ineffective at upholding rights.[39] The new governance somewhat unsettles this democratic argument. It suggests that representative institutions struggle to hold accountable the complex policy process let alone to ensure it respects individual rights. Thus, juridification now appears to many observers to be needed as both a constraint on infringements of individual rights and a way of securing public trust and so performance legitimacy. The new governance inspires skepticism about the claims made on behalf of representative democracy. This skepticism then makes juridification seem an attractive addition to representative institutions.

The stark debate about the rival merits of representative democracy and judicial review presents a greatly restricted range of options. It is

[39] For a recent example, see R. Bellamy, *Political Constitutionalism: A Republican Defence of the Constitutionality of Democracy* (Cambridge: Cambridge University Press, 2007).

true that the new governance pushes us to rethink the effectiveness of representative democracy. But we could look elsewhere than to juridification for solutions to the problems associated with the new governance. We might have to reject the cozy image of a representative democracy in which a sovereign parliament debates and promotes the general good and passes legislation that dictates policy outcomes—politics is more chaotic than that. But we need not turn to liberal constitutionalism and the courts to tame the chaos, protect rights, and secure tepid accountability through public acceptance of outcomes. Instead of forsaking democracy for a formal rights-based legalism in a hollowed-out state, we might turn to new forms of opportunities for participation in a more decentered system of governance.

Alternatives to juridification appear once we rethink the lingering attachment to representative democracy and seek instead to build on the new governance so as to develop new styles and spaces of democratic participation. The courts might be part of governance networks, popular participation, and social pluralism.[40] Let us briefly examine each in turn.

First, the courts might be part of governance networks. Historically, the law has often been regarded as a formal system of rules standing above politics and society. The new theories of governance suggest that we might see the law as part of a broader pattern of decision making in which disputes are negotiated and renegotiated by diverse actors. The law is open to contest and uncertainty. It is important to emphasize that a view of the law as open in these ways is quite compatible with a belief in the rule of law. Collective liberty requires that we be ruled by known and consistent laws, as well as requiring us, as a community, to make those laws. Yet, even granted the rule of law, the law itself can be seen as open to contest and contingency, for no law or rule determines its own application to new circumstances, and, moreover, laws can be overturned. The application and the reform of law are political practices, typically located at the border of state and civil society. Individuals and groups routinely negotiate and settle disputes through the courts.

Second, the courts might facilitate popular participation. Historically, the emphasis has often been placed on either a legislature or judges determining laws. Yet, other individuals and groups already play active roles in negotiating legal outcomes. There are indeed some ways in which the law appears to be more participatory than does representative government. Whereas citizens elect their political representatives only

[40] The interested reader might note significant similarities and differences between my views here and the more individualistic concept of law as akin to a market order. For the latter, see Trägardh and Carpini, "The Juridification of Politics in the United States and Europe."

intermittently, they can enter the legal system more or less at will, at least in principle. And whereas the legislature is under no obligation to take up grievances or pursue issues raised by particular citizens, the courts must hear the cases that come before them. The two main roles for popular participation in the legal system are those of litigant and juror. Tort law in particular enables litigants peacefully to deliberate and resolve disputes in a fairly open-ended process. The most democratic feature of the legal system is, however, the jury. The involvement of citizens in judicial decisions means that the application of the law can reflect changes in social norms and values. But this involvement could be extended. Jurors need not be restricted to deciding the facts, bringing in a verdict, and assessing damages. They could do more to decide cases and outcomes. They could play a more active, interrogatory role in at least some legal proceedings.

Third, the courts might uphold and extend social pluralism. Historically, the central state has often been thought to have a monopoly on the making of laws. A more plural view would recognize that other groups formulate rules and laws that are binding to their members. Distinct "courts" and "tribunals" even decide on the application of laws in many corporate bodies, including churches and universities.

So, a radical democratic response to the new governance might build further on the open, participatory, and pluralist nature of the law. From this radical democratic perspective, the type of representative democracy associated with Dicey, the Westminster model, and many critics of juridification is a misguided attempt to ignore the virtues and vices of the new governance; it privileges voting over active citizenship exercised at all kinds of entry points in civil society, the state, and the courts. Equally, from this radical democratic perspective, the turn to formal legal rights associated with legal constitutionalism and juridification is a misguided attempt to limit and control a more open-ended process of debate; it privileges judicial expertise and formalized rights over public deliberation and collective decision making.

Conclusion

Juridification is intimately linked to the new governance. New theories of governance increased awareness of the role courts have always played. New worlds of governance made judges and courts more significant. Finally, politicians, judges, and citizens responded to the new governance by giving a greater role to law and the courts. New Labour's judicial reforms are an example of this latter active promotion of juridification.

To recognize the extent to which juridification has been actively promoted as a response to the new governance is to challenge its aura of inexorability. When social scientists link juridification to globalization and the new governance, they give it an aura of historical inevitability. Earlier I mentioned that Trägardh and Carpini recognized the links between juridification and the wider processes that were eroding national democracy and creating new forms of governance. Unfortunately, however, they describe these processes as if there were no alternative. They write, "from this point of view, the juridification of politics is a more or less unavoidable fact of modern political life."[41] Yet, to associate juridification with the new governance is to suggest it is unavoidable only if one assumes, first, that the new governance is unavoidable and, second, that the association between them is necessary rather than contingent. Both these assumptions are questionable. We can question the inexorability of the new governance by emphasizing the extent to which it has been actively crafted in accord with new theories that undermined older images of politics. Likewise, we can question the necessary association between the new governance and juridification insofar as we regard juridification as having been actively promoted in response to the new governance, rather than merely revealed by new theories of governance or conjoined to new worlds of governance. Far from juridification being more or less unavoidable, other responses to the new governance might be possible.

The possibility of other responses gains piquancy from the irony of New Labour clinging to the vestiges of Dicey's constitutional ideas even as it enacts reforms in response to the very forms of governance that have undermined Dicey, the Westminster model, and arguably our inherited concept of representative democracy. One alternative response to the new governance would be to give up even our lingering attachment to these ideas. We might turn instead to more participatory forms of democracy and more dialogic forms of policymaking.

Alas, even if participatory democracy and dialogic policymaking offer an alternative response to the new governance, there are few signs of their likelihood. In Britain, the main political parties all remain captured by visions of representative democracy leavened with the alleged expertise of judges and social scientists. Juridification—especially judicial review with reference to codified rights—appears to have become an unquestioned doxa of British politics. Gordon Brown began his campaign to become leader of the Labour Party with a speech that included hints of further constitutional and judicial reforms.[42] After Brown became prime

[41] Ibid., 42.
[42] *Guardian*, September 25, 2006.

minister, his government issued a green paper, significantly titled *The Governance of Britain*, which proposed a distinct British Bill of Rights and Duties.[43] The Liberals are even more committed to such proposals, and the Conservatives now accept some such ideas. David Cameron, the current leader of the Conservative Party, supports the repeal of the Human Rights Act, but, unlike his predecessors, he proposes replacing it with an alternative bill of rights for Britain. It would take a dramatic change for radical democracy and deliberative policymaking to emerge from the shadow of codified rights and alleged expertise.

[43] *The Governance of Britain*, Cm 7170 (2007).

PART III

Public Administration

CHAPTER EIGHT

Public Policy

THE CONCEPT OF governance spread as new theories and new worlds undermined older analyses of the state, casting doubt on the inherited view of representative democracy. They highlighted problems associated with the relationship between principles and agents and with the declining ability of the center to control the networks and markets through which policies and services are increasingly delivered. Part 1 of this book explored the rise and content of these new theories and worlds. Part 2 examined the problems they posed for constitutional democracy. I also argued there that policy actors had responded to these problems largely by drawing on the old view of representative democracy along with the very theories that had made it so problematic: policy actors responded to the challenge of governance in ways that remain constrained by the image of representative democracy and a faith in policy expertise. Now, in part 3, I want to extend this argument to public administration.

Broadly, part 3 will argue that reforms of public policy and the public sector are often inspired by the new theories of governance. To be more precise, they are inspired by rational choice theory, and above all, by mid-level social science associated with the new institutionalism. They neglect more interpretive approaches to social science. As such, they represent a quest for efficiency based on new forms of expertise. They do not pursue participatory, deliberative, or dialogic alternatives.

This chapter focuses on the different approaches to public policy associated with the new theories of governance. The following chapters rely on British and comparative cases to show how policy actors have drawn on new forms of expertise associated with some of these theories to try to address the problems associated with the new worlds of governance. Chapter 9 offers a genealogy of joined-up governance, whole of government, and related policy agendas that arose out of the new institutionalism. Similarly, chapter 10 shows how police reform oscillates between a neoliberal expertise that privileges markets and an institutionalist expertise that privileges networks and community. These chapters all demonstrate how the institutionalist discourse of networks and community is less a turn to participatory democracy than the imposition of a new form of expertise. The pursuit of networks and community is less a reflection of democratic ideals than of an expertise that suggests they will promote efficiency.

Public policy refers very generally to the set of actions—plans, laws, and behaviors—adopted by a government. The literature on the new governance draws attention to the extent to which these actions are often performed now by agents of the state rather than directly by the state. There are a growing number of studies of specific policy areas, and even specific policy problems and governmental responses to them, that offer detailed accounts of the impact of the new public management and the rise of the new governance in particular policy sectors, such as health care, social welfare, policing, and public security. However, policy analysis often includes a prescriptive dimension as well as a descriptive one. Students of public policy attempt to devise solutions to policy problems as well as to study governmental responses to them. Of course their solutions are sometimes specific proposals aimed at a particular policy problem. At other times, however, they concern themselves with the general question: how should the state try to implement its policies?

The new governance inspires the more specific question: how should the state try to implement its policies given the proliferation of markets and networks in the public sector? Answers to this question typically seek to balance concerns over efficiency with ones over ethics. This chapter will argue that the leading answers reflect the leading theories of governance. Table 8.1 provides a summary of this argument. Rational choice theory tends to promote market solutions; its exponents typically want to reduce the role of the state in implementing policies. Institutionalists tend to concentrate on strategies by which the state can manage and promote particular types of organizations; its exponents typically offer advice on how the state can realize its policy agenda in a largely given institutional setting. Interpretive theory tends to promote dialogic and deliberative approaches to public policy; its exponents typically want to facilitate the flow of meanings, and perhaps thereby the emergence of a consensus.

STEERING AND SERVING

The stereotype of the "old governance" is of a bureaucratic state trying to impose its plan on society. Formal strategic planning did indeed play a prominent role in much state activity in the late twentieth century, but there is still a widespread recognition that strategic planning is an integral feature of government. Plans help to establish the goals and visions of the state and its agencies, and they facilitate the concentration of resources in areas where they are thought to be most likely to improve an organization's efficiency in relation to its dominant goals. Of course plans

TABLE 8.1
Rethinking Public Policy

	Rational choice	*Institutionalism*
Basis of policymaking	Expertise (markets)	Expertise (networks)
Role of state in governance	Steering (and marketization)	Network management
State oversight	Audit and regulation	Policy learning
Examples	1. Osborne and Gaebler	1. Kickert
	2. Majone	2. Nutley, Davies, and Smith

are not set in stone. Rather, they are made on the basis of assumptions that might prove inaccurate and visions that might change in ways that require the plan to be modified.

Planning remains an integral feature of government.[1] Yet, there has been much debate over how the state should implement its plans and policies. By the late 1970s many commentators were arguing that the state could no longer manage all the tasks assigned to it. Many neoliberals also argued that the state was inherently inefficient at implementing policy and especially at delivering public services. Neoliberals hoped to solve the problems of the overloaded and inefficient state by means of privatization, marketization, and the introduction to the public sector of techniques of management from the private sector. The state tried to divest itself of various functions. But it still needed to promote its policies. How was it meant to do so?

Steering, Not Rowing

The neoliberals wanted the state to concentrate on steering and not rowing. Sometimes they argued that a focus on steering would enable the state to plan more effectively: when state actors step back from the delivery of policies, they have more time to consider the big picture. Neoliberalism represented less a repudiation of planning than an attempt to contract out the delivery of policies to nonstate actors. Typically its advocates suggested that devolving service delivery would do much to foster a more entrepreneurial ethos in the public sector; they said that the new public management would free managers to manage.

---

[1] With the rise of the new governance, styles of planning have often focused more on collaboration and transnationalism. See P. Healy, *Collaborative Planning: Shaping Places in Fragmented Societies* (London: Macmillan, 1997); and P. Newman and A. Thornly, *Urban Planning in Europe: International Competition, National Systems and Planning Projects* (London: Routledge, 1996).

David Osborne and Ted Gaebler led the way in arguing that the state would function better if it focused on "steering" public policy as opposed to "rowing."[2] Steering involves the laying out of a broad strategy for public policy, perhaps including the specification of policy goals. Rowing consists in the actual implementation of policy, and especially the delivery of services. A notable feature of Osborne and Gaebler's book is their inclusion of case studies from local governance to illustrate the benefits of contracting out. For example, they tell us the story of mental health projects and services in Ohio. The Ohio state government uses local boards to oversee mental health policy, but it relies on nonprofit health organizations to operate the relevant facilities and programs. The local boards do not provide the services to the population at whom their policies are aimed. Instead they concentrate on ensuring that their policies are being implemented, trusting the professionals of nonprofits to provide quality care. The short case studies that litter Osborne and Gaebler's book are intended to suggest that contracting out makes public policy more efficient.

We might ask: why would a focus on steering enable the state to make better public policy? Osborne and Gaebler argue, first, that contracting out services enables the state, and also those service providers who win the contracts, to focus on what they do best. The service providers can focus on ensuring efficient and quality service delivery, while the state and public agencies can focus on policymaking.

Osborne and Gaebler argue, second, that a focus on steering facilitates a more adventurous style of policymaking. In their view, potential policies can come to a grinding halt when the issue of logistics comes up. But when state actors do not have to worry about how a plan will be implemented, they can be bolder and more creative in their ideas. They can create policies without getting bogged down in logistical questions about how the policies will be put into practice. It is left to the private sector bodies that win the relevant contracts to decide how best to implement the services.

Finally, Osborne and Gaebler argue that a focus on steering facilitates a more holistic approach to policymaking. In their view, when state actors worry about rowing, they typically adopt a Band-aid approach to policymaking. When state actors become involved in the operation of existing programs, they tend to concentrate on ways of improving or fixing these programs. They look at the programs themselves, rather than the societal problems that the programs are meant to address. A focus on rowing thus encourages state actors to ignore underlying social problems, making it impossible for those problems to be eradicated. What is more, Osborne and Gaebler continue, a focus on rowing leads state agencies

---

[2] Osborne and Gaebler, *Reinventing Government.*

to approach policy problems in a fragmented manner. Large-scale social problems such as drug abuse and poverty have many causes and cannot be cured by a single government program. But when state actors are preoccupied with questions of implementation, they typically concentrate on the operation of one policy at a time, even when the underlying problems are large and need to be dealt with through a range of varied policies. Here too, Osborne and Gaebler associate a focus on steering with a more holistic approach to public policy. By contracting out service delivery, state actors free themselves to craft more comprehensive programs that deal with the various aspects of a complex social problem. State actors can approach the problem from all angles. They have multiple private agencies ready to work on a variety of different programs, each tackling one source of the problem.

Leadership and Trust

Osborne and Gaebler clearly want to trumpet the virtues of contracting out for public policy. Yet even they acknowledge that the positive features they identify with a focus on steering cannot be guaranteed. Other commentators have been noticeably more skeptical of the claims made on behalf of the first wave of public sector reform. Indeed, once we turn our attention away from the overt advocates of contracting out and the new public management, we find most commentators believe that the consequences of these reforms bore strikingly little resemblance to those for which their advocates had hoped.[3] Many commentators argue that the success of the reforms, and so a focus on steering, depends on other aspects of the policymaking process. In their view, the reforms require different agencies to collaborate in ways they have not done previously, so their success presupposes the conditions under which such collaborations can flourish.

Most commentators point to the importance of conditions such as leadership, communication, and trust either in cementing the success of the first wave of reforms or at least in mitigating some of their unexpected consequences.[4] Leadership consists here of a strong central authority that is both listened to and respected. Analysts suggest that if the state is on an equal footing with other organizations, then the organizations all tend to undermine one another's authority, and if they undermine one another's authority, public policy is likely constantly to oscillate back and forth;

---

[3] Compare, on public policy generally, D. Marsh and R. Rhodes, eds., *Implementing Thatcherite Policies: Audit of an Era* (Buckingham: Open University Press, 1992).

[4] E.g., C. Huxham, "The Challenge of Collaborative Governance," *Public Management* 2 (2000): 337–57.

thus, policy remains unstable. In contrast, if the state assumes a strong leadership role, it can ensure consistency across the process of policy implementation. Analysts also suggest that strong leadership by the state is a requirement for proper democratic accountability: accountability requires that elected politicians have the ability to oversee the nongovernmental organizations involved in the delivery of public services.

The viability of public sector reform depends not only on leadership but also on the existence of strong and open lines of communication. Many commentators have found that policy actors from the public and private sectors have different working styles. Pertinent differences include goals, language, and relationships at work. The differences typically lead to misunderstandings and frustrations. They undermine collaboration and service provision. The most often mentioned way of overcoming these differences is by communication. Communication enables the different policy actors to articulate their goals and strategies, it fosters a dialogue, and it can facilitate the creation of an overarching language and culture in which the different policy actors are able to establish a productive work relationship.

Yet another condition for the success of public sector reform is the presence of trust among the different policy actors to which it has given rise. To some extent, of course, policymaking has always involved different types of actors. While the differences between elected politicians and career bureaucrats are arguably found in theory more than practice, it remains true that the two often have different time frames, look for different results, and have different concerns about the status of their jobs. Politicians often want instant results that they can take to their constituents. Bureaucrats are more likely to temper immediate goals with long-term ones. Scholars of public administration have long recognized the importance of personal relations—of trust and loyalty—in easing the tensions that arise from such differences. Today the new governance gives a far greater role to private and voluntary sector bodies in public policy, and it is arguable that they too need to be glued to politicians and especially public sector officials in relations of trust. Alas, such sentiments can come across as trite, since the concept of trust often remains very abstract. There is little clear-cut advice on how to generate it.

An Ethic of Service

Some critics of the first wave of reforms argue that they create problems even when there is leadership, communication, and trust. Even when these conditions are met, the number of organizations now involved in the policy process places high costs in time and energy on those concerned to ensure coordination and consistency in public policy, and these costs can undermine the quality of service provision. The rolling back of the state has led to a fragmentation of policy. There has been a proliferation and splintering of the organizations involved.[5]

Critics also argue that the fragmentation of the policy process can erode public service ethics. Often they are less concerned with the conditions under which contracting out can be made to work than with reinvigorating ideas of democratic citizenship and public service. Many of them argue that instead of either steering or rowing, policy actors should define their task as "serving." A decent public policy requires those involved to value the public interest over their personal gain. It requires them to give priority to the needs of society. In doing so, they might even help to create a more effective policy process. According to Robert Denhardt and Janet Denhardt, for example, a shared commitment to public service can sustain effective collaboration among the diverse actors involved in making and implementing policy.[6] They argue that if everyone's goal is to serve, many of the problems that arise between different agencies will fade away; elected politicians, public servants, and nongovernmental actors will work together as civic-minded individuals whose only desire is to serve the public well. Calls for a revived ethic of public service thus have a kind of janus-faced quality. Sometimes they look back to the old concept of public service that was once thought to inspire public bureaucracies. At other times they appear to be interested in the ways in which a rejection of neoliberalism, a renewed recognition of the role of the public sector, and a new ethic of collaborative engagement might provide an effective response not only to the problems that faced the state in the 1980s but also to the new problems that have been created by the neoliberal reforms themselves.

NETWORK MANAGEMENT

Social scientists often conclude that the withdrawal of the state from service delivery led to a proliferation of networks. The spread of networks appears further to undermine the ability of the state to control and coordinate the implementation of its policies. Social scientists, notably institutionalists, argue that effective public policy now depends on mechanisms for controlling and coordinating networks. There are a number of different approaches to the management of policy networks.[7] Some ap-

---

[5] E.g., Rhodes, *Understanding Governance.*

[6] Denhardt and Denhardt, "The New Public Service."

[7] Consider the diverse positions discussed and even advocated in W. Kickert, E-H. Klijn, and J. Koppenjan, eds., *Managing Complex Networks: Strategies for the Public Sector*

proaches focus on improving the ability of the state to direct the actions of networks by means of law, administrative rules, or regulation. Others focus on the ability of the state to improve the cooperative interactions between the organizations in networks; typically they suggest the state can promote cooperation by altering the relevant incentive structures. Yet other approaches concentrate on negotiating techniques by which the state might promote incremental shifts in the dominant norms and cultures that operate in a network.

The different strategies of network management can be seen as complementing one another. In this view, the state should deploy different policy styles as appropriate in different settings. This perspective returns us to something like the older idea that public policy is an incremental process of muddling through.[8] Public officials respond to specific problems in concrete settings. Generally public officials have to bear in mind multiple objectives, including meeting quality standards, promoting efficiency, remaining democratically accountable, and maintaining public trust and legitimacy. Their responses to problems are typically pragmatic ones: they aim to satisfy all these objectives, rather than to maximize their performance in relation to any one of them.

When Do Networks Succeed?

It is often difficult in practice to distinguish between advocacy of strategies for network management and advocacy of networks as such. Their advocates claim, for example, that networks provide at least as much flexibility and creativity as would a public sector based on markets.[9] Within networks, agencies can draw on their expertise and their knowledge base so as to respond quickly to unexpected situations. Again, the very division of labor in networks is said to promote innovation. Each network actor can concentrate on a few specialized areas, thereby developing a strong knowledge base of the sort that facilitates the development of creative new ideas and practices.

The distinction between networks as partnerships and contracting out as marketization suggests some of the particular settings in which networks are likely to succeed. Whereas contracting out requires clear divisions between different actors, partnerships often rely on an extensive overlap between actors. Whereas contracting out generally pits actors

---

(London: Sage, 1997); and M. Mandell, ed., *Getting Results through Collaboration: Networks and Network Structures for Public Policy and Management* (Westport, CT: Quorum Books, 2001).

[8] The classic account of incrementalism is C. Lindblom, "The Science of 'Muddling Through,'" *Public Administration Review* 19 (1959): 79–88.

[9] For a nuanced example of such advocacy, see R. Arganoff and M. McGuire, "Managing in Network Settings," *Policy Studies Review* 16 (1999): 18–41.

into competitive relations, partnerships rely on collaborations in which the actors genuinely share the workload with one another. Whereas market-based systems can make one organization's success another's failure, partnerships are typically such that the organizations involved share the profits or other benefits of success. Thus, we might associate contracting out and partnerships with different styles of management. Contracting out typically goes with project management: its success depends on defining the project, tendering, and monitoring costs and quality. Partnerships are associated with process management: their success depends on the contexts in which actors are included, the quality of their interactions, and the nature of the mediations between them. Erik-Hans Klijn and Geert Teisman conclude, on just these grounds, that partnerships are most appropriate for long-term projects that require considerable interactions among a range of actors.[10] These projects are ones in which process management is most needed.

Some social scientists express skepticism about the possibility of formulating rules for the success of networks. Rod Rhodes suggests, for example, that organizations operate in multiple networks simultaneously, that no two networks are the same, and that each network encounters experiences that arise from their unique makeup, structure, and goals.[11] However, while Rhodes is right to insist that each network is as unique as the reason for its creation, even he points toward guidelines for the successful management of networks. It seems to most observers that the main characteristics of successful networks, and so network management, are collaboration, negotiation, flexibility, and trust. Let us look briefly at each in turn, although it is important to remember that because these characteristics intersect with each other, there is something artificial about treating them separately.

The significance of collaboration arises because each organization typically has specific strengths and weaknesses. Besides, it is often considered dangerous to rely on a single organization for a particular task. No doubt there are times when organizations find it easier simply to divide work up, with each being delegated complete control over a particular task. But if organizations go it alone, they fail to take advantage of the skills and resources possessed by their counterparts. One aspect of network management thus consists of the attempt to build collaboration. Policy makers should attempt to promote unity and teamwork—trust and collaboration—among the participants in a network. Policy will improve,

---

[10] See E-H. Klijn and G. Teisman, "Managing Public-Private Partnerships: Influencing Processes and Institutional Context of Public-Private Partnerships," in O. van Heffen, W. Kickert, and J. Thomassen, eds., *Governance in Modern Societies: Effects, Change and Formation of Government Institutions* (Dordrecht: Kulwer, 2000), 329–48.

[11] R. Rhodes, "From Marketization to Diplomacy: It's the Mix That Matters," *Australian Journal of Public Administration* 56 (1997): 40–53.

it seems, if agencies are given tasks that develop collaboration between different groups.

Negotiation is the preferred way by which policy makers interact with actors from other organizations in a network. It is thought that hierarchic bureaucracies rely on laws and rules. In bureaucracies, public officials get other actors—typically their juniors—to act appropriately by utilizing stringent rules to specify the appropriate action. Such rules are thought to be of far less use to network managers. Typically, network managers are seeking to foster a latitudinal organizational structure, not a hierarchical one. Rules and regulations can stifle the collaboration and innovation that networks require and inspire; they can undermine the free-flowing exchange of ideas so important to networks. Again, networks are believed to offer a system of efficient service delivery that is quick to adapt to new situations, and strict codes are believed to interfere with such efficiency and, in particular, with adaptation to change. There is also a tension between stringent rules and the interdependence and trust that characterize networks. Whereas rules imply that one actor has the authority to tell others what to do, networks arise when actors are dependent upon cooperation with one another in a way that implies the exercise of authority should be minimally invasive so as not to weaken the basis of cooperative behavior. Policy will improve, it seems, if managers rely on negotiation rather than the specification of rules and regulations.

Flexibility consists of the ability to adjust and react when unexpected situations arise. Perhaps networks are an especially flexible form of organization. Nevertheless, if a network is inflexible, it might struggle to adapt to its unique circumstances. Some network analysts think in terms of a nonagreement point—an outcome that arises when actors do not compromise and which then satisfies none of them.[12] Flexibility is crucial to the avoidance of such outcomes. A flexible approach to negotiation can lead the actors to reach a new, agreed plan. In the absence of flexibility, the project might come to a halt, and the partnership or network may disintegrate. Policy will improve, it seems, if managers remain flexible about how to achieve the desired outcomes.

A final characteristic of successful networks is trust among the actors. Yet there are numerous definitions of trust, as well as different judgments as to its necessity.[13] Trust need not require that actors hold the same

[12] "Nonagreement point" is a technical concept derived from rational choice theory (specifically game theory) that is most often found in related discussions of justice. For an example of its application to networks, see A. Hindmoor, "The Importance of Being Trusted: Transaction Costs and Policy Network Theory," *Public Administration* 76 (1998): 25–43.

[13] "Trust" has become such a mainstay of the literature on governance that it is hard to know where to begin, but how about V. Braithwaite and M. Levi, eds., *Trust and Governance* (New York: Russell Sage Foundation, 1998). Measurements of trust are increasingly

beliefs and values. Typically it requires, rather, that actors have similar expectations, especially about their respective roles and goals. Rational choice theorists are especially likely to argue that successful networks arise when the benefits of such trust outweigh the costs. Institutionalists are more likely to argue that trust is learned and shaped through constant interactions.

Problems with Networks

The idea that different organizational forms and strategies are appropriate for different projects suggests that there may be disadvantages to network governance. Some of these disadvantages concern possible inefficiencies that arise in particular contexts. Observers worry that networks, and also markets, may weaken state control in ways that threaten democratic accountability, and specifically, that markets and networks have spread to such an extent that the state is no longer able to steer, let alone row. In this view, elected officials no longer can exercise any effective control over the nonelected actors who actually provide many public services. This lack of control precludes proper evaluation of policy implementation. Perhaps more important, it compromises our democratic integrity. In the case of networks, the fact that all the actors are interdependent might imply that none is accountable for the end results. More generally, the proliferation of markets and networks arguably means that governance is now simply too complex for the state to retain any effective oversight of the provision of public services. Concerns about how to control markets and networks have led to an explosion of audits and regulatory agencies.

AUDIT AND REGULATION

Perceptions of a decline in the ability of the state to exercise control have been one of the main impetuses behind the expansion of regulations and audits.[14] The two waves of public sector reform have increased the role of nonstate actors in public policy: NPM tried explicitly to remove the state from service delivery, and the rise of networks left the state increasingly

---

used as official and unofficial indicators of good governance. For a critical discussion, see G. Bouckaert and S. van de Walle, "Comparing Measures of Citizen Trust and User Satisfaction as Indicators of 'Good Governance': Difficulties in Linking Trust and Satisfaction Indicators," *International Review of Administrative Sciences* 69 (2003): 329–43.

[14] See J. Jordana and D. Levi-Faur, eds., *The Politics of Regulation: Institutions and Regulatory Reforms for the Age of Governance* (Cheltenham: Edward Elgar, 2004); and Power, *The Audit Explosion*.

dependent on other actors to secure its policies. Because nonstate actors are playing an increasingly important role in public policy, the state has struggled to find ways of retaining control and ensuring accountability; after all, even if markets and networks are supposed to be more efficient than hierarchic bureaucracy, the state still has a responsibility to ensure certain standards and to hold nonstate actors accountable for meeting these standards. Audits and regulatory agencies appear to be its preferred means of so doing.

So, while some neoliberals appear to think that market mechanisms can ensure that nonstate actors will do as the state (or citizens) wish (or should wish), others recognize that the state still has to structure and oversee the policy process. The state still has to set the goals for other actors, and it still has to audit and regulate these actors in relation to those goals. Even as the state has forsaken direct intervention, it has expanded its arms-length attempts to control and coordinate other actors. The new governance includes expanded regimes of regulation. A growing number of agencies, commissions, and special courts enforce rules to protect rights, competition, and standards of service.

A Regulatory State?

Some social scientists even talk of a shift from a positive state to a regulatory state.[15] They point to an increase in the number of specialized actors involved in the policy process. Power is now diffused among numerous such actors. The central state has tried to come to terms with these changes by expanding its regulatory powers. The new governance lies behind the rise of a whole new branch of the state—a branch that attempts to oversee specialized agencies. This new regulatory branch of the state concentrates on ensuring that the actions of the agencies are in line with the plans of elected politicians. It has to be specialized enough to understand the actions of the agencies.

There are surprisingly few detailed empirical studies of the changing size and resources of the regulatory branch of the state. In one empirical study Christopher Hood, Oliver James, and Colin Scott conclude that in Britain the size and scope of regulation increased dramatically between the 1970s and the 1990s.[16] In those years alone, the number of oversight

---

[15] For a loosely rational choice example, see G. Majone, "From the Positive to the Regulatory State: Causes and Consequences of Changes in the Mode of Governance," *Journal of Public Policy* 17 (1997): 139–67. For a more institutionalist one, see M. Moran, *The British Regulatory State: High Modernism and Hyper-Innovation* (Oxford: Oxford University Press, 2003).

[16] C. Hood, O. James, and C. Scott, "Regulation of Government: Has It Increased, Is It Increasing, Should It Be Diminished?," *Public Administration* 78 (2000): 283–304.

agencies increased by over 20 percent, while the number of staff jumped up about 90 percent, with extra funds and expenditure also accompanying this growth. Many states are developing extensive and technocratic systems of regulation to oversee the role of nongovernmental agencies in governance.

Advocates of the regulatory state ascribe to it various advantages. The main advantages are interconnected with one another. To begin, because regulation gives the state some oversight of public policy, it helps to reintroduce a measure of control. The central state can monitor the performance of its devolved agencies and also nonstate actors so as to make sure that they are providing services that meet or exceed minimum standards. Indeed, regulation and audits are sometimes thought to be the only way by which the contemporary state can make sure that its policies are being implemented. Likewise, audits constitute one of the main techniques by which the central state might try to monitor the outcome of its policies. Audits and regulatory agencies provide an important feedback mechanism. The state takes information from them about the effects of its policies, and it can then use this information in an attempt to improve its policies. Finally, regulation is, in some people's opinion, a way of reinstating some of the democratic safeguards that are lost in the new governance. It provides a way of making executive agencies and nonstate actors answerable to elected politicians and thus to citizens. The rise of the regulatory state restores accountability and returns power to the people.

Problems of Regulation

It would be eminently reasonable to ask if the explosion of audits and regulatory agencies is truly as beneficial as some commentators claim. It certainly seems plausible, for example, to suggest that regulatory bodies rarely restore accountability as opposed to measuring performance. They can even look suspiciously like a kind of contracting out of democratic accountability.

Even neoliberals generally agree that the regulatory state has its drawbacks. They worry that it replicates some of the problems they associate with the bureaucratic welfare state. Giandomenico Majone, writing in a distinctly neoliberal vein, argues that audits and regulations are tainted by an old hierarchical and bureaucratic politics.[17] The positive side to such a politics is that the center can force a change to take place. But Majone wants to highlight what he regards as the negative side of this politics. He argues that the very changes that the center forces through

[17] Majone, "From the Positive to the Regulatory State."

can be damaging to the smaller bodies in the system. The European Union provides him with an illustration of how a governing system might force subunits to adopt specific laws in an attempt to ensure that certain minimum standards are met but with the effect of undermining the ability of the subunits to handle their own problems and issues. In his view, the regulatory regime imposed by the EU stifles the capacity of member states to handle impending problems and crises. The implication is that regulations, benchmarks, and standards are bureaucratic barriers to efficiency and effectiveness.

Other social scientists often point to a related but rather different critique of the rise of regulatory agencies. They argue that regulatory agencies can have excessive costs for private sector companies.[18] When companies are forced to comply with specific rules, they begin almost automatically to accrue costs. Each time the rules change, they have to bear the costs of changing their manuals and practices to satisfy the new codes. In this view, some regulations might have positive benefits—those that enforce health and safety are often mentioned—but many are denounced as unnecessary burdens on the dynamism and profitability of the private sector. What is more, the critics add, these financial demands do not apply only to private companies. To the contrary, the explosion of regulatory agencies entails an increase in the amount of public expenditure that goes on such oversight as opposed to the delivery of services.

Regulation typically places a financial burden on both the private and public sectors. However, some social scientists argue that it need not do so. Hood and his collaborators have proposed various ways of cost-effectively securing oversight and regulation.[19] One option is to decrease costs through various forms of self-inspection. Self-inspection provides for the internal enforcement of a set of externally defined standards and rules. Advocates of self-regulation suggest that it allows the state's voice to be heard while giving agencies and companies the power to deal with their own internal workings. There is a case for the state combining self-inspection with a policy of unscheduled inspections. If the state relies on scheduled inspections, it commits itself to the costs of making them, and it also usually gives agencies and companies forewarning of the checks thereby enabling them to rely on superficial, last minute measures to ensure compliance with relevant standards. In contrast, if the state relies on unscheduled checks, agencies and companies constantly have to rely on

---

[18] Some even argue that regulation is more costly than monopoly. See R. Posner, "The Social Costs of Monopoly and Regulation," *Journal of Political Economy* 83 (1975): 807–28.

[19] Hood et. al., "Regulation of Government."

permanent measures to ensure compliance with the standards while the state can undertake only a few random checks, thereby saving resources. A similar case can be made for the state combining self-inspection and unscheduled inspections with a policy of "zero tolerance" towards failure. If the state zealously punishes every failure in an unscheduled check, it substantially enhances the prospects of agencies and companies taking self-inspection seriously; it does so simply by increasing the consequences of failure. Finally, a case can be made for the state adopting a "running-tally" approach to regulation. This approach would involve the state concentrating its time and energy on those agencies that fail to meet minimum standards while relaxing its oversight of those agencies that have a strong performance record.

No matter what judgment we make on the growth of government audit and regulatory agencies, few signs point to their disappearance. The rise of the new governance finds the state grasping for levers of control. The state has few ways in which to force through its policies. Audit and regulation are among the few that remain. They represent attempts to bind policy actors, and especially non-governmental agencies, to the will of the state. It is this that makes them so appealing to state actors no matter how much they drain away resources and no matter how imperfectly they are set up.

POLICY LEARNING

Skeptics argue that the successive waves of public sector reform have created as many public policy problems as they have solved. They point to the rise of audits and regulatory frameworks as evidence for this argument. Some of the skeptics echo earlier accounts of policymaking as an incremental process of muddling through. Others attempt to systematize something akin to incrementalism as a rational (even scientific) basis for public policy. Pertinent examples include the vogue for policy learning, and more especially for evidence-based policy-making.

Policy learning refers to a process of policy formation that relies primarily on the knowledge, skills, and habits already gained through just that process.[20] The process can be broken down somewhat schematically into various stages from the introduction of new information, through

---

[20] Some commentators imply that policy learning is especially relevant to the new governance and the social world that has given rise to it. See G. Room, *The European Challenge: Innovation, Policy Learning, and Social Cohesion in the New Knowledge Economy* (Bristol: Policy Press, 2005).

the interpretation of past policies and the inclusion of new ideas, on to the modification of the policy. Its advocates suggest that it institutionalizes a form of bounded rationality in which policy actors reduce levels of uncertainty by drawing on past routines and past experiences to respond to novel situations.

Evidence-Based Policy

Recently policy learning has become increasingly closely tied to concepts such as evidence and benchmarking.[21] These concepts represent a fairly conscious backlash against the theoretical agendas associated with planning and with neoliberalism.[22] Their advocates regularly complain that public policy has been too reliant on just such grand theories. These advocates suggest that academics and politicians are all too likely to rely on abstract and unproven ideas when formulating public policy. They call instead for a form of policy learning based on practical experience and evidence-based research. They argue that the resulting policies are more likely to succeed, or at least less likely to fail disastrously.

Benchmarking is in many ways an archetypal example of policy learning.[23] In its simplest form, benchmarking occurs when policy actors compare their activities and outcomes. The idea is that actors thereby come to adopt the best practices of their contemporaries in an effort to match their performance. Proponents of benchmarking argue that, unlike vague and abstract objectives written on paper, it gives policy actors concrete models to follow. Benchmarking enables policy actors to learn from the ways in which each other operate; it encourages them to consider new policy options and to explore new possibilities.

Calls for evidence-based policy and benchmarking can overlap with claims that distinct policy styles are appropriate to specific local contexts in that both validate policy makers developing policies in accord with their hands-on experience of specific cases.[24] The general idea is that grand theories are bound to fail insofar as they purport to have universal applicability. They fail because the impact of any given policy or policy style actually varies across different regions or other contexts. Each

---

[21] Compare S. Nutley, H. Davies, and P. Smith, eds., *What Works? Evidence Based Policy and Practice in Public Services* (Bristol: Policy Press, 2000).

[22] E.g., I. Sanderson, "Evaluation, Policy Learning, and Evidence-Based Policy Making", *Public Administration* 80 (2002): 1–22.

[23] For a study of EU benchmarking, see C. De la Porte, P. Pochet, and G. Room, "Social Benchmarking, Policy Making and New Governance in the EU," *Journal of European Social Policy* 11 (2001): 291–307.

[24] The earlier literature on policy styles included J. Richardson, ed., *Policy Styles in Western Europe* (London: Allen and Unwin, 1982).

region has its own culture, value set, and problems that prohibit over-arching policies or regulations. Policy learning is thought to offer the possibility of tailoring policies to fit different regions and contexts with their specific problems and demands.

Policy styles and cultures are the contexts in which policy learning takes place. Even when cultures appear similar to an outsider, they often have significant differences. One moral of their diversity is that there are advantages to implementing many policies on a small scale.[25] A small-scale approach makes it easier to handle problems that arise. It also respects the variations between different countries and population segments. For example, a law implemented by the EU has jurisdiction over almost the entire continent of Europe, yet because the member states vary in history, geographic size, demographic makeup, and economic conditions, it is often difficult to serve the best interests of all these states through one uniform pattern of law. Recognition of the diverse policy cultures in Europe may improve public policy by encouraging the EU to give its member states the flexibility to formulate and implement policies to suit their particular circumstances. The logic of the argument suggests that member states too might do well to provide a similar degree of flexibility to their internal localities and regions. In short, the smaller the program, the better its probable fit to the local context.

DIALOGUE AND DELIBERATION

Skepticism about grand theories of public sector reform can inspire not only attempts to base policy on experience (particularly local experience) but also radical democratic attempts to involve citizens more fully in the processes of policymaking and policy implementation. Radical democrats are less focused than many advocates of policy learning on offering advice to policy makers about how best to ensure their policies are effective. Rather, they advocate dialogue and deliberation in large part as a means to give greater control of the policy process to citizens. Some of them argue that the direct involvement of citizens has become both more important and more plausible as a result of the rise of the new governance and the emergence of new information technologies. Of course, radical democrats do sometimes advocate greater participation as a way of securing more effective policies. However, they also advocate more

[25] Compare F. van Waarden, "Persistence of National Policy Styles: A Study of Their Institutional Foundations," in B. Unger and F. van Waarden, eds., *Convergence or Diversity? Internationalisation and Economic Policy Response* (Dartmouth: Ashgate, 1995), 333–72.

participatory forms of public policy on ethical grounds. They tie participation to democratic ideals.

The Limits of Expertise

When radical democrats argue from effectiveness, they generally rely on a similar skepticism to that informing many defenses of policy learning. Radical democrats argue here that there is an inherent flaw in the idea of a technocratic science of society.[26] Social scientists cannot predict human behavior, so technocratic policies based on grand theories or models always have unexpected results, and these unexpected results often undermine the effectiveness of the policies. No doubt to reject technocratic approaches to public policy is not necessarily to advocate greater participation. Recall, though, that the rejection of technocratic approaches stems here from the claim that we cannot predict human behavior. This claim reminds us that the effectiveness of policies depends on the organizations and citizens who are their targets responding to them in the ways in which policy makers expected. Thus, greater participation leads to more effective policies inasmuch as it gives policy makers a better understanding of how the targets of their policies will react to those policies. Dialogue enables policy makers to frame their policies so as to allow for the way citizens feel about them and so are likely to respond to them. It also enables policy makers to explain policies to citizens in a way that might help them to modify the ways in which citizens respond to the policies. Some theorists even suggest that we should allow organizations and individuals to devise their own policies in dialogue and deliberation with one another.

Advocates of dialogue and deliberation argue, in other words, that they facilitate social learning. Public problems are not technical issues to be resolved by experts but rather questions about how a community wants to act or govern itself. Dialogue and deliberation better enable citizens and public officials to resolve these questions as they appear in concrete issues of public policy. They enable a community to name and frame an issue, thereby setting an agenda. They can inform the various policy actors about each others' concerns, preferences, and ideas for solutions. They can help to establish trust and cooperative norms in a community. Perhaps most important, they can reveal common ground, and even help to generate a consensus on the public good. They facilitate common action by the citizens of a society.

[26] E.g., J. Dryzek, "Policy Analysis and Planning: From Science to Argument," in F. Fischer and J. Forester, eds., *The Argumentative Turn in Policy Analysis and Planning* (Durham: Duke University Press, 1993), 213–32.

Critics point to various problems with dialogic and deliberative policy-making.[27] They argue that it is unrealistic given the size of modern states, it ignores the role of expertise in making policy decisions, it inevitably excludes groups or viewpoints, and it is slow and cannot respond to crises. Critics also suggest that some policy areas—such as national security—are particularly inappropriate for direct citizen involvement. Despite such criticisms, calls for citizen involvement in the policy process remind us that policymaking should reflect our ethical ideals as well as being reasonably effective.

Ethical Considerations

Theories of policy learning portray the policy process as a kind of piecemeal social engineering based on trial and error.[28] No doubt there is some value in experts forming and reforming policies to make them more effective. But this kind of piecemeal social engineering presupposes that society has a fixed set of values and goals. Thus, even when policy analysts adopt evidence-based approaches, they are likely to falter when they have to decide what is best for society. Generally the members of a society have different values, and they disagree about the goals of policy. Their disagreement means that policymaking cannot be treated simply as a kind of experiment. To the contrary, satisfactory policymaking requires free democratic debates about goals. Even after the experts voice their opinions about policy options, there has to be a free argument about which policy citizens want to adopt.

No doubt we could associate free democratic debate over goals with the electoral process. However, advocates of dialogue and deliberation often suggest that it would be a mistake to do so. They argue that deliberative conversations act not only as fertile sources of ideas but also as a transformative experience for many of those involved.[29] In this view, dialogue and deliberation themselves provide settings for a form of learning; it is through them that organizations and citizens learn about what is and is not true, and, perhaps more important, about membership, identities, shared memories, competencies, and collaborative and cooperative forms of behavior.

---

[27] Some even argue that it is undemocratic. See L. Sanders, "Against Deliberation," *Political Theory* 25 (1997): 347–76. For an attempt to adapt deliberation to nonideal circumstances, see A. Fung, "Deliberation before the Revolution: Toward an Ethic of Deliberative Democracy in an Unjust World," *Political Theory* 33 (2005): 397–419.

[28] Compare Dryzek, "Policy Analysis."

[29] E.g., J. Forester, *The Deliberative Practitioner: Encouraging Participatory Planning Processes* (Cambridge: MIT Press, 1999), esp. chap. 5.

Rethinking Citizenship

Even if policy makers wanted to foster deliberation and dialogue, they still would need to find organizations and citizens who were willing to collaborate with them. It seems that participatory approaches to public policy require the creation and maintenance of especially high levels of civic engagement. Alas, moreover, they do so at a time when social scientists and politicians alike are preoccupied by an apparent decline of social capital and political participation as evidenced by falling rates of voting in many democracies. Perhaps we could no longer craft a deliberative policy community even if we wished to do so.

Some social scientists argue, however, that today's apathy and disillusion with politics in part reflects the absence of deliberative and dialogic processes in many democracies. Henrik Bang and Eva Sørensen have found some evidence for this more optimistic scenario.[30] They suggest that a new kind of active citizen is emerging under the new governance. Their "Everyday Maker" is found in the Nørrebro district of Copenhagen. Everyday makers do not necessarily vote, but they are establishing new forms of political action and new forms of governance. Typically, everyday makers are prompted into action by policy failures, and especially local problems. They work in local communities to alleviate problems through cooperative policies. Their principles are that people should make changes for themselves in their own neighborhood, so they favor voluntary organizations over politicians and public officials. Their activities resemble a deliberative, cooperative, and self-governing ideal. Perhaps, however, a note of caution is needed. Bang and Sørensen admit that the everyday maker is an ideal type, and, we might add, it is an ideal type based on citizens in what is arguably the most politically active district in Denmark. We should be cautious of generalizing from such a narrow base.

If we do not find everyday makers, we might be left confronting a decline of active citizenship. Some commentators would not worry about such a decline. They might even welcome it on the grounds that democratic participation merely gets in the way of good policy decisions and efficient policy implementation. Perhaps they will commend nonmajoritarian institutions and contracting out as superior, rational forms of policymaking. In doing so, however, they would place good governance conceived as efficiency before good governance conceived as democratic

---

[30] H. Bang and E. Sørensen, "The Everyday Maker: A New Challenge to Democratic Governance," *Administrative Theory & Praxis* 21 (1999): 325–41.

and accountable. Thus, even if we agreed with them about the road to efficiency—and we reasonably might not do so—we still may conclude that it is a road we do not want to travel.

CONCLUSION

The new governance poses issues of efficiency and democracy in public policy. Different theories of governance encourage different responses to these issues. Rational choice theorists are more likely than others to persist with the idea that markets can solve such problems when they can be introduced and made to function properly. Neoclassical economics and rational choice theory sometimes combine to inspire visions of public administration in which the state largely steers, regulates, and audits other organizations that implement policies and deliver services in ways that are governed by contracts and markets. The rational choice strand of the new institutionalism can inspire similar visions. It often leads to an account of the ways the state can steer networks that focuses primarily on manipulating the incentives and regulations that apply to the relevant organizations. Other institutionalist theories lead to noticeably different visions of public administration and public policy. While they too often concentrate on network management, they focus more on the state steering by manipulating things such as the relations between actors, the distribution of resources, or the dominant values and perceptions. Typically these institutionalist theories place more emphasis on the particular context of a network, policy, or program. Sometimes they are suspicious of grand theories or models that neglect these contexts. Thus, they advocate more gradual processes of policy learning based on past experience and evidence and sensitivity to different policy styles and cultures. Despite their differences, rational choice theorists and institutionalists generally share a continuing attachment to the idea that social science generates an expertise that is capable of informing public policy. Some radical democrats are suspicious of just this idea. They defend theories that highlight the contingency and contestability of social life, and so the limitations and dangers of expertise. And they deploy these theories to defend more deliberative and dialogic approaches to public policy.

   The different theories of public policy are not just rival academic positions. To the contrary, like the new theories of governance, they are beliefs that people have acted on so as to establish the new patterns of governance and administration to which they refer. Once again, then, I am drawing attention to the interaction of theories and worlds. This chapter concentrated on how the different theories of governance typically give rise to different approaches to public policy. The next chapter will argue that much recent public sector reform—joined-up governance, whole of government approaches, and the like—is informed by broadly institutionalist theories. The chapter after next will explore the way in which theories based on both economic and sociological concepts of rationality have similarly informed successive waves of police reform. The goal of the next two chapters is thus to illustrate the broad claim that policy actors have responded to the new governance by drawing on forms of expertise based on the new theories, and that they have thereby neglected democratic possibilities.

CHAPTER NINE

Joined-up Governance

HOW DOES THE PREVIOUS chapter on theories of public policy help us to make sense of recent administrative reforms? Once again my approach relies on the idea that the theories helped inspire the reforms. This approach suggests that we can better understand the reforms if we identify the intellectual traditions that led people to introduce them. More particularly, this chapter will argue that institutionalist approaches to the new governance lie behind the Third Way and joined-up government.

The claim that social science informs administrative reforms may appear less plausible than the one that democratic theories inform constitutional reform. It would be difficult, for example, to claim that institutionalism is a dominant commitment in the Labour Party in quite the same way as is representative democracy. Nonetheless, the role of social science becomes more apparent once we consider not only leading traditions in the Labour Party but also those among the think tanks and policy experts on whose advice the party depends. Many commentators have pointed to the role of think tanks and policy wonks in developing the first wave of public sector reforms. We know that neoliberal think tanks and policy advisers have acted as a transmission belt, taking ideas from the academic social sciences to the politicians and public officials who formulate policy. This chapter argues that the second wave of reforms emerged similarly. Think tanks and policy advisers have carried institutionalist ideas from the academic social science to politicians and other policy actors.

To avoid misunderstanding, I should emphasize that the ties between social science theories and public policies are not invariant ones. Just as there are rational choice theorists who do not advocate marketization and the new public management, so there are institutionalists who do not advocate networks and joined-up governance. Again, just as the New Right merged neoliberal ideas with older conservative motifs, so New Labour is notably eclectic, taking ideas from all kinds of sources even as it introduces institutionalist reforms in the public sector. Despite these qualifications, however, we can recognize the broad debts of the New

Right to neoliberalism and of New Labour to institutionalism, and we can explain these debts in part by referring to the impact of think tanks and policy advisers.

SOCIAL DEMOCRACY AND SOCIAL SCIENCE

As we saw in chapter 6, the dominant tradition in the Labour Party fused Fabianism and ethical socialism to defend a representative democracy in which the state acts aggressively to pursue social justice. Fabianism particularly emphasized the role of the social sciences as sources of expert knowledge on how the state best can manage social, economic, and administrative affairs. Public officials and other policy advisers (including the Fabians themselves) would use social science to formulate appropriate policies, while elected politicians oversaw the policy process, thereby ensuring that the bureaucratic state remained trustworthy.

The dominant tradition in the Labour Party thus synthesized a commitment to representative democracy with one to social science as a source of policy expertise. New Labour inherited this tradition in a way that helps to explain its faith in expertise. When it turned to think tanks and policy advisers for expert advice, they provided it with advice derived from a broad institutionalism.

New Labour's Think Tanks

The leading actors in this chapter are a diffuse, intersecting group of social scientists, policy advisers, and politicians. Together they effectively combined institutionalism, network theory, and the Third Way into a recognizable package of public policies. The most important of these actors worked in center-left think tanks such as Demos, the Foreign Policy Centre, and the Institute for Public Policy Research. These think tanks carried ideas and concerns back and forth between institutionalists and the government in much the same way as the Adam Smith Institute and the Centre for Policy Studies did in the Thatcher years. Let us briefly look at some of the actors.

Geoff Mulgan was the cofounder and first director of Demos, and he is still chairman of its Advisory Council. Before founding Demos in 1993, he worked from 1990 to 1992 as a senior policy adviser to Gordon Brown. Later he worked in the prime minister's Policy Unit under Tony Blair. Demos's current director, Tom Bentley, took up the post after working from 1998 to 1999 as a special adviser to David Blunkett, then secretary of state for education and employment. Its deputy director, Beth Egan, spent a secondment assisting Brown while he was chancellor of the exchequer. Several of the researchers at Demos also have been employed in New Labour: for example, Charles Leadbeater wrote a White Paper entitled *Our Competitive Future.*[1]

Perri 6 is a Demos researcher who straddles both the academy, where he defends neo-Durkheimian institutionalism, and government, where he provides New Labour with regular policy advice on holistic governance. Similar connections tie Demos to other center-left think tanks and these think tanks to New Labour. Daniel Stedman Jones was a Demos researcher who had already worked in the prime minister's Policy Unit and also the Institute for Public Policy. Mark Leonard became the director of the Foreign Policy Centre after having been a senior researcher for Demos, and he advised New Labour as a member of the Foreign and Commonwealth Office Panel.

Institutionalist Theory

Various think tanks and policy advisers brought institutionalist ideas to New Labour. As we saw in chapter 3, the new institutionalism is amorphous, consisting of rational choice, historical, and sociological strands. The latter two strands themselves consist of a diverse cluster of attempts to preserve mid-level analysis by emphasizing our social embeddedness and thereby the role of institutional structures and cultural norms as determinants of social life. Whereas rational choice deploys assumptions about utility-maximizing agents—thereby generally postulating a properly functioning market as the form of organization that best expresses our rationality—institutionalists argue that agents are embedded in institutions, and they thereby suggest that networks are the organizations best suited to our nature.

Institutionalism overlaps with network theory in complex ways. On one hand, institutionalists use the concept of a network to describe the inevitable nature of all organizations given that individuals are socially embedded. They thereby imply that hierarchies and markets are networks. Concepts such as embeddedness and network suggest that human action is always already structured by social relationships. Thus, these concepts provide institutionalists, such as Mark Granovetter and Walter Powell with a rebuttal of economic concepts of rationality and rational choice theory in social science.[2] On the other hand, institutionalists

---

[1] *Our Competitive Future: Building the Knowledge Driven Economy*, Cm 4176 (1998).

[2] M. Granovetter, "Economic Action and Social Structure: The Problem of Embededness," *American Journal of Sociology* 78 (1973): 1360–80; and Powell, "Neither Market nor Hierarchy." For what follows, also see M. Granovetter, "Business Groups," in N. Smelser and R. Swedberg, eds., *Handbook of Economic Sociology* (Princeton: Princeton University Press, 1994), 453–75; and W. Powell, K. Koput, and L. Smith-Doerr, "Interorganiza-

suggest that networks are better suited to many tasks than are hierarchies or markets. Thus, the concepts of embeddedness and network provide institutionalists with a rebuttal of the neoliberal policies of the New Right. They imply that states often should promote networks not markets, trust not competition, and diplomacy not the new public management. Typically institutionalists combine these two ways of conceiving of networks by suggesting that although all organizations take the form of embedded networks, those that best resemble the ideal type of a network reap the benefits of so doing.

Today many institutionalists accept neoliberal arguments about the inflexible and unresponsive nature of hierarchies. But instead of promoting markets, they appeal to networks as a suitably flexible and responsive alternative based on recognition that social actors operate in structured relationships. Institutionalists argue that economic efficiency and success derive from stable relationships characterized by trust, social participation, voluntary associations, and friendship, at least as much as from markets and competition. In their view, while hierarchies can provide a context for trust and stability, the time for hierarchies has passed: hierarchies were useful for the routinized patterns of behavior that dominated Fordist economies, but they are far less suited to the new knowledge-driven global economy in which states must foster innovation and entrepreneurship if they are to compete effectively. Institutionalists argue that this new economy requires networks in which trust and participation are combined with flexibility, responsiveness, and innovation. The appeal of network theory often lies in its apparent ability to account for economic successes that are difficult for neoliberals to explain by reference to competition, such as Japanese Alliance Capitalism and the high-tech sectors in Silicon Valley and north-central Italy.

Institutionalism suggests that social scientists should study the first waves of reform not through abstract models based on assumptions about utility-maximizing agents but in terms of their impact on socially embedded actors. Institutionalists such as Rod Rhodes and Gerry Stoker argue that the first wave of reforms had unintended consequences as a result of entrenched institutional patterns and norms.[3] These reforms fragmented service delivery, thereby weakening central control without establishing proper markets. They created networks instead of either the

---

tional Collaboration and the Locus of Innovation: Networks of Learning in Biotechnology," *Administrative Science Quarterly* 41 (1996): 116–45.

[3] Rhodes, *Understanding Governance*, esp. chaps. 1 and 3; and G. Stoker, "Introduction: The Unintended Costs and Benefits of New Management Reform for British Local Governance," in G. Stoker, ed., *The New Management of British Local Governance* (London: Macmillan, 1999), 1–21.

old hierarchies or the neoliberal vision of markets. According to many institutionalists, the state now acts as one of several organizations, albeit the dominant one, that interact within networks to formulate policies and deliver services. From this perspective, the administrative tasks that now confront the state are primarily ones of fostering and managing networks.

THE THIRD WAY

New Labour's Third Way arose as it tackled dilemmas such as state overload against the background of a socialist tradition and with the aid of institutionalism and network theory. Of course, neither institutionalism nor network theory is inherently socialist. In practice, however, institutionalism and network theory found a home in New Labour due to personal ties, a similar concern to rebut the New Right and the economic ideas with which it was associated, and a shared, if unrecognized, debt to a lingering Christian idealism.

Constructing Dilemmas

New Labour stands at the juncture where a socialist tradition confronts issues initially highlighted by the New Right. The dominant tradition of British socialism inherited from the early ethical socialists a belief that the individual exists and attains the good only in the context of community. Blair often expressed this belief, insisting, for example, that we are "citizens of a community," not "separate economic actors competing in the marketplace of life."[4] Socialists thus joined institutionalists in arguing that sociality and solidarity are integral features of human life. They argued that people make sense of the world, including their own interests, in the context of social institutions that constrain them, enable their creativity, and bind them to one another in community.

Historically, socialists used a belief in our socially embedded nature to defend commitments to social justice, citizenship, and fellowship. They often identified people's social nature and responsibilities with social rights to a minimal standard of living, including adequate food, clothing, and housing, as well as protection from ill health and unemployment. For much of the postwar period, socialists tried to realize these rights through the Keynesian welfare state. They wanted the state to promote equal-

---

[4] T. Blair, *New Britain: My Vision of a Young Country* (London: Fourth Estate, 1996), 300.

ity by demand management, welfare provision, and progressive taxation. The resulting welfare state also embodied the command model of public service provision that had become so popular with socialists between the two world wars.

New Labour and the New Right. During the 1970s and 1980s, a number of dilemmas confronted socialists: worries about the underclass challenged the welfare state, worries about state overload posed questions of the command model of public service provision, and worries about inflation undermined the Keynesian macroeconomic framework. Typically these dilemmas were highlighted by the New Right, which eventually established hegemony over discussion of them. This hegemony appeared later in New Labour's adoption of positions resembling those of the New Right.

Perhaps New Labour most significantly resembles the New Right in that it conceives of the global economy as a competitive setting that renders economic efficiency and success absolute prerequisites for almost everything else. When institutionalists invoke costs of learning to explain the persistence of otherwise inefficient institutions, and when New Labour represents flexible labor markets and welfare reform as economic imperatives of the global economy, they tacitly accept the neoliberal idea of an unavoidable, universal, and tyrannical economic rationality—a rationality operating at the micro level to create structural constraints to which one has no option but to bow. In bowing to an allegedly unavoidable economic rationality, New Labour adopted themes that spread out to alter other aspects of its heritage. For example, the socialist ideal began to focus less on cooperation aimed at securing the good life for all, and more on economic partnerships to secure prosperity for all in the context of a robust competition in which everyone has a chance to compete.

Another significant similarity between New Labour and the New Right lies in their rejection of the bureaucratic hierarchies associated with Old Labour. New Labour accepts that the state suffered a crisis because hierarchies were inefficient in the new global economy. In this respect, New Labour again transforms the socialist tradition to mirror the New Right. Peter Mandelson and Roger Liddle explicitly rejected the "municipal socialism" and "centralized nationalism" of Labour's past. They insist that New Labour "does not seek to provide centralised 'statist' solutions to every social and economic problem."[5]

Despite the similarities between New Labour and the New Right, we should be wary of interpreting the former as a capitulation to the latter.

---

[5] P. Mandelson and R. Liddle, *The Blair Revolution* (London: Faber and Faber, 1996), 27.

To do so would be to neglect the constructed and contingent nature of social life in a way that would leave us few resources with which to explain their differences. Even if New Labour and the New Right conceived the dilemmas confronting the state in broadly similar fashion, they did so against the background of different traditions, and the continuing influence of these traditions explains the differences in their thinking and policies. Again, even if New Labour represents a response to the New Right, socialists constructed the dilemmas facing the welfare state, public services, and economy against the background of their tradition and so in a way different from the New Right.

The welfare state. In the case of the welfare state, socialists sometimes express worries about the underclass, but they generally portray this class as trapped on welfare not because of psychological dependency, but because of institutional facts, such as the way in which welfare payments are reduced once claimants start to earn even modest wages. Some of New Labour's policy advisers even suggested that the welfare state traps people in poverty because it fails to conceive of poverty as social exclusion or "network poverty." New Labour conceptualizes dependency in institutionalist terms of insufficient or inappropriate social embeddedness. According to Perri 6, for example, the most common way of getting a job is through informal networks of friends, former colleagues, and acquaintances.[6] Thus, the welfare state traps people in unemployment by lumping them together and thereby undermining their ability to enter the social networks where jobs are typically found. If unemployed people volunteer, they are treated as being unavailable for work, and yet, Perri 6 continues, volunteering is an important way of entering the networks and making the kinds of contacts that result in employment. Likewise, training schemes for the unemployed are provided by specialist bodies that deal with them alone, instead of by companies that connect them to the employed.

Public services. In the case of public services, when socialists deplore the inefficiency and rigidity of the provision of goods by a hierarchic bureaucracy, they rarely describe such inefficiency and rigidity as inherent consequences of public ownership, as does the New Right. On the contrary, the Third Way embodies a rebuttal of the New Right since it implies that the New Right's faith in markets ignored social embeddedness. Advocates of the Third Way argue that public services should reflect

---

[6] Perri 6, *Escaping Poverty: From Safety Nets to Networks of Opportunity* (London: Demos, 1997). Also see M. Granovetter, *Getting a Job: A Study of Contacts and Careers* (Cambridge: Harvard University Press, 1974).

our sociability; public services should reflect an ethic of mutual coop-eration, even if, when appropriate, they rely on market mechanisms to increase choice and promote responsibility. While New Labour accepts that markets can be an appropriate means of delivering public services, it insists that markets are not always the most efficient way to deliver services, for they can go against the public interest, reinforce inequali-ties, and entrench privilege, all of which damage economic performance. For New Labour, the problem with public services is one of adapt-ing them to new times, not rolling back the state to promote market competition.

The economy. In the case of the economy, socialists might have re-jected Keynesian macroeconomics, but they have rarely adopted the mon-etarist doctrines associated with the New Right. New Labour follows the New Right in identifying macroeconomic stability, and especially low inflation, as the main prerequisite of growth and high, long-term levels of employment; it believes that "government's first job is to ensure a stable macroeconomic environment."[7] New Labour also follows the New Right in concentrating on supply-side reforms, not demand man-agement. Nonetheless, New Labour's supply-side rests on institutional-ism rather than neoliberalism. New Labour follows the institutional-ists in suggesting that the problem is not one of removing barriers to competition but of coming to terms with the new economy. Leadbeater wrote here of a thin-air economy in which knowledge is all-important, and in which the vital ingredients for success are flexibility and innova-tion.[8] Mulgan similarly suggested that a revolution in communications and technology had produced a new "connexity" that involved a shift from liberal individualism and old-style social democracy to new forms of interdependence.[9]

So, for New Labour, the problems facing Britain's economy derive from a short-term outlook that neglects investment in the supply-side as much as they do from inflation. By constructing the dilemma facing the economy differently from neoliberals, New Labour opens up another space in which to denounce the New Right. This denouncement, like the institutionalist response to neoliberalism, highlights the dangers of ne-glecting social embeddedness and fetishizing the market. According to New Labour, the New Right failed to recognize that firms are social or-ganizations, and its policies thus encouraged an excessive individualism, privileging short-term issues, creating unnecessary economic volatility,

[7] *Our Competitive Future*, Cm 4176, 12.
[8] C. Leadbeater, *Living on Thin Air* (Harmondsworth: Penguin, 1999).
[9] G. Mulgan, *Connexity* (London: Jonathon Cape, 1997).

and exacerbating divisions in society. The Third Way begins with our social nature and the importance of a community composed of mutual rights and obligations and then suggests these considerations show social cohesion to be integral to economic prosperity.

New Labour's Response

New Labour trumpeted several "big ideas"—stakeholder society, social capital, communitarianism, and the Third Way—to express its distinctive response to the crisis of the state. Whatever the label, New Labour's response to the crisis of the state draws on institutionalism and network theory. New Labour accepts aspects of the New Right's challenge to the old bureaucratic welfare state but rejects the turn to markets and monetarism, advocating instead networks based on trust. New Labour does not exclude bureaucratic hierarchy or quasi-market competition. Rather, it advocates a mix of hierarchies, markets, and networks, with the choice between them depending on the nature of the service—"services should be provided through the sector best placed to provide those services most effectively," where "this can be the public, private or voluntary sector, or partnerships between these sectors."[10]

The welfare state. In the case of the welfare state, a belief in our social embeddedness encourages New Labour to envisage a world of citizens linked together by reciprocal duties and responsibilities. These citizens join the state in a cooperative enterprise aimed at producing an economically and socially vibrant nation. The state acts not as a safety net but as an enabler: it provides citizens with opportunities for advancement, leaving to the citizens the responsibility for taking advantage of these opportunities. New Labour thus seeks to promote individual responsibility through cooperation. Frank Field, former minister for welfare reform, wrote, for example, of an "age of mutuality" during which "self-interest . . . will also promote the common good," before emphasizing the importance of locating responsibility for self-improvement with individuals.[11] Blair too said that "the modern welfare state is not founded on a paternalistic government giving out more benefits but on an enabling government that through work and education helps people to help themselves."[12] The enabling state represents an allegedly new type of partnership—a new contract between citizen and state.

---

[10] *Modern Public Services for Britain: Investing in Reform*, Cm 4011 (1998).

[11] F. Field, *Reforming Welfare* (London: Social Markets Foundation, 1997), 78–80.

[12] Blair, *New Britain*, 302. For the impact of such sentiments on public policy, see especially *New Ambitions for Our Country: A New Contract for Welfare*, Cm 3805 (1998).

One clear aim of this new partnership is to overcome social exclusion and network poverty. New Labour's New Deal for the Unemployed sought to make work pay by eradicating the institutional disincentives to employment created by the rules governing taxation and benefits. The Working Families Tax Credit supplemented earnings from paid employment with cash benefits so that every family containing a full-time worker would have a guaranteed minimum income of a 190 pounds a week. The New Deal also sought to connect the unemployed to the employed. The young unemployed were given four options, including volunteering as well as paid work, training, and participation in an environmental task force. And the government offered a subsidy to employers lasting six months for each worker they recruited from among the long-term unemployed.

Public services.   In the case of public services, the Labour government conceives of networks as peculiarly appropriate to its ideals of partnership and an enabling state. The Service First program, in particular, promoted Quality Networks composed of local organizations from all areas and levels of the public sector working together in partnerships based on trust. The purposes of these networks included the development of principles of best practice, the sharing of troubleshooting skills, and the building of partnerships between relevant organizations. They were intended to encourage public services to work together to improve the efficiency and especially coordination of public services.

While New Labour's emphasis on individual involvement recalls themes found in the New Right, its model of service delivery is quite different. New Labour argues that many features of the new public management, such as quasi-markets and contracting out, maintained an unhealthy dichotomy between the public and private sectors: public bodies did not connect properly with private companies so much as merely contract out services to them. In contrast, the Third Way seeks to develop networks that enable public and private organizations properly to collaborate. In more concrete terms, the government revived Private Finance Initiatives in an attempt to create mechanisms by which public and private organizations might form partnerships and networks in order to finance and undertake projects. Typically these projects constitute a form of investment in the supply-side, such as the construction and repair of schools or the transport infrastructure.

New Labour's networks for public service delivery are supposed to be based on trust. Blair described trust as "the recognition of a mutual purpose for which we work together and in which we all benefit."[13] Trust

[13] Blair, *New Britain*, 292.

matters, New Labour tells us, because we are interdependent social beings who achieve more by working together than by competing. Effective and high-quality public services are thus best achieved through cooperative relations based on trust. Blair has often spoken of building relationships of trust between all actors in society. Under New Labour, trust is promoted between organizations by means of the Quality Networks program; it is promoted inside organizations through "management within boundaries," and it is promoted between organizations and individuals by means of the Service First program.

The economy. New Labour tells us that in the case of the economy the state should become an enabling institution oriented around self-organizing networks. Proponents argue that "the Government has a key role in acting as a catalyst, investor, and regulator to strengthen the supply-side of the economy."[14] The state can best fulfill this role, moreover, by entering into partnerships and networks with individuals, voluntary bodies, and private companies. Thus, for example, New Labour promoted Individual Learning Accounts in which the state and employers provide individuals with a grant to be used toward training on the condition that the individuals themselves provide a small initial sum. Similarly, New Labour formed a partnership with the Wellcome Trust to spend nearly 1.5 billion pounds to improve the technological base of British industry.

New Labour clearly regards networks as good institutions in terms of ethics (they reflect our place in a community that gives us rights and responsibilities) and in terms of efficiency (they promote competitiveness in the global economy). Both the moral revival and the prosperity of community depend on clusters of self-governing institutions, such as schools, housing associations, and local councils, working together in networks. New Labour's original models here were the economic success stories once beloved of institutionalists—the Asian Tigers, Silicon Valley, and north-central Italy. Leadbeater pointed to lessons learned from California.[15] He argued that economic competitiveness depends on entrepreneurship and knowledge, especially of software, the Internet, and biotechnology. California promotes a culture of creative individualism that fosters the openness and experimentalism essential to such entrepreneurship and knowledge. The high-tech companies of Silicon Valley form networks in which they share information and collaborate on projects. The networks of high-tech firms are models of stakeholding: they have large schemes of employee-ownership; they focus on building loyalty among employees

---

[14] *Our Competitive Future*, Cm 4176, 7.

[15] Leadbeater, *Living on Thin Air*; and C. Leadbeater, *Britain: The California of Europe?* (London: Demos, 1999).

and customers; and they set high standards of corporate responsibility. If Britain builds networks of social entrepreneurs and civic leaders, Leadbeater implies, it will share the flexibility, responsiveness, and prosperity that California enjoys.

For New Labour, investment in the supply-side and creation of networks are the solutions to Britain's economic ills. The new, knowledge-driven, global economy offers opportunities and constraints. It allows and requires us to develop innovative ideas and to turn them into jobs and economic growth. New Labour believes that Britain must become an outward-looking, flexible, and creative center, developing its networks, connexity, and social capital. Thus, Blair, following policy advisers such as Leonard, tried to rebrand Great Britain as "cool Britannia"—a people and society characterized by "know-how, creativity, risk-taking, and, most of all, originality."[16]

Thus, we see how New Labour's Third Way draws on institutionalism and network theory to "modernize" socialism and thereby address the crisis of the state. Of course, politicians and policy advisers of New Labour often disagree among themselves: Leadbeater and Mulgan have suggested that the idea of stakeholding proposed by Will Hutton and John Kay is too cumbersome to meet the demands of the entrepreneurial, knowledge-driven economy of today.[17] Nonetheless, the disagreements occur within a broadly shared framework: Leadbeater and Mulgan allow that stakeholding remains a viable idea. The elite of New Labour rely on an institutionalist language of social embeddedness, sociality, community, social capital, networks, and partnership.

JOINING-UP

New Labour's response to the crisis of the state overlaps with, and draws on, institutionalism. Against the background of a socialist tradition, New Labour constructed the dilemmas facing the state in a way that pointed to a rejection of Old Labour and the New Right and to an affirmation of social embeddedness, partnership, networks, and trust. Blair glossed this vision, saying, "joined-up problems need joined-up solutions."[18] Joined-up governance refers to New Labour's vision of the public sector reformed in accord with its Third Way. The idea of joined-up governance

---

[16] Cited in J. Heastfield, "Brand New Britain," *LM Magazine*, November 1997. Also see M. Leonard, *Britain: Renewing Our Identity* (London: Demos, 1997).

[17] C. Leadbeater and G. Mulgan, *Mistakeholding: Whatever Happened to Labour's Big Idea?* (London: Demos, 1996).

[18] *Observer*, May 31, 1998.

thus invokes networks as a solution to both the perceived crisis of the old-fashioned bureaucratic state and the additional damage that institutionalists suggest has been wrought on the state by the first wave of reforms.

Constructing Dilemmas

The Third Way deploys institutionalism to challenge the neoliberal narrative. It suggests that the neoliberals neglected our social embeddedness and fetishized markets in a way that damaged the efficiency, flexibility, and responsiveness of the public sector and the economy. This challenge implies that the New Right created additional problems for the state—fragmentation, steering, and managerialism. Joined-up governance attempts to resolve these problems.

Fragmentation.   A lack of coordination is one of the most widely invoked consequences of the first wave of public sector reform. Services are delivered by a complex combination of government, special-purpose bodies, and the voluntary and private sectors. In Britain there are over five thousand special-purpose bodies that spend about forty billion pounds and to which ministers make about seventy thousand patronage appointments. It is no wonder the critics complain that marketization led to excessive fragmentation.

According to institutionalists, the fragmentation associated with the New Right merely exacerbates a lack of coordination also characteristic of hierarchies. Perri 6 argues, for example, that the organization of government into separate departments with their own budgets undermines attempts to deal with wicked problems that cut across departmental cages.[19] He then suggests that the reforms of the New Right made it even harder to deal adequately with wicked problems since they created a plethora of agencies only too willing to pass a problem on to someone else in an attempt to ensure that they themselves meet the quasi-market criteria of success under which they operate. Examples include schools excluding difficult children who then turn to crime, or mentally ill patients being returned to the community where they are liable to become a problem for local law and order. Government, Perri 6 concludes, needs to be holistic.

While the New Right has exacerbated the problem of coordination, institutionalists and New Labour often suggest that the external fact of globalization makes this problem such a pressing one. The Foreign Pol-

---

[19] Perri 6, *Holistic Government* (London: Demos, 1997); and Perri 6 et al., *Governing in the Round: Strategies for Holistic Government* (London: Demos, 1999).

icy Centre declares, for example, that the problems of today flow across boundaries between nation states and the departments of state within them. In this view, we live in a smaller, faster, global world in which factories in Cardiff shut down because of troubles in the economy of South Korea. Thus, the argument continues, we need to move away from traditional bureaucratic modes of coordination toward networks formed around particular issues; we need to reorganize government around cross-cutting issues and joined-up solutions.

The Labour government indicated sensitivity to issues of coordination in its White Paper *Modernising Government*. The White Paper illustrates the problem by pointing to the large number of organizations involved in providing long-term domiciliary care.[20] It also follows Perri 6 in its analysis of the rigidity and limits of central departments. It too calls for holistic, joined-up governance.

Steering. A lack of control is another problem associated with the first wave of reforms. Institutionalists generally suggest that fragmentation has led to an increasingly diverse range of institutions being involved in the process of governance, in turn, creating a particular need for the central core to provide leadership. The New Right exacerbated this problem by getting rid of functions through privatization and regulation. The unintended consequence, institutionalists tell us, was a loss of control and even a hollowing out of the state. The New Right created numerous special-purpose agencies that were difficult for the state to steer. There is even a suspicion that some privatized companies have captured their regulatory bodies. New Labour often echoes the institutionalists' account of the issue of control. Efforts by New Labour to increase the strategic capability of central government have included a turn toward a corporate approach, attempts to strengthen horizontal policymaking, and the increased role given to the Cabinet Office.

Managerialism. Excessive managerialism is yet another problem often liked to the first wave of reforms. Although views differ on the extent to which the senior civil service has acquired more than a veneer of managerialism, socialists and institutionalists typically worry that creeping managerialism erodes public-service ethics. The apparent spread of patronage under the Thatcher governments in Britain provoked fears about falling standards of public conduct. In addition, the new public management was seen as undermining the sense of public duty associated with the generalist tradition of the civil service.

[20] *Modernising Government* Cm 4310 (1999), 24.

New Labour's Response

Institutionalists and social democrats have drawn on their traditions to ascribe problems of fragmentation, steering, and managerialism to the first wave of public sector reforms. They also draw on the same traditions to prescribe joining-up as a solution to these problems. The bold claim is that joined-up government can tackle wicked problems; it can establish a revitalized public sector that will be responsive, flexible, entrepreneurial, and efficient—a public sector that will be in tune with the new knowledge-based global economy.

Fragmentation. In response to fragmentation, institutionalists appeal to networks as offering flexible yet effective co-ordination. New Labour similarly claims that the delivery of services depends as never before on linking organizations together through responsive connections in an unstructured framework. In so far as networks are decentralized and characterized by an indirect and diplomatic style of management, New Labour hopes that they can co-ordinate departments in a way that will not just produce a new system of cages.

New Labour quickly identified one of the main challenges facing the civil service as "improving collaborative working across organisational boundaries," and it set out to meet this challenge by "ensuring that policy making is more joined-up and strategic."[21] In particular New Labour immediately created a Social Exclusion Unit to "develop integrated and sustainable approaches to the problems of the worst housing estates, including crime, drugs, unemployment, community breakdown, and bad schools."[22] The unit founded employment, education, and health zones operating under a single regeneration budget. These action zones are meant to enable the state to operate across departmental cages when dealing with wicked problems.

Later New Labour turned to networks again to promote coordination within distinct policy areas, including employment, education, and health. Addressing unemployment, the government established action teams to focus on network poverty conceived as a cycle of decline in which children from poor households are less likely to stay at school and so less able to secure employment. Addressing national health care, it initiated a new statutory duty for NHS Trusts to work in partnership with other NHS organizations so that the various bodies that deliver services

[21] Ibid., 56 and 6.
[22] *Bringing Britain Together: A National Strategy for Neighbourhood Renewal*, Cm 4045 (1998).

might work together to develop integrated systems of care.[23] Addressing education, it created zones composed of about twenty schools, covering all age ranges and operating under an action forum composed of the local education authority in partnership with businesses, parents, and community groups.

Steering. Because institutionalists often champion networks as a superior form of organization, they have paid considerable attention to the question of how best to control them. They generally concentrate on presenting the styles of management they believe best fit different types of network, guided by allegedly objective social facts such as the structure of relations. Almost all the popular management styles seek to provide scope for central government to steer networks while promoting a culture of trust through greater diplomacy and negotiation. Stoker, for example, lists techniques for steering urban governance that clearly strive to avoid hierarchy. They include indirect management through cultural persuasion, communication, and monitoring, as well as more direct steering through financial subsidies.[24]

New Labour too promotes a culture of trust while attempting to deploy a range of techniques to enhance central control. The Local Government Act (2000) increased the powers of local government, but it did so at a time when the central government was increasingly deploying persuasion and "naming and shaming" to make councils respond to its agenda in the way it thought appropriate. Elsewhere New Labour combined a decentralization that gave more scope to other organizations with attempts to specify in great detail what these other organizations should do, to persuade them to do what is specified, and to regulate them in relation to the relevant specifications. In the case of employment, the government might conceive of action teams as flexible and rooted in local initiatives, but it still relies on direct financial control to hold them to the criteria that it uses to assess them—a rise in the proportion of people in work, an improvement in the employment rates of disadvantaged groups, and the number of people employed through the direct efforts of the team. In the case of health, New Labour suggested that local variations in standards of care could be adequately dealt with simply by having organizations share principles of best practice, but it specifies national standards and preferred models for specific types of service. In the case of education, even as schools acquired more powers, so the center defined specific measurements and targets of literacy and numeracy.

---

[23] *The New National Health Service: Modern, Dependable,* Cm 3807 (1997), 45.

[24] G. Stoker, "Urban Political Science and the Challenge of Urban Governance," in Pierre, ed., *Debating Governance,* 98–104.

Generally New Labour adopts an instrumental approach to network management. It assumes that the center can devise and impose tools to foster integration in networks and thereby realize the objectives of the center. Measures such as the creation of action zones have a centralizing thrust. They seek to coordinate departments and local authorities by imposing a new style of management on other agencies and especially by evaluating them against criteria defined at the center. Indeed, the government openly says that while it does "not want to run local services from the centre," it "is not afraid to take action where standards slip."[25] The center owns zones, and local agendas are recognized only if they conform to those of the center.

Managerialism. Fears about the erosion of the traditional public service ethos quickly inspired interest in a code of ethics. The Treasury and Civil Service Committee proposed such a code complete with an independent appeal to the Civil Service commissioners. New Labour moved to give this code statutory force. The *Ministerial Code* states that ministers have "a duty to uphold the political impartiality of the Civil Service" and "to ensure that influence over appointments is not abused for partisan purposes."[26]

Joining-up. Clearly New Labour hopes that networks can resolve the problems of coordination and control and so, in conjunction with a suitable ethical code, establish a responsible and efficient public sector. The government and its policy advisers equate networks with the flexibility and responsiveness they believe are so important in the new economy. They argue that the flexibility of networks means joined-up governance will be able to identify and tackle problems before they become acute. It also means that governmental bodies will be able to work in partnership with private sector ones to generate additional finance and expertise. The alleged responsiveness of networks implies that joined-up governance will tackle issues in the round instead of through numerous, separate agencies. It also implies that the state will focus on changing cultural habits through information and persuasion instead of changing behavior through coercion and control. More generally, networks are invoked as organizations peculiarly conducive to the growth of, in Leadbeater's words, a "civic enterprise culture."[27] The flexibility and responsiveness of joined-up governance allegedly encourages an innovative, people-focused

---

[25] *Modernising Government,* Cm 4310, 55.

[26] Cabinet Office, *Ministerial Code: A Code of Conduct and Guidance on Procedures for Ministers* (London: Cabinet Office, 1997), 21, para. 56.

[27] Compare C. Leadbeater and S. Goss, *Civic Entrepreneurship* (London: Demos, 1998).

culture that attracts civic entrepreneurs—visionary individuals whose skills lie in building networks and establishing trust.

Of course, there are disagreements and debates among the politicians and policy advisers of New Labour: Perri 6 called on the government to learn from its early mistakes and to devolve more.[28] Yet the disagreements occur in a shared framework: Perri 6 elides his concept of holistic government with joined-up governance while appealing to action zones and single regeneration budgets as concrete examples of his vision. The elite of New Labour relies on an overlapping consensus derived from an institutionalist language of networks, zones, steering, partnership, trust, and civic entrepreneurship.

What happened next? It would be foolish to assume that New Labour's second wave of reforms worked as intended, or even that New Labour's commitment to the reforms has been unchanging. To the contrary, we might distinguish several stages in New Labour's development. The first stage would be the formative one prior to its victory in the 1997 election. During this stage, the party transformed its internal organization and its policy commitments and aggressively promoted images of novelty and modernization in order to signal a break with its own history. A second stage from 1997 until about 2003 saw New Labour in government and implementing reforms associated with the Third Way and joined-up government. This delivery stage began with a time of caution in which the government felt constrained by its fiscal and financial legacy. It moved through a time of modernization in which policies were meant to make Britain more innovative and dynamic and then ended with a time of redistribution in which the emphasis fell as much on using limited budgetary resources to tackle the poverty and social exclusion of targeted groups. Finally, we might identify a third stage, from about 2003 onward, during which New Labour seemed increasingly tired. During this stage, the government faced mounting criticisms, spent more and more time dealing with events and disasters and seemed to lose much of its faith in its own agenda. Arguably, a distinctive "Blairism" arose, combining the Third Way and joining-up with a foreign policy characterized by muscular interventionism, and this new foreign policy then split New Labour apart, setting the scene for Gordon Brown to take over as prime minister.

During New Labour's tired stage, public sector reforms still drew on buzzwords and programmatic ideas tied to community, social capital, networks, partnerships, and trust. Yet there were changes. For a start, the government had less scope for policies based on these ideas. Policy disasters provided distractions that sometimes discredited the government:

[28] Perri 6 et. al., *Governing in the Round.*

examples range from the millennium dome to the Hutton Inquiry. Events sapped the government's energy: examples range from Joe Moore's claim that September 11 was a good day to bury bad news to the much more serious appearance of new terrorist threats. Foreign policy from Kosovo to Iraq became increasingly time-consuming, and used up vast amounts of goodwill within the party and among the electorate. In addition, the government lost some of its faith in its own programmatic agenda, a loss that continues to affect current policy. On one hand, institutionalist themes continue to inspire public policies, as evidenced by foundation hospitals and the leading-edge partnership program for schools. But, on the other hand, there is a growing sense that some policies have not lived up to expectations; they have not created the dynamic, innovative, and responsible citizens, organizations, and society promised by institutionalism.

New Labour's declining scope and faith in its agenda has altered the practice of governance. Consider, for example, the relationship of the Prime Minster's Office at No. 10 Downing Street to the rest of Whitehall. After 1997 New Labour introduced a number of centralizing measures to increase the role of the Cabinet Office and the strategic capability of the center. Yet, since about 2003, there has been a shift from regular and routine interactions in the context of these centralizing measures, to what we might call No.10 as "searchlight." Government departments are largely left alone by No. 10, save that they are intermittently and suddenly subject to intense scrutiny and a flurry of activity. The altered relationship between No. 10 and the rest of Whitehall reflects the declining scope for programmatic policymaking: the searchlight typically focuses on departments when they are involved in a policy disaster or newsworthy event. The altered relationship also reflects New Labour's declining faith in its programmatic agenda. Departments are generally left to go their own way in part because No. 10 is less sure about where it thinks they should be going.

COMPARATIVE PERSPECTIVES

The British case suggests that the new governance cannot be assimilated to the neoliberal promotion of markets. Public sector reform has come in two waves. The first was dominated by neoliberal emphases on markets and a new public sector management. In contrast, the second owed more to the new institutionalism and its emphases on networks, partnerships, and joining-up. Social scientists would do well to take note of at least a transformation of neoliberalism and arguably its demise. Contemporary patterns of rule increasingly instantiate ideas and practices in which networks are deliberately promoted as a means of bringing together public and private organizations on multiple levels and in multiple policy sectors. Comparative cases that illustrate the dramatic rise of joined-up governance include Australia's whole of government approach, homeland security in the United States, aid to fragile states, and the response to the recent financial crisis.

Australia: Whole of Government

Australia's whole of government approach has much in common with joined-up governance. Australia aims to improve governance and in particular to overcome fragmentation by building networks. "The distinguishing characteristic of whole of government work is that there is an emphasis on objectives shared across organizational boundaries, as opposed to working solely within an organization."[29]

The whole of government agenda rose against a background of growing dissatisfaction with the unresponsiveness of bureaucracy. In 1976 the Coombs Report, published by the Royal Commission on Australian Government Administration, called for a comprehensive service at the local level so that the public sector seemed more in touch with citizens.[30] Attempts to make public services more responsive initially reflected a faith in markets, the new public management, and an increasing use of task forces and other special agencies. But over time the emphasis shifted to partnerships, joining-up, and networks. In 1992 the Council of Australian Governments was formed specifically to promote cooperation between various levels of government. In the late 1990s the Howard administrations also encouraged the creation of broader networks or "social coalitions" that brought public sector organizations together with voluntary and private ones.

Like joined-up governance, Australia's whole of government approach is indebted to the new institutionalism and other sociological theories of governance. This debt is manifest in appeals to the advantages of networks in delivering services, securing coordination and control, and tackling wicked problems.

Service delivery. The whole of government approach consists in large part of using networks to improve service delivery. Australia, like Brit-

---

[29] Australian Public Service Commission, *Connecting Government: Whole of Government Responses to Australia's Priority Challenges*, Management Advisory Committee Report No. 4, Department of Prime Minister and Cabinet (2004), 3.

[30] For discussion and debate, see C. Hazlehurst and J. Nethercote, eds., *Reforming Australian Government: The Coombs Report and Beyond* (Canberra: ANU Press, 1977).

ain, introduced one-stop shops to help citizens more easily navigate and combine the various services of relevance to them. One-stop shops intend to reduce complexity by consolidating the delivery of diverse yet related services. A particularly clear example is Centrelink.

Centrelink was created in 1997 under the Department of Human Services to consolidate the delivery of a range of welfare benefits and related services that had earlier been provided by a number of different agencies. By 2007 Centrelink had over a thousand delivery points serving an estimated 6.5 million Australians. It has made payments on behalf of thirty-one departments and agencies, including the Department of the Attorney-General, the Department of Education, Science and Training, the Department of Foreign Affairs and Trade, and the Department of Health and Ageing. In all, it provides 119 different services with a total value of AU$66.3 billion.

Coordination and control. Australia's whole of government approach promotes network solutions to coordination and control. For a start, it strives to coordinate public sector actions across multiple organizations operating at multiple levels. Centrelink, for example, is meant to enhance coordination of welfare payments and related services. In addition, this coordination is meant to enhance the ability of the center to control or at least steer other actors so as to realize its policy goals. The ambition is not only to link various public sector actors but also to keep them "focused on the [central] government's policy and operational agenda."[31] Networks are meant to increase the strategic leadership role of the cabinet by driving agency and department heads to follow up on decisions made at the center. Centrelink and other organizations created under the whole of government approach are typically meant to work in accord with priorities determined by the center.

Britain's joined-up governance and Australia's whole of government approach both give a powerful steering role to the center. However, the tools by which the center steers differ. In Britain, the center, notably the Cabinet Office and the Treasury, steers primarily by setting and monitoring targets. In Australia, steering depends less on explicit targets than on the prime minister and cabinet monitoring performance through output budgets. Arguably, the Australian approach leaves room for a greater variety of policy outcomes, albeit that these outcomes must remain within priorities determined by the center.

Wicked problems. The Australian Public Service makes explicit use of the term "wicked problem." As we saw in chapter 4, "wicked prob-

[31] *Centrelink Annual Report 2006–2007* (2007).

lems" is a technical concept that arose in planning theory before spreading across institutionalism and organization theory, where it was picked up by policy actors. In its official paper *Tackling Wicked Problems*, the Australian Public Service specifies that wicked problems are not only peculiarly resistant to resolution but also a challenge to bureaucratic ways of working and solving problems. Wicked problems, including climate change, obesity, and indigenous disadvantage, require "thinking that is capable of grasping the big picture" and "more collaborative and innovative approaches"; they allegedly require actors to operate "across organizational boundaries" in a whole of government approach.[32]

Land management provides an example of a wicked problem tackled within the whole of government framework. In 2002 the Australian government established the Natural Resource Management Team (NRM) to promote sustainable agricultural production and environmental protection. The NRM is tasked with securing cooperation and coordination in the administration of government programs such as the Natural Heritage Trust and the National Action Plan for Salinity and Water Quality. Policy is formed by a multijurisdictional committee, the Natural Resource Management Ministerial Council, which consists of environment and agricultural policy makers from the federal level, the states, and local territories, and which is cochaired by the heads of the Department of Environment and Heritage and the Department of Agriculture, Fisheries, and Forestry. The NRM is an attempt to secure coordination through a network. It is also an attempt to facilitate central steering of the network through a strong federal presence.

The United States: Homeland Security

The terror attacks of September 11, 2001, prompted a massive overhaul of American security apparatuses. The resulting reforms sought to foster networks aimed at preventing other terrorist attacks. Initially the main language was that of "interagency coordination," but policy actors increasingly relate this to whole of government and joined-up approaches.[33] Homeland security is another example of an attempt to foster joined-up governance in order to promote coordination and central control in an otherwise increasingly fragmented environment. The main difference is

[32] Australian Public Service Commission, *Tackling Wicked Problems*, iii.

[33] E.g., D. Kilcullen, "Three Pillars of Counterinsurgency," paper presented to the U.S. Government Counterinsurgency Conference, Washington, DC, September 2006; and F. McDonough, "Whole of Government: Visions, Strategies, and Challenges," paper presented to the 40th Conference of the International Council for Information Technology in Government Administration, Guadalajara, Mexico, September 12 –14, 2006.

that in this case joining-up is discussed in relation to national security more than managerial reform.[34]

At the federal level, the Bush administration responded to the 9/11 attacks by creating a new cabinet-level department. The Department of Homeland Security (DHS) brought together a diverse patchwork of twenty-two agencies responsible for diverse territories and activities. These agencies included the Coast Guard, the Citizenship and Immigration Services, the Customs and Border Protection, the Federal Emergency Management Agency, Immigration Customs Enforcement, the Secret Service, and the Transportation Security Administration. The rationale for the DHS explicitly mentions "collaborating and coordinating across traditional boundaries, both horizontally (between agencies) and vertically (among different levels of government)" with the equally explicit aim of creating a "cohesive, capable and service-oriented organization whose cross-cutting functions will be optimized" so as better to protect the "nation against threats and effectively respond to disasters."[35]

The DHS focuses on the gathering and analysis of intelligence. It gathers information by cooperating with intelligence assets on federal, state, and local levels, as well as private and voluntary sector organizations. Inside the DHS, the Office of Intelligence and Analysis collates and analyzes this information so as to enable the DHS to advise policy makers and disseminate information back to its federal, state, local, and private sector partners. The DHS is thus meant to act as a cache for intelligence that is accessible to policy makers and law enforcement agencies. It is meant to break down barriers between agencies, promoting a free flow of intelligence.

Joined-up approaches to security and emergency are spreading in the United States at the local as well as the federal level. Many local authorities have initiatives to foster cooperation and coordination among agencies involved in emergency management and response. For example, Arlington County, Virginia, has established an emergency management team composed of the police and fire departments as well as various officials from the public works and public health departments.[36] In addition, the county has negotiated with its neighbors to establish aid agreements under which they all share resources across jurisdictional boundaries. The idea of shared resources here extends to protocols and practices: it includes the interoperability of radio systems and the use of standard

[34] For discussion of this difference, see D. Brook and C. King, "Civil Service Reform as National Security: The Homeland Security Act of 2002," *Public Administration Review* 67 (2007): 399–407.

[35] *Securing Our Homeland: Department of Homeland Security Strategic Plan* (2004), 6

[36] C. Anderson, "Pentagon in Peril," *Securing the Homeland*, a special supplement to *Governing* (October 2004), 22.

emergency response equipment so that any agency's tools will work when responding to an emergency anywhere in the region; and it includes a uniform incident management system covering issues such as which agency will take the lead in responding to particular types of emergency.

Fragile States: Aid and Intervention

Security concerns have also influenced the growing popularity of joined-up approaches to aid and intervention in fragile states. Before September 11, 2001, debates about aid were conducted mainly in terms of underdeveloped states and their economic needs. But since the terrorist attacks, greater attention has been paid to fragile states and the wicked problems they confront. Fragile states are defined not just by poverty but also by related problems of weak governance and violent conflict. Donor states increasingly conceive of aid as requiring a whole of government approach that sets out to address all these problems simultaneously. They argue that effective aid to fragile states depends on networks that combine actors and issues associated with foreign policy, security, and development.

The whole of government approach. Donor states increasingly approach fragile states through a whole of government approach that emphasizes the importance of coordination among policy actors involved with diplomacy, defense, and development. By 2005 Australia, Britain, Germany, and the United States had established dedicated units to coordinate departmental efforts to aid reconstruction in fragile states. Several states had also explored novel funding arrangements to encourage greater interdepartmental collaboration.

Unsurprisingly the whole of government approach quickly took root in the Organisation for Economic Co-operation and Development (OECD). In 2005 the Fragile States Group of the OECD Development Assistance Committee devised Principles for Good Engagement in Fragile States that highlighted the importance of developing coherent programs that spanned the administrative, economic, political, and security domains. The group then set up a workstream, chaired by Australia and France, to devise a framework for an explicitly whole of government approach.[37]

The international community even appears to be moving toward support for a whole of government approach to aid more generally. From February to March 2005 a high-level forum on joint progress toward enhanced aid effectiveness met in Paris. It brought together over a hundred countries as well as international institutions such as the African

---

[37] Organisation for Economic Co-Operation and Development, *Whole of Government Approaches to Fragile States* (2006).

Development Bank, the Asian Development Bank, the European Bank for Reconstruction and Development, the OECD, the World Bank, and the United Nations Development Programme. The forum resulted in the Paris Declaration, which calls for greater harmonization, alignment, and managing aid in relation to a set of monitorable indicators.

All cases of a whole of government approach to fragile states and aid more generally emphasize the alignment of expertise and actions concerned with economics, governance, and security. In addition, many organize funding to encourage such alignment. Pooled funding and joint budget lines allow resources to be oriented toward specific problems and goals rather than following established bureaucratic domains or agency affiliations. For example, Britain has established an Africa Conflict Prevention Pool and a Global Prevention Pool to prompt collaboration among a wide range of policy actors in the creation of integrated strategies. Finally, some whole of government approaches try to build aid strategies in partnership with private sector actors. One example is the involvement of private companies in the reconstruction of war-torn societies.

Canada and Haiti. The OECD points to Canada's operations in Haiti as a good example of the whole of government approach. Canada has been a leading proponent of this approach since adopting it in an international policy statement of April 2005. The approach lies behind the formation of interorganizational networks in Ottawa and on the ground in Haiti.

Canada's policies toward Haiti and its operations in Haiti are devised and planned by an Interdepartmental Steering Group and an Interdepartmental Working Group. The steering group brings together the agencies involved in the operations: the Canadian International Development Agency, the Department of Foreign Affairs and International Trade, the Department of National Defence, the Privy Council Office, and Public Safety and Emergency Preparedness Canada. This steering group defines broad procedures and budget for the operations in Haiti. Within this broad framework, an Interdepartmental Working Group manages the operations. This working group brings together the expertise involved in the operations, including specialized departments such as Correctional Services Canada, Elections Canada, and the Department of Justice, all of which possess different aspects of the expertise needed to realize the objectives defined by the steering committee.

Operations on the ground in Haiti are primarily executed by the diplomatic corps and security personnel. The whole of government approach appears again in the emphasis placed on coordinating between these groups and between them and other relevant actors. The presence of security personnel and peacekeepers is a collaborative effort among the Canadian International Development Agency, the Department of Foreign Affairs and International Trade, and Royal Canadian Mounted Police, which collectively provide about a hundred personnel to the United Nations Stabilization Mission in Haiti. In addition, the diplomatic corps in particular collaborates with the international community and especially with Haitian officials, providing a channel for local ideas and inputs.

It is extremely early to assess the whole of government approach to fragile states. There is surely something intuitively appealing about it. Yet the few assessments available highlight some of the challenges that remain.[38] Donors talk about combining economics, governance, and security, and they send experts from all these fields, but they often fail to develop comprehensive strategies that unify the aid and services they provide.

The Financial Crisis

I am reluctant to offer an opinion about the current financial crisis or political responses to it, but it looms so large in many people's concerns that it is perhaps an unavoidable topic.[39] The financial crisis rose from the collapse of credit, banking, and the housing market. The extent of the crisis remains uncertain. The International Monetary Fund (IMF) predicts that debt originating in the United States will reach 1.4 trillion dollars. American and European banks will loose $10 million. Credit growth will collapse from a postwar annual average of 9 percent to a mere 1 percent.[40] The question for us is: how will this affect patterns of governance? I am reluctant to hazard an answer partly because it is too early to tell and partly because I suspect much of what has happened just shows policy actors are panicking and grabbing for anything that has the slightest chance of mitigating the crisis. To attempt to describe a coherent policy agenda may be to overly intellectualize.

Still, the question remains: what does the experience of the credit crisis mean for my broader argument about changes in governance and democracy? Some observers see the crisis as heralding a return to the state and state action, a move from governance back to government. I doubt it. The crisis may stand as the final end of the first wave of public sector reforms. Neoliberalism may have run its course even as economic policy.

[38] E.g., S. Patrick and K. Brown, *Greater than the Sum of Its Parts? Assessing "Whole of Government" Approaches to Fragile States* (New York: International Peace Academy, 2007).

[39] The referees of the original manuscript of this book certainly thought I could not avoid discussing the financial crisis!

[40] *Economist*, October 2008.

Certainly few people currently defend deregulation, liberalization, and easy credit. Nonetheless, the end of neoliberalism and greater skepticism toward markets need not entail a return to the bureaucratic state. To the contrary, I suspect that policy actors will generally respond to the financial crisis with policy instruments associated with the second wave of reforms. Typically policy actors will look for solutions in regulation, networks, and partnerships, rather than hierarchic controls and state ownership.

Already the response to the financial crisis seems to owe more to ideas such as joined-up governance than to bureaucratic control and rational planning. Reregulation is among the most persistent demands to have risen from the crisis. Policy actors appear determined to rely on regulation to try to prevent the banking sector from becoming swamped with risky credit. Even the IMF acknowledges the failings of a regulatory regime that relied so heavily on self-disclosure and market discipline.[41] In September 2008 central bankers endorsed the Basel Committee's proposals for increased liquidity regulation. The Financial Stability Forum consists of finance ministries, central banks, regulators, and supervisory authorities from the G7 plus five, and it has begun to examine new regulatory proposals.

The Financial Stability Forum is itself an example of the role of transnational networks in the response to the crisis. Similar networks surely played a role in diverse states coordinating their announcements of stimulus packages. Particular states have also promoted more local networks. Networks—and especially public-private partnerships—have become the main way by which states try to steer collapsing institutions to safety. States have generally avoided taking ownership or even direct control of failing financial institutions. Innocent observers might gasp at the willingness of policy actors to hand over large amounts of money while asking for so little in return. There has been little evidence of states controlling or even directing financial institutions to ensure they act for the public good. Even when states have taken ownership of a failed financial institution, the plan almost always is to return the institution to the private sector as soon as possible. The American response to the financial crisis in particular has involved less a return to the bureaucratic state than a notable reluctance even to mention nationalization.

A reluctance to take over institutions means that state funding to failed institutions has led to public-private hybrids or, if we are willing to stretch the term, "partnerships." States are partners with failed and vulnerable private sector organizations, collaborating, for example, to purge

---

[41] International Monetary Fund, "Lessons of the Financial Crisis for Future Regulation of Financial Institutions and Markets and for Liquidity Management," February 4, 2009.

bad loans. Similarly, the United States government is trying to unlock frozen credit markets through a "public-private investment program for legacy assets." The program uses public funds to encourage private sector actors to invest along with the taxpayer in taking over legacy loans. The state and the private sector then more or less share the risks and profits of buying up these loans.

CONCLUSION

I have spent some time relating New Labour and joined-up government to institutionalism in the same way that social scientists often relate Thatcherism and the new public management to neoliberalism. I have also spent some time exploring how similar ideas and policies appear in other policy agendas aimed at creating whole of government approaches to problems or simply connecting government. One of my main aims in doing so has been to draw attention to the role played by expertise from the social sciences in the new governance. New theories of governance may have made us see the world differently, thereby contributing to the rise of new problems of governing and democracy. Equally, however, policy makers have often drawn on just these theories to craft responses to the relevant problems.

Insofar as social scientists tend to use economic and sociological concepts of rationality to forge explanations that bypass studies of contingent beliefs and desires, they often suggest that there is just the one story to tell—a story of objective facts and reason and norms, about social pressures and entrenched institutions, and so about suitable policy outcomes. In contrast, I have suggested that social scientists and policy makers construct their conceptions of pressures, institutions, and outcomes very differently, depending on their inherited traditions and their respective concepts of rationality. From this perspective, the institutionalist narrative and the joined-up policies of New Labour are by no means the only options available. Arguably, they are less pure and neutral accounts of a given world than they are historical events with their own problematic genealogy. To denaturalize institutionalism and New Labour in this way is to ask, who is telling this story and why? What alternative stories might be told? Which stories do we want to be governed by?

CHAPTER TEN

Police Reform

THIS CHAPTER continues to explore the way in which public sector reforms rely on expertise from the social sciences to address problems associated with the new governance. Here the focus shifts, however, from joined-up government to the narratives and cultures that inform police reform, where police reform refers broadly to the formal and informal attempts to change the policing practices of public and private sector actors. My main aim is to draw attention to the differences between the elite forms of expertise that inspired the reforms, and the local cultures of the rank-and file-officers who typically implement the reforms. Recognition of these differences highlights and helps explain the incomplete and continuing nature of police reform. More important, an appreciation of local cultures and local reasoning may point the way to more bottom-up and participatory approaches to police reform. The recent reforms may have made policing more efficient, and they may even have managed to increase the extent to which individuals and civic associations are able to participate in policing. But, even if they have, their neglect of local cultures appears in a series of unintended consequences that are now barriers to the democratization of policing.

This chapter begins by returning to familiar themes. It argues that the history of police reform may be understood in terms of cultures and narratives derived in part from the new theories of governance. Police reform embodies the two overlapping waves of public sector reform with their respective bases in neoliberalism and institutionalism. Thereafter the chapter turns to ethnographic evidence of the local cultures and local reasoning through which rank-and-file officers have responded to the reforms. This ethnographic evidence points to what I will call the fallacy of expertise: the gap between the reformers' intentions and local police cultures is less a result of the intransigence of serving officers than of the hubris of social science and policy expertise. Finally, the last part of the chapter will offer a democratic assessment of the different narratives of reform and their impact on policing.

CULTURE AND REFORM

Calls for the study of cultures of police reform should be clear about how they conceive of policing, police reform, and especially culture. A broad concept of policing refers to all efforts to develop agents of crime control whether they are governmental or nongovernmental. Over the last fifty years policing has undergone significant reforms that have much in common with the broader trend away from bureaucracy and toward markets and networks. During much of the last century policing became increasingly bureaucratic and professional. In both Britain and the United States, it became more or less the exclusive purview of centralized, state-sponsored departments. But in the 1980s and 1990s the rise of neoliberalism and other social changes brought both a proliferation of private security forces and the outsourcing of some government services related to law and order. More recently still, the creation and maintenance of quasi-markets has given way to new approaches to community policing. While community policing has been a slogan for reformers since at least the 1960s, it has recently taken on a distinctive concern with organizational forms such as networks and partnerships.

The broad contours of police reform are, of course, widely known, as is their resemblance to public sector reform more generally. Less attention has been paid to the conflicts between elite narratives of reform and the local cultures of policing in which the reforms are enacted. The agency and resistance of local police means that the reforms have had a series of unintended consequences. If we are to develop a more thorough account of the process of reform, we need to examine not just elite cultures and their narratives of reform, but also the ways in which these narratives have been practically understood and enacted in various local cultures.

Culture is, of course, a widely used term that can have many meanings. In this context, "culture" will denote a collective based wholly on the intersubjective beliefs and routine actions of a group of individuals. In this view, cultures are not constitutive of an individual's beliefs and actions. To the contrary, they are just aggregations based on people's beliefs and actions. People adopt their beliefs against the background of inherited traditions, and they modify traditions in response to dilemmas. Tradition and culture are pragmatic concepts, not essentialist ones. Thus, traditions and cultures of policing are not monoliths with fixed cores; rather, we distinguish them from one another in various ways in accord with the particular topics that interest us. Likewise, traditions and cultures of policing are not static; rather, they constantly change as police officers respond to dilemmas, altering their beliefs and practices to accommodate new experiences and new ideas. In short, police cultures are both contested and contingent.

The intersubjective beliefs that make up a culture include narratives about human actions and the social world. Some narratives deal specifically with police, their attitudes, their behavior, their interactions with criminals and citizens, and the problems they face. Generally these narratives point to particular sets of policies that are meant to make policing more efficient, more just, and even more democratic. Narratives provide an orientation, vocabulary, and history with which to tackle questions about appropriate ways to prevent crime and enforce the law.

Of course, I am offering my own narrative about policing. My story focuses on the elite narratives that informed successive attempts to reform policing, and on the ways in which local police cultures influenced the implementation of the reforms. It is a story that highlights the gap between the elite narratives of reform and the everyday experience of implementing the reforms. Thus, my narrative is not just a review of other narratives. To the contrary, the whole point of exploring narratives and cultures lies in their impact on policies, actions, and outcomes. To put the same point more abstractly: whereas many social scientists think of governing structures as formal institutions, I argue that we should conceive of institutions as practices composed of actions based on narratives and beliefs generally. Thus, my narrative of narratives is an attempt to identify and explain the beliefs and actions that inform contemporary policing. We can better explain police reform and its consequences by explicating the beliefs of policy makers and rank-and-file officers.

NARRATIVES OF REFORM

Police reform generally consists of initiatives developed by political and administrative elites with expert advice from social scientists and then imposed on local departments and rank-and-file officers. Yet, the experts do not agree among themselves. Rival elites draw on rival traditions of expertise to propose quite distinct reforms. Police reform is contested. There are multiple narratives of reform.

Three particular reform narratives have had a profound impact on policing since the latter half of the twentieth century. Table 10.1 summarizes them. Each narrative arose out of a particular elite culture with a distinct intellectual ethos. Each narrative privileged a particular mode of governance, and each narrative has a characteristic vision of democracy, accountability, and choice.

TABLE 10.1
Narratives of Police Reform

	Progressive	Neoliberal	Community
Intellectual ethos	Empiricist and technocratic	Rationalist and deductive	Empirical social theory (e.g., new institutionalism, communitarianism)
Mode of governance	Bureaucratic	Market-orientated	Networks and partnerships
Democratic ideal	Representative, with democratic pluralism	Representative, with empowered consumers	Representative, with state sponsored networks
Examples	Blue-ribbon crime commissions	UK—Police and Magistrates' Courts Act (1994)	UK—Police Reform Act (2002) U.S.—Violent Crime and Control Act (1994)

The progressive, neoliberal, and community narratives are all familiar in the public sector more generally. They overlap respectively with the bureaucratic paradigm and the first and second waves of reform. A full history of these narratives will not be provided here. Instead, the intellectual ethos, preferred mode of governance, and democratic ideal of each narrative will be identified and illustrated by reference to exemplary policy initiatives.

The Progressive Narrative

The intellectual ethos of the progressive narrative is one of empiricism and technocratic expertise. This ethos influences judgments about who should make policy and about what constitutes an appropriate response to any given policy problem. Decisions are made by elected politicians on the advice of public officials, social scientists, and other experts. Suitable advice responds to a problem by analyzing empirical data, discovering correlations and trends, and recommending policies based on such knowledge.

Advocates of the progressive narrative find a bureaucratic mode of governance appealing in part because bureaucracies facilitate the flow of expert advice up to elected politicians and down to subordinate actors. Indeed, the hierarchic and functional divisions of bureaucracies mirror the elitist and specialist approach to knowledge that dominates the progressive narrative. Advocates of the progressive narrative also favor bureaucracies on the grounds that they are especially effective at implementing the policies that experts recommend. In this view, bureaucracy insulates policymaking from community leaders and political factions, leaving it to impartial specialists who possess the appropriate methodological training.

We have already seen how Fabianism and other traditions of progressive politics combined the bureaucratic paradigm with a representative concept of democracy. In this view, democracy consists mainly of periodic elections and a system of government in which elected politicians are able to hold public officials accountable. Now, we may add that when social scientists began to focus more on political behavior, they sometimes rethought democracy in terms of an elite pluralism.[1] Elite pluralism allows for policies typically being made by networks of major interest groups interacting with public officials, leaving elected politicians formally responsible for making decisions. Typically, elite pluralists remain profoundly distrustful of citizens; they think that citizens lack the training and expertise needed for the impartial collection and analysis of empirical data. Thus, elite pluralists restrict mass participation to elections: experts develop policy, political elites make decisions, and citizens periodically use the ballot to pass judgment on politicians and policies.

Police forces in Britain have never been under the direct control of political operatives.[2] The Police Act (1964) established a tripartite system in which the governance of police forces was shared among the home secretary, chief constables, and local police authorities, the latter of which comprise two-thirds elected councilors and one-third unelected magistrates. This tripartite arrangement reflected the progressive narrative's emphasis on insulating the police from political pressure. Broadly speaking, it left the home secretary in charge of promoting greater efficiency, chief constables in charge of operational policy, and local police authorities in charge of maintaining an adequate and efficient police force. Rank-and-file officers were meant to follow policies that emerged from in-house decisions by chief constables with occasional interference from the Home Office. There was little political consultation with the local authorities, citizens, or rank-and-file officers. As a result, the progressive narrative often led to a creeping professionalism and centralization. In Britain, the Police Act (1964), the Local Government Act (1972), and the Police and Magistrates' Courts Act (1994) all decreased the number of

---

[1] See, for example, R. Dahl, *Pluralist Democracy in the United States* (Chicago: Rand McNally, 1967); and, for a more jaundiced view, E. Schattschneider, *The Semisovereign People: A Realists' View of Democracy in America* (New York: Holt, Rinehart, and Winston, 1960).

[2] But see the nuanced discussion of this widespread idea in C. Emsley, *The English Police: A Political and Social History* (London: Longman, 1996).

provincial departments while further insulating police forces from political and social influence.[3]

In the United States, the progressive narrative was even more closely entwined with second-wave professionalism. The second wave of police professionalism sought to increase efficiency through a range of measures, including, in David Sklansky's words, "streamlining operations, strengthening lines of command, raising the quality of personnel, leveraging personnel with technology, clarifying the organizational mission, and building public support."[4] This second-wave professionalism still dominated the main blue ribbon crime commissions as late as the 1960s and 1970s. These commissions were created as cities, states, and the federal government responded to urban riots and campus protests by bringing various experts together to examine the available evidence and to propose suitable reforms. The Commission on the Los Angeles Riots, the National Advisory Commission on Civil Disorders, and the President's Commission on Campus Unrest all consisted of members with an expertise based not just on practice but more often still on the scientific study of crime and civil disorders. The commissions proposed various reforms that were adopted somewhat selectively by policing agencies. An alleged scientific expertise thus lay behind a host of regulations and rules that were implemented through and on rank-and-file officers. The progressive narrative inspired a top-down bureaucracy in which rules and procedures were increasingly supposed to limit the discretion of field agents.

The Neoliberal Narrative

As we saw in chapter 4, the neoliberal narrative arose as people responded to dilemmas such as state overload by drawing on neoclassical economics and rational choice theory. Often it also overlapped with specific concerns about law and order. In Britain, the industrial strife associated with the Winter of Discontent in 1978–79 and later the miners' strike of 1984–85 brought policing issues to the forefront of public debate. Some people denounced the excessive use of force by police. Others combined the impression of civil disorder with the themes of economic decline and state collapse to project a sense of crisis.[5] In the United States too, urban riots and campus protests led to a reexamination of policing practice.

---

[3] Compare B. Loveday, "Reforming the Police: From Local Service to State Police?," *Political Quarterly* 66 (1995): 141–56.

[4] D. Sklansky, "Police and Democracy," *Michigan Law Review* 103 (2005): 1743.

[5] Compare C. Hay, "Narrating Crisis: The Discursive Construction of the Winter of Discontent," *Sociology* 30 (1996): 253–77; and P. Wallington, "Policing the Miners Strike," *Industrial Law Journal* 14 (1985): 145–59.

Whereas the progressive narrative relied on inductive empiricism, the neoliberal one drew on neoclassical economics with its more rationalist and deductive ethos. Neoliberals characteristically favor markets over bureaucracy. The neoliberal reforms of the Thatcher and Reagan governments were primarily attempts to promote efficiency through marketization and the spread of private sector management techniques to the public sector. However, while the neoliberal narrative typically emphasizes the goal of market efficiency, it also contains a normative strand about choice and participation in public services. Many neoliberals argue that markets and quasi-markets provide greater scope for personal choice than do the one-size-fits-all solutions of large bureaucracies. Similarly, they argue that markets enable people to hold service providers accountable simply by withdrawing their custom from any service provider with whom they are not satisfied. By turning citizens into consumers of public services, neoliberals hoped both to expand opportunities for choice and to ensure that public officials were accountable to those they served. For neoliberals, democratic values are better served by the spread of markets than by bureaucratic hierarchies.

Over the last three decades, neoliberal reforms in Britain and the United States have led to a dramatic rise of marketization in policing and even to private police.[6] Market-oriented reforms have altered the role of the police and the relationship of the police to private sector security services. The privatization of security forces and public safety has taken various forms. For a start, the number and roles of for-hire private security firms have risen dramatically. Moreover, the state increasingly provides official certification to private sector security agents. In Britain, for example, police now certify private sector bouncers working at clubs and pubs. Finally, police forces increasingly employ civilians to perform activities that used to be the role of officers. In Britain, for example, the Police Reform Act (2002) facilitated the rise of accredited community safety officers and community support officers. By 2006 there were over six thousand police community support officers, and the government was committed to raising the number to over twenty thousand by the end of 2008. These officers are usually part of community action teams that provide a highly visible uniformed presence to offer reassurance to the public but that are restricted to tasks that do not require the experience or powers of police officers. The contracting out of public services is, of course, an increasingly popular way to maintain levels of service while decreasing costs. Policing is no exception to the trend.

---

[6] See, respectively, D. Bayley and C. Shearing, "The Future of Policing," *Law and Society Review* 30 (1996): 585–606; and L. Johnston, "Private Policing in Context," *European Journal on Criminal Policy and Research* 7 (1999): 175–96.

Neoliberals also spread private sector managerial techniques to polic-ing. Like many public sector organizations, police departments experi-enced aspects of the new public management. In policing, NPM generally involved the publishing of performance targets and the evaluation of pro-grams in relationship to these targets, the introduction of fees for services that may or may not have been provided otherwise, the decentralization of administrative structures, and the use of performance budgeting.[7]

In Britain, the neoliberal concern with marketization and NPM in-spired a range of inquiries and acts right up to the mid-1990s. The Inquiry into Police Responsibilities and Rewards (the Sheehy Inquiry) reported in 1992.[8] Patrick Sheehy, a leading businessman, led the inquiry, focusing on the internal management of police forces. The inquiry made 272 recom-mendations for reform, many of which drew notably on private sector management techniques. The most contentious recommendations were those involving performance-related pay, fixed-term posts, and reduced starting salaries. These met with heavy resistance from the police unions.

Soon after the Sheehy Inquiry, the government published a White Paper on *Police Reform*.[9] This White Paper focused on broader issues of gov-ernance in British policing. It claimed that policing suffered overlapping and confused lines of responsibility and accountability, suggesting that the tripartite structure of policing had led to police forces becoming in-flexible, resistant to change, fiscally unaccountable, and ineffective. Like the Sheehy Inquiry, the White Paper recommended introducing private sector management practices. It also recommended devolving decision-making responsibility to local police commanders in order to provide au-tonomy and choice to localities in setting their own priorities and funding programs.

Many of the White Paper's recommendations were incorporated into the version of the Police and Magistrates' Courts Act (PMCA) that was introduced into the House of Lords. The more controversial reforms were cut from the final legislation following stiff resistance from police officers and their unions. Nonetheless, the act still introduced a number of neoliberal reforms. It gave police authorities the duty of establishing an "efficient and effective" police force for its designated area, clearly associating efficiency with the creation of local policing plans and even more specifically the implementation of performance targets. At the be-ginning of each fiscal year, each police authority had to establish a set of

---

[7] See S. Cope, F. Leishman, and P. Starie, "Globalization, New Public Management and the Enabling State: Futures of Police Management," *International Journal of Public Sector Management* 10 (1997): 444–60.

[8] *Inquiry into Police Responsibilities and Rewards*, Cm. 2280 (1993).

[9] *Police Reform: A Police Service for the 21st Century*, Cm. 2281 (1993).

local policing objectives, taking into account national and local goals. At the end of the financial year, it had to compile an annual report showing how the local policing plan had been carried out and to what degree of success. In this way, the PMCA gave a legal basis to the neoliberal concern with private management strategies based heavily on financial planning, performance targets, formal evaluations, and managing by results. As Stephen Cope and his coauthors wrote, "despite a parliamentary mauling, the PMCA further centralized the 'steering,' while decentralizing the 'rowing' of the police."[10]

Finally, the Home Office Review of Police Core and Ancillary Tasks (the Posen Inquiry) examined the services being delivered by public police forces.[11] The inquiry's findings, published in 1995, divided the services being performed by public police into two categories: core and ancillary. It recommended that police promote cost-efficiency by changing their delivery systems for their core tasks and by transferring responsibility for many of their ancillary tasks to other public or private agencies.

Collectively these inquiries and acts introduced neoliberal reforms that went some way toward turning police departments into providers of services in competition with other agencies for resources and customers. The reforms also fragmented police departments, creating teams and groups, some of whom were again in competition with one another for resources. The police are increasingly required to meet performance measures in order to demonstrate their effectiveness in deterring crime, enforcing the law, and using resources appropriately. Nonetheless, we should not overestimate the extent to which the neoliberal reforms work as they were intended to. For a start, the reforms have often turned out to depend on just the kind of top-down managerial authority that they purportedly set out to overcome: the new managerialism often strengthens the oversight and control of administrators and managers over rank-and-file officers even if it alters the mode of control from formal rules to financial audits.[12] In addition—as we will see in some detail—the rank and file rarely implemented the reforms in the ways that neoliberals intended.

---

[10] Cope, Leishman, and Starie, "Globalization, New Public Management and the Enabling State," 450.

[11] Home Office, *Review of Police Core and Ancillary Tasks: Final Report* (London: Stationery Office, 1995).

[12] For a more nuanced discussion of the changing modes of control over the police, see M. Bowerman, H. Raby, and C. Humphrey, "In Search of the Audit Society: Some Evidence from Health Care, Police, and Schools," *International Journal of Auditing* 4 (2000): 71–100. Perhaps, however, the center is especially likely to grab for historical levers of control when dealing with the police. Compare J. Chan, "Governing Police Practice: Limits of the New Accountability," *British Journal of Sociology* 50 (1999), 251–70.

The Community Narrative

The community-oriented narrative of police reform renews a belief in empirical social science. Like the more general shift to networks and part-nerships, it draws heavily on the new institutionalism, communitarian-ism, and organization theory. These theories reject the deductive ethos of neoclassical economics. They also attempt to broaden the concept of an institution to cover informal ones based on norms as well as more formal ones defined by laws or rules. They thereby shift attention somewhat from hierarchies to networks. The community narrative draws on these theories to portray networks as often preferable to both bureaucracies and markets.

In the last chapter, we saw how institutionalism and network theory lurk behind the increasingly popular strategies of joined-up government. The proponents of network governance argue that it combines the flex-ibility of markets with the long-term stable relationships that character-ize hierarchies. They argue that networks are thus peculiarly conducive to the kind of innovation needed in a globalizing world. In policing, the community narrative has inspired networked approaches to security and especially new visions of partnerships between police, community, and public. It is fast becoming commonplace that police, whether they like it or not, now have to operate in and through local, national, and interna-tional networks.[13]

Advocates of community-oriented approaches argue that the police fight crime more effectively if they involve community actors in their activities. They claim that, at least in contemporary society, a compre-hensive strategy toward crime prevention must combine the resources of many different public, voluntary, and private sector groups. Policing thus appears to require the formation and management of networks based on partnerships among the police, other public agencies, community groups, and citizens.

Like neoliberal reformers, community-oriented reformers combine concerns about efficiency with normative, democratic themes. They argue that networks and partnerships can increase public participation and promote social inclusion.[14] Policy documents often now laud commu-nity policing for being sensitive and responsive to the needs and fears of citizens. For example, in Britain, the National Policing Plan for 2005 to 2008 appealed to a "citizen-focused police service which responds to the

---

[13] Compare J. Fleming and J. Wood, eds., *Fighting Crime Together: The Challenges of Policing and Security Networks* (Sydney: University of New South Wales Press, 2006).

[14] For some limited evidence to the contrary, see K. Kerley and M. Benson, "Does Community-Orientated Policing Help Build Stronger Communities?," *Police Quarterly* 3 (2000): 46–69.

needs of communities and individuals, especially victims and witnesses, and inspires public confidence in the police, particularly among minority ethnic communities."[15]

Community policing arose in the 1960s and 1970s as something of a grassroots movement by rank-and-file officers who felt powerless in the face of rising crime rates and increasing social unrest. It was developed at the local level in American cities such as Detroit, New York, Madison, Oakland, and Portland.[16] Recently, community policing has become more closely associated with networks and partnerships, often in part as a result of the evaluation research of the 1970s and 1980s. It is this type of community policing that is now championed as a reform program by policy makers.[17] In the United States, this new community policing came to prominence following an Executive Session on the Police held at Harvard University from 1985 to 1990. This executive session was funded by the National Institute of Justice, which is itself part of the Department of Justice. The session brought together social scientists and police chiefs with the explicit aim of devising new styles of policing and crime prevention. Today, although community policing can refer to different visions, it is commonly associated with increased consultation with members of the community, increased flexibility through decentralization, increased partnerships with other agencies and community organizations, and a problem-oriented approach to crime prevention.

This new type of community policing has already had an impact on legislation. In the United States, the Violent Crime Control and Law Enforcement Act (1994) led to the federal government funding community policing through the Office of Community Oriented Policing Services (COPS). COPS has now handed out more than $11 billion in grants to local communities to implement community policing, including the hiring of extra officers to patrol neighborhoods. In Britain, the Police Reform Act (2002) expanded not only the powers of the secretary of state but also the role of the local community in policing. Part 4 of the act allows for the creation of new community safety accreditation schemes that seek to combat crime and increase safety by having civilian officers patrol the streets. These community schemes allow for many of the law enforcement powers that are given to official constables being given to civilian

[15] Home Office, *National Policing Plan 2005–08: Safer, Stronger Communities* (London: Stationery Office, 2004). Also see *Confident Communities in a Secure Britain*, Cm 6287 (2004); and, for an American example, L. Brown, *Community Policing: A Practical Guide for Police Officials* (Washington, DC: Department of Justice, 1989).

[16] Compare J. Greene, "Community Policing in America: Changing the Nature, Structure, and Function of the Police," in J. Horney, ed., *Policies, Processes, and Decisions of the Criminal Justice System* (Washington, DC: National Institute of Justice, 2000), 299–370.

[17] See D. Bayley, ed., *What Works in Policing* (Oxford: Oxford University Press, 1998).

employees provided that these civilians identify themselves by means of a uniform badge and work under guidelines set by the chief officer overseeing the scheme. [18] More generally, the recent Home Office Green Paper, *Policing: Building Safer Communities Together*, clearly emphasized the importance of "joint working" and "policing by cooperation" while identifying the private sector as a key "partner" in tackling crime. [19]

LOCAL PERSPECTIVES ON REFORM

Policing has been subject to a host of reforms based on neoliberal and community narratives. Yet the mere fact that elites enact reforms does not mean that those affected by the reforms respond as expected. Properly to understand the effects of the reforms, we have to examine the ways in which local officers and others have responded to them from within their own local cultures. The suspicion must surely be that the reform narratives have relied on deductive models or sweeping social theories that do not allow sufficiently for local cultures and so have generated false expectations about the consequences the reforms are likely to have. All too often reform initiatives simply do not fit with the day-to-day experiences of police officers. Thus, serving officers necessarily adapt and modify the reforms in an attempt to respond to the dilemmas thrown up by their experiences. The everyday practice of policing is thus a "constant process of adaptation, subversion and reinscription" of meanings. [20] Far from the narratives of reform remaking policing in their own image, they have created dilemmas for police officers, and policing has then been remade by the diverse ways in which officers have responded to these dilemmas.

An Ethnographic Taster

Police officers themselves have had strong responses to the reforms. As a taste of these responses, I offer a set of quotations from two ethnographic studies, followed by a more general discussion of themes prevalent in these studies. [21] While these themes are all oversimplifications of

[18] *Building Communities, Beating Crime: A Better Police Service for the 21st Century*, Cm 6360 (2004).

[19] Home Office, *Policing: Building Safer Communities Together* (London: Stationery Office, 2004).

[20] Compare A. Davies and R. Thomas, "Talking Cop: Discourses of Change and Policing Identities," *Public Administration* 81 (2003): 681–99.

[21] The study by Jenny Fleming is based on interviews with senior officers and focus group meetings with officers of all ranks in Britain and Australia in 2003. For details, see J. Fleming, "Working through Networks: The Challenge of Partnership Policing," in Flem-

complex worlds, they suggest—in contrast with the idea that the reforms have remade policing—that bureaucracy still exists, markets are resisted, community reforms are neglected, and constant reform has become self-defeating.

Here are sample quotations from serving police officers.

On bureaucracy:

1. There is still a command and control mentality within the service and [a sense] that the police have no ownership of what goes on.

2. They pay a lot of lip service to the notion that we have a corporate mentality—no rank distinction—everyone can say what they want, but believe you me when you step out of line, the military line comes right back and if you want to get on you are not going to be part of a frank discussion.

On neoliberal reforms:

3. When I arrived, in the order of 110 performance measures were being proposed! We got it down to 75 in the end but it was difficult. I couldn't believe it when I saw the rising crime figures and this ongoing preoccupation with things like how many forensic tests we might perform in any one year. There didn't seem to be a concern about crime at all at this point.

4. I think we shouldn't sort of minimize just how serious it is and I keep saying to officers, you know "to actually arrest somebody and take somebody's liberty away is a very, very major event" and so to see them if you like, in consumerism terms, it sort of wears a little bit thin, probably for them more than us.

5. I think the thing is, for me, that the public actually as a rule have to take the service that they get, they can't actually go out and say, I don't actually like the way X Police do this so I'm going to see if I can phone through and get Y Police to come and do it, because on such and such scales they deal with my type of incident in a far better way.

On community policing:

6. I think your biggest problem will be the culture. It's still isolated, a "boy's own" club—community policing means beat policing to them [rank-and-file officers] and they don't do that well. They don't like all this touchy feely stuff.

ing and Wood, eds., *Fighting Crime Together*, 87–115. The study led by John Clarke and Janet Newman is based on interviews and other ethnographic techniques involving all kinds of public service providers and citizens in Britain. For details, see J. Clarke et al., *Creating Citizen-Consumers: Changing Publics and Changing Public Services* (London: Sage, 2006). I am grateful for permission to draw on these studies.

On continuous reform:

7. [The force] is change weary. Since 1990, it has been one major upheaval after another. The [last commissioner] had big ideas, and [so did] the commissioner before him. They would go around telling it how it was but every time there was a change of management, there was another reorganization. Police are so fed up with this, that the [current] commissioner has decreed that any further change must be incremental.

Bureaucracy Still Exists

As the first two quotations suggest, bureaucratic modes of governance are still pervasive in policing.[22] Command and control continues in many ways to be the guiding principle of police departments even after decades of reforms aimed at breaking down the walls of bureaucracy and eliminating red tape. Many police officers do not think that markets or networks are appropriate to what they still regard as core parts of their job. At least parts of policing involve a kind of danger that, in their view, is best dealt with by having clear lines of command and clear decision makers.[23] Consequently, when police officers perceive themselves as facing a dilemma between the dictates of the job and the rhetoric of markets and networks, they are likely to fall back on the kind of command-and-control bureaucracy that they know and often think is appropriate. While this conclusion might seem to lend credence to complaints about police resistance to change, these complaints too often ignore the lived experience of the police. For police officers, the question is rarely whether or not to embrace change; it is how to make a proposed change work given the nature of their duties and job environment. Bureaucracy still exists because it has a number of very clear advantages. Perhaps the main advantage is that it imposes order in a world composed of seemingly incompatible demands.

Markets Are Resisted

Police officers may well resist all kinds of reforms, but they seem to be especially hostile to neoliberal reforms. They are notably skeptical of the relevance of private sector management practices to crime prevention. Some of them believe that neoliberal reforms question not only how

[22] For evidence of the general persistence of bureaucratic hierarchies, see Hill and Lynn, "Is Hierarchical Governance in Decline?"

[23] On the differences and relationships of beat officers and their managers, see E. Lanni-Reus and F. Lanni, "Street Cops and Management Cops," in M. Punch, ed., *Control in the Police Organisation* (Cambridge: MIT Press, 1983).

police officers go about their business but also the very identity of the police. Thus, while performance indicators and outcome measurements have been introduced to policing, many officers treat them as words without meaning—a type of rhetoric to which they need to pay lip-service without modifying their practices. The third quotation above highlights police skepticism of NPM. The officer clearly takes high-level talk of performance measures to be more or less irrelevant to law enforcement. Some police officers believe that the neoliberal reforms have taken resources and time away from the battle against crime. They do not necessarily deny that performance measurements are important. But they do believe that the neoliberal reforms have introduced performance measurements that fail to provide an adequate picture of crime prevention programs. In their view, productivity (filings and fingerprinting operations) fiscal status (per capita costs of service) and performance (crime rates in the Uniform Crime Report) may be easy to quantify, but they are not adequate measures of police effectiveness or efficiency.[24] This skepticism means that NPM is unlikely to be effectively implemented. Perhaps it is doomed to fail.

Neoliberals need to make the case to police officers that managerial reforms are linked to crime prevention. Alternatively, they need to make the case that officers should conceive their job in terms that pay less attention to crime prevention. Part of the issue here is, as the fourth and fifth quotations suggest, that most police officers perceive a tension between the need to ensure public safety and the neoliberal ideal of promoting choice for consumers. They are far from convinced by attempts to redefine the police as service providers and citizens as their consumers. At the very least this redefinition ignores the authority and power that are built into the law, and at times it also seems to ignore the idea that law and order constitute public goods, not just private ones. Policing is, at least to many of those engaged in it, not a commodity but a public service vital to a functioning society. Once again, then, we see a gap between the narratives that inspire the reforms and the local police cultures in which the reforms must be made to work.

Community Reforms Are Neglected

Community policing has not faced as much resistance from rank-and-file officers as have neoliberal reforms. One reason for the greater acceptance of community policing is, however, that police officers often believe that they are already involved in networks and partnerships. Problems arise

[24] Compare R. Wadman and S. Bailey, *Community Policing and Crime Prevention in America and England* (Chicago: Office of International Criminal Justice, 1993).

here from the vagueness of the very concepts of network and partnership. Do visits to local schools count as building a network? If police officers talk regularly with local businesses, does that constitute a partnership? The current vogue for community policing has seen a lot of rhetoric encouraging police officers to work in networks and partnerships, but it has often remained perilously thin on concrete proposals on how and when to do so to what degree and in what ways. Thus, it is all too easy for police officers to define their existing activities as meeting the proposals of the reformers. When they do so, however, they domesticate the reforms, removing any sense of the need for dramatic changes to their existing practices.

Resistance to community reforms arises when police officers perceive them as placing additional emphasis on parts of the job with which they are unsympathetic. As the sixth quotation suggests, community policing is associated with routine patrols and the personal touch. Yet, police officers generally consider such activities to be not only unexciting but also ineffective in combating crime. It is perhaps worth adding that many social scientists would agree with them. The evaluation research of the 1970s and 1980s often suggested that having a lot of highly visible officers on the streets is not necessarily an effective way of reducing crime and may even be inappropriate in some situations.[25] Thus, police officers confront a dilemma in trying simultaneously to meet the demands of community policing and neoliberal reforms. Community-minded reformers need to make the case that community activities are an effective way to combat crime. Alternatively, they need to convince officers to rethink their job in terms that put more emphasis on, for example, promoting a sense of personal security among the public. When neither case is made, the rank and file does not buy into the reforms, so the reforms remain top-down initiatives that are ignored if not actively resisted.

Constant Reform Is Self-defeating

The responses of police officers to first- and second-wave reforms help to explain the fates of the reforms. The reforms drew heavily on forms of expertise that rely on formal models and social theories, rather than dialogue with those whom they will affect. The reforms embody a top-down approach: reformers rarely took seriously the task of securing widespread acceptance of their proposals among rank-and-file officers; they rarely explored whether the reforms had a suitable fit with the lived experience of police officers. Thus, police officers have had to negotiate dilemmas that arise from the tensions between the reforms and their own

[25] E.g., Bayley, ed., *What Works in Policing.*

local cultures, interpreting the reforms to make them fit with their experience. Crucially, when the police interpret the reforms, they transform them, resisting them or domesticating them in ways that have unintended consequences. All too often, moreover, this whole process becomes reiterative. The reforms meet with police skepticism, the police respond to them in ways that have unintended consequences, and the negative consequences then inspire another round of reform, which again meets with local skepticism.

The continuous process of reform soon will reach—if it has not already reached—a point at which the police's weariness makes them immovable. Constant reform undermines morale and breeds ever-greater skepticism about reform. Declining morale and growing skepticism, especially when combined with confusion among officers about what is required of them and how that translates into their daily practice, may erode the ability of the police to enforce the law and protect the public. It would be foolish to ignore the extent to which police forces need to change. But the quotations suggest that too many different waves of reform following one another too quickly may lead not to change but to exhausted inertia.

THE FALLACY OF EXPERTISE

The gap between elite narratives of reform and local police cultures helps to explain the limited impact of the reforms, their unintended consequences, and even the continuous nature of reform. To some readers, this gap may resemble an implementation gap.[26] Nonetheless, the concept of an implementation gap may miss key issues. There is nothing wrong with a broad concept of an implementation gap between the top-level strategists who formulate policies and the midlevel managers and street-level bureaucrats who implement policies. The problems start only if this broad concept of an implementation gap carries the narrower connotation that the gap is the result of the failings, intransigence, conservatism, or self-interest of those working at the mid level and street level. To dramatize my doubts about this narrower connotation, I might say that whereas an implementation gap points to failings at the local level, I am pointing to failings in the elite narratives of reform.[27] Perhaps we should talk less of an implementation gap and more of the fallacy of expertise.

[26] See A. Dunsire, *Implementation in a Bureaucracy* (Oxford: Martin Robertson, 1978).
[27] Contrast E. Silverman, "Community Policing: The Implementation Gap," in P. Kratcosky and D. Dukes, eds., *Issues in Community Policing* (Cincinatti: Anderson, 1995).

Narrower concepts of the implementation gap locate the problem as a lack of follow-through by street-level bureaucrats. They imply that policies are poorly implemented due to the intransigence or vested interests of lower-level public officials. The practicality of elite policymaking based on expert knowledge goes more or less unquestioned. Indeed, the solution often appears, in this view, to be further to limit the discretion of field agents, specifying their actions by more precise rules and procedural requirements in order to make sure that they do as the elites and experts intend. I would suggest, in contrast, that the problems arise not because of the unreasonable or self-interested nature of street-level bureaucrats but because of the limitations of elite policymaking based primarily on the formal models and abstract theories of social scientists.

The fallacy of expertise consists of the assumption that discretion might be avoided, or, to put it differently, that public policy can be comprehensive, clear, and self-defining. Policy makers generally adopt the fallacy of expertise whenever they ignore the contingent and contestable nature of action and, consequently, the open-ended diversity of the cases to which street-level bureaucrats might have to respond. The fallacy arises when policy makers assume, as social science often encourages them to, that contingency and contest can be tamed and action can be predicted by means of knowledge of, for example, formal models, statistical correlations, or social laws. Policy makers assume that suitable expertise provides them with knowledge of human action, institutions, and their effects, and that they can apply this knowledge to construct policies that will apply and have certain effects more or less irrespective of local cultures and local circumstances. Certainly, police reform has often been defined by narratives that purport to establish how expertise, bureaucracy, markets, or networks will operate, and the benefits they will bring, largely irrespective of things such as particular policy fields, diverse traditions of citizenship, and local cultures.

In the case of police reform, the reformers have not recognized the particularity of their own narrative, the importance of including police officers in the policy development process, or the variable and open-ended nature of the cultures and actions within which and to which the reforms will have to apply. Again, the fallacy of expertise neglects:

- The competition among elite narratives
- The limited acquiescence of the rank and file to elite narratives
- The impossibility of narratives fixing their own application to particular cases.

Consider, first, the competition among elite narratives. Reformers often overlook the particularity of their own narrative. They forget that other reformers, policy actors, and citizens have different narratives about the nature of policing, its failings, and how to improve it. Yet, as we have seen, police reform has often consisted of incompatible measures inspired by competing narratives. Given competing narratives and reforms, police officers simply are not confronted by a consistent and coherent agenda. To the contrary, they are confronted with conflicting elite narratives and demands. Thus, they must interpret and negotiate among these narratives to try to forge a single perspective that is consistent enough for them to act. What is more, police officers generally have their own narratives, and they necessarily deploy their understanding of their job and what it requires in an attempt to make sense of the demands of the competing reform narratives. Rank-and-file officers interpret the often conflicting policies that are passed down from the elite in ways that reflect their own cultures and experiences. Police officers resist or reinterpret reforms because they are struggling to make sense of conflicting demands in order to act as they believe their job requires.

Now consider the limited extent to which police officers accept elite narratives. The top-down view of the policy process held by many reformers means that local police departments and rank-and-file officers are often only cursorily consulted about reform programs, which can inspire resistance from rank-and-file officers. The rank and file does not appreciate being told what to do by outsiders, especially outsiders who they perceive as out of touch with the daily demands of their job. No doubt reforms imposed by outsiders are likely to spawn resistance in any occupation. Resistance is especially likely, however, in an occupation such as policing where there is an established and entrenched culture of in-group preference and out-group hostility.[28] Local police cultures encourage the view that reforms have been developed by individuals who have never "worn the badge" and do not understand the daily challenges facing officers. Thus, reformers need to do more to secure prior buy-in from rank-and-file officers if they want the police to have a sense of ownership over the reforms.

Consider, finally, the impossibility of narratives fixing their application to cases. How reforms operate depends on how people interpret them from within local cultures, where how people interpret them is not fixed in advance but rather emerges as a product of their situated agency. Thus, the reformers simply cannot know in advance what kinds of circumstances rank-and-file police will confront. They cannot specify a complete set of rules telling officers how they should act in all possible circumstances. What is more, the rules they do provide are necessarily

[28] On this aspect of police culture, and other problems it causes, see T. Cox, "The Implementation of Cultural Diversity in Police Organizations," *Journal of Police and Criminal Psychology* 10 (1994): 41–46.

somewhat abstract, so the application of these rules to any given police force or any given situation necessarily involves a creative moment of interpretation. Police officers are bound to interpret the reforms if only in an attempt to apply them to particular situations.

The narrow concept of an implementation gap embodies an oversimplified account of the policy process that leads to a largely negative view of local discretion. I have suggested, in contrast, that local discretion is inevitable as the policy process is contested, incomplete, and open-ended. Police officers have to act creatively in attempts to address the dilemmas presented by the gap between policies and their experiences.[29] When they do so, they are no more bound to be conservative and self-interested than they are to be communal and other-regarding. We should no more demonize them than romanticize them.

DEMOCRACY, CITIZENSHIP, AND PARTICIPATION

The fallacy of expertise encourages policy makers to underestimate the importance of involving the targets of a policy in its formulation. The participation of street-level bureaucrats and citizens in the policymaking process might increase the effectiveness of policymaking. More important for us, it raises new ways of thinking about citizenship and democracy. Unfortunately, most reform narratives downplay such democratic considerations in part because of their overriding concern with efficiency and in part because they take for granted a representative concept of democracy. Thus, while, as we saw earlier, the reform narratives are linked to somewhat different views of democracy, they share a commitment to representative democracy as the primary way of holding accountable a policymaking process that is largely left to elected politicians, public officials, and experts. The clearest example is no doubt the progressive narrative: it presents citizens as voters who judge politicians and their policies in periodic elections, thereby locating the democratic endorsement of reform proposals in regular, free, and fair elections. Neoliberal and community narratives may rethink this view of citizenship, but they do relatively little to promote greater participation in policymaking.

The neoliberal narrative redefines the citizen as being also a consumer. It suggests that people exercise choice and hold others accountable

---

[29] Compare M. Lipsky, *Street Level Bureaucracy: Dilemmas of the Individual in Public Services* (New York: Russell Sage Foundation, 1980); and M. Brown, *Working the Street: Police Discretion and the Dilemmas of Reform* (New York: Russell Sage Foundation, 1981).

through acting as consumers in market settings as well as through voting. Citizens choose or buy the services they prefer, and they punish those who behave badly by withdrawing their custom. However, while the neoliberal narrative offers a different vision of citizenship, it still leaves it up to others to construct policies: others produce the policies and services that citizens then choose whether or not to buy. What is more, neoliberals rely on expert assertions of the benefits of the market. They are often more than willing to impose markets on citizens even if the citizens dislike their doing so.

The community narrative stresses the role of partnerships and networks in increasing public involvement in the policy process. Citizen review boards, task forces, and community support officers form partnerships that involve rank-and-file officers and the general public. Citizens are meant to be active. They are meant to provide democratic input and endorsement to policing activities by meeting and talking to their beat officer and their local police department. Performance measurements often include the local community's opinion of the police. However, the community narrative calls for this greater participation in policy implementation precisely because institutionalists and other policy experts claim that such participation leads to more efficient public policies and services. The formulation of public policies is still based on expert discourses about networks, partnerships, and inclusion. There is, after all, a difference between engaging in dialogue with community members and granting citizens actual powers of policymaking or policy oversight.

I do not want to deny that the neoliberal and, more especially, the community narrative can lead to significantly greater public choice and involvement in policing. I do want to point out, however, that the extent and moment of choice and involvement are restrained by the fallacy of expertise. Typically choice and involvement act as ways of endorsing and evaluating reform programs, not formulating them. Likewise, choice and involvement typically apply to how local police forces are doing in the context of a national agenda based on relatively fixed assumptions about the importance of either markets or networks and partnerships. Thus, although each reform narrative has its own view of how police reform might be endorsed by the community, they give limited roles to rank-and-file officers and citizens in the process of policy formation. They rely on technocratic expertise to craft reforms that are then imposed on local police cultures.

The restrictions that the reform narratives place on choice and involvement help explain the skepticism with which they have often been met. Skeptics view community policing, for example, as little more than an exercise in public relations. They argue that community policing neglects any genuine concern to integrate police departments into their communities in favor of a concern to secure public support for policing activities. Perhaps community policing has become little more than an exercise to improve the public image of policing.[30]

The privileging of expertise, effectiveness, and efficiency by reform narratives has also led to inadequate attention being paid to the democratic implications of the reforms. Consider the relationship of the neoliberal reforms to ideals of accountability and equity. Private police are not under the same legal and constitutional restrictions as public police forces.[31] Often they are not even indirectly accountable to voters by way of politicians. Sometimes the only way of holding them to account is to cancel their contract or license. Moreover, citizen-consumers enter the market for policing with very different levels of wealth and power. The current distribution of wealth in advanced democracies means that well-to-do citizens, neighborhoods, and commercial interests are far more able to afford private security than are poorer ones, but it is typically the latter who suffer the worst effects of crime. Consider, likewise, the relationship of the community-orientated reforms to ideals of accountability and equity. Networks and partnerships generally blur lines of authority and responsibility. Moreover, police officers and citizens are likely to have different resources (time, money, knowledge) that influence the likelihood of their becoming members of commissions, task forces, and citizen boards, let alone having a decisive impact on them.

The fallacy of expertise has led to reforms that neglect both local police cultures and democratic ideals. Perhaps it is time we turned instead to more participatory forms of policymaking, allowing citizens and rank-and-file officers a far greater role. Perhaps a more bottom-up approach to police reform will bring greater success in implementing reforms. Perhaps it also will provide a participatory solution to some of the problems that now confront attempts to reconcile increasingly complex policing networks with concepts of accountability associated with representative democracy.

Workplace democracy in particular remains, of course, an alien practice to most police forces. Nonetheless, a few police departments, mainly in the United States, have begun to reorganize their leadership structures so as to increase the opportunities for participatory decision making. The Broken Arrow Police Department in a suburban area of Oklahoma

[30] Compare I. Loader, "Policing and the Social: Questions of Symbolic Power," *British Journal of Sociology* 48 (1997): 1–18.

[31] For a related but different perspective, see D. Sklansky, "Private Police and Democracy," *American Criminal Law Review* 43 (2006): 89–105.

has introduced what appears to be a successful expansion of participatory management techniques.[32] The local chief of police has given rank-and-file officers a say in departmental procedure, including extensive decision-making powers, and the result seems to have been increased morale and efficiency and a greater willingness to engage in community policing. Arguably, the best account of a participatory democracy involving rank-and-file officers and citizens is, however, Archon Fung's study of Chicago.[33] Starting in 1994, the Chicago Police Department began to develop its alternative policing strategy. It opened up operations to rank-and-file innovation and scrutiny by local residents. In each of 280 neighborhood police beats, residents now meet with their serving police officers in open "beat meetings." These monthly meetings constitute forums in which the officers and residents deliberate and develop policing strategies to meet local needs. Together they decide which safety issues to prioritize and how to deal with them.

CONCLUSION

This chapter has extended the examination of the new governance beyond the new theories of governance and the forms of expertise and new worlds to which they have helped give rise. It has drawn attention to the local cultures and local reasoning that inform the responses of police officers to reform. It has argued that these local cultures led the police to resist NPM and attempts at marketization, and to domesticate initiatives that promoted community policing. I do not want to suggest that the effects of local cultures mean reformers should halt community policing. To the contrary, the lesson seems to be that awareness of local cultures can contribute to the development of such reforms.

More abstractly, this chapter implies that local reasoning means the consequences of public sector reform are inherently contingent. Modernist social science hides this contingency behind expertise couched as formal models, statistical correlations, and social laws. Again, modernist social science relies on economic and sociological concepts of rationality that downplay the contestable and contingent nature of social life. Thus, neoliberal and institutionalist policy makers often deny or forget the con-

---

[32] See B. Steinheider and T. Wuestewald, "From the Bottom up: Sharing Leadership in a Police Agency," *Police Practice and Research* 9 (2008): 145–63.

[33] A. Fung, *Empowered Participation: Reinventing Urban Democracy* (Princeton: Princeton University Press, 2004), 31–68. Also see the earlier account by W. Skogan and S. Hartnett, *Community Policing, Chicago Style* (New York: Oxford University Press, 1999).

testability and contingency associated with local cultures. They too rarely pause to consider how police officers, other street-level bureaucrats, and citizens may resist, domesticate, and transform public policies.

Expertise is unsettled by contingency. Economic and sociological concepts of rationality are unsettled by local reasoning. Perhaps, therefore, contingency and more especially local reasoning provide alternative concepts with which not only to narrate police reform but also to respond to the new worlds of governance and the democratic issues they pose. It is this possibility that will occupy us in the final chapter.

After Modernism

THE WORD "governance" is often used in confusingly diverse ways. Governance can point to changes in the state and the public sector. It refers to the state's abandonment of hierarchical structures by which to develop and implement public policy. It captures the shift from bureaucratic hierarchies to markets and networks. In this view, the state has a diminished capacity to act, and it thus increasingly enlists the aid of private and voluntary sector organizations in its attempts to realize its goals. Similarly, "governance" can refer to the consequent rise in the public sector of self-organizing policy networks. The rise of such networks means that the state has to concern itself less with direct action and more with the tasks of managing and steering networks. While "governance" can refer to the state or the public sector, its range of meanings extends more broadly. The word "governance" is used to discuss transnational and global orders. Yet other people use the word "governance" in ways that utterly break the link between it and political regimes. For example, the widespread discussions of corporate governance capture concerns about the ethical norms that govern private sector businesses, especially concerns about how to make businesses properly accountable to their shareholders.

The diverse uses of the word "governance" can appear to have little in common. Yet, many of them, especially those associated with political regimes, have some connection to narratives about changes in the world since the mid- to late twentieth century. From these perspectives, the word "governance" arose alongside the "new governance," which, in turn, arose in large part due to global pressures and changing international economic trends.

Many observers suggest that global trends undermined the hierarchic welfare state, leading political actors to search for alternative organizational forms and patterns of rule. In this view, even if globalization developed gradually, it accelerated over the last decades of the twentieth century when there was a rapid increase in capital accumulation and a growing predominance of international financial markets. Thus, the state found itself confronted by old and new problems brought on by a blurring of borders among markets and peoples. Neoliberals often suggest that states had little power to shape this process: they had no option but to liberalize their economies, reduce state expenditure, and create more efficient public sectors. Others argue that although states were affected by globalization, they still had the power to influence global trends. Both camps generally agree that states had to explore new models of governance by which to respond to the dilemmas facing the state.

MODERN GOVERNANCE

This book has explored the nature of the new governance and its implications for democracy. It has argued the following.

- The concept of governance, in contrast to that of government, evokes a pattern of rule characterized by networks in which the state overlaps with actors from civil society.
- The concept of governance rose both as new theories led people to see the world differently and as policy makers drew on these theories actively to promote markets and networks.
- The new governance poses dilemmas for representative democracy, and policy makers have responded to these dilemmas with policies based on the very theories that lurk behind governance.

At times I have also pointed toward another argument, which will be the main concern of this concluding chapter.

- Interpretive political science provides an alternative to the main theories of governance, and it may encourage a more participatory and dialogic response to the dilemmas facing representative democracy.

Governance as Networks

A concept of governance as rule by and through networks draws on themes from the earlier literature on policy networks.[1] One theme is networks as interorganizational analysis. The literature on interorganizational analysis emphasizes the structural relationship between political institutions as opposed to the interpersonal relations between individuals in those institutions.[2] These structural relations are taken to be the cru-

---

[1] Recent overviews of the literature on policy networks include Bevir and Richards, *Decentring Policy Networks*; and R. Rhodes, "Policy Network Analysis," in M. Moran, M. Rein, and R. Goodin, eds., *The Oxford Handbook of Public Policy* (Oxford: Oxford University Press, 2006), 425–47.

[2] E.g., D. Knoke, *Policy Networks: The Structural Perspective* (Cambridge: Cambridge University Press, 1990).

cial element in any given policy network. The focal organization of the network tries to manage the more dependent organizations using diverse strategies. The other organizations use similar strategies to attempt to manage each other and the focal one. A network consists, therefore, of numerous overlapping relationships, each of which depends to a greater or lesser degree on the others.

The concept of governance by and through networks also draws on earlier studies of networks as interest intermediation. The literature on interest intermediation is part of a broader tradition of pluralism that has devoted much attention to subgovernments.[3] Pluralists disaggregate the study of policymaking into subsystems in which bureaucrats, legislators and their staff, and the representatives of interest groups all interact with one another. These clusters of individuals make most of the routine decisions in any given area of policy. Typically the pluralists concentrate on a few elite groups who have especially close ties to government and who often exclude other groups from access. In this view, government confronts innumerable interest groups. Some groups are considered to be extreme and unrealistic; they are kept away from the policy process. Others are deemed significant and responsible; they become insiders on whom government relies to ensure its policies work appropriately. Over time the interactions between government and the insiders become institutionalized. An "iron triangle" develops between the central agency, the legislative committee, and the elite interest group, all of which develop symbiotic relationships with each other.

Just as policy network analysis has inspired public sector reforms, so it has informed strategies for managing the products of such reforms. Recognition of networks as constraints on the state's ability to act has fueled research on techniques by which the state might manage policy networks. There are three leading approaches to network management, namely, the instrumental, the interactive, and the institutional.[4] The instrumental approach concentrates on top-down steering with government exercising its legitimate authority. It typically presumes a governmental department to be the focal organization in a network. The central state then devises and imposes tools that foster integration in and between policy networks and so enable it to attain its objectives. One problem with this instrumental approach is the clear tension between its suggestion that government can exercise effective control and its recognition of the control deficits associated with networks and governance. The interactive approach to network management moves away from hierarchic modes of control. It presumes the mutual dependence of actors in networks: collective action depends

---

[3] E.g., P. Schmitter and G. Lehmbruch, eds., *Trends towards Corporatist Intermediation* (Beverly Hills: Sage, 1979).

[4] Compare Kickert, Klijn, and Kooppenjan, eds., *Managing Complex Networks*.

on cooperation, and goals and strategies arise out of mutual learning. Management thus requires negotiation and diplomacy. This approach highlights the need to understand others' objectives and to build relations of trust with them. Chief executive officers are thus urged to develop interpersonal, communication, and listening skills. Yet, an interactive approach is often costly since cooperation is time-consuming, objectives can be blurred, and outcomes can be delayed. Finally, the institutional approach to network management focuses on the rules and structures against the background of which interactions take place. Management strategies seek to change relationships between actors, the distribution of resources, the rules of the game, and even values and perceptions. The aim is incremental changes in incentives and cultures. One problem with this approach is that institutions and their cultures are notoriously resistant to change.

The New Governance

A concern with governance rose in part as social scientists adopted new theories that led them to a more pluralist view of the state. Yet, while concepts of governance draw on an earlier literature on policy networks, they also transform important aspects of this literature. Earlier studies of policy networks typically concentrated on analyzing relations of power around the central state. In contrast, concepts of governance are often tied to the idea of a decline in the power of the central state. Accounts of governance usually focus on the boundary between state and civil society rather than on policymaking in specific areas. They explore the increasing diffusion of state power and authority onto other organizations. Governance is a broader term than government because it points to the diverse ways public services are delivered by any combination of public, private, and voluntary sector organizations. Similarly, concepts of governance often invoke international factors that contributed to the decline in the power of the central state. Whereas earlier studies of policy networks concentrated most commonly on policymaking in national policy sectors, concepts of governance are more likely to point outward to transnational networks. However, this last difference is perhaps not that great; after all, transnational policy networks have long been recognized as a feature of policymaking, especially in the European Union.

The differences between concepts of governance and the earlier literature on policy networks often reflect the impact of public sector reforms in the late twentieth century. The reforms attempted to extend and manage first markets and then networks. As policy makers promoted markets and networks, however, they also weakened the central state, diffusing some of its power and authority among various public agencies and even voluntary and private sector organizations. This process created new networks and increased the membership of existing networks. The state swapped direct for indirect controls. Central departments are no longer as likely to act as the fulcrum of a network. The government can set the limits to network actions. It still funds many services. But it has increased its dependence on multifarious networks.

Obviously we should not exaggerate the decline of the state—as if it had become a hollow shell. Several commentators argue that the central state remains strong.[5] Some argue that in Britain power actually became more centralized under Tony Blair.[6] In this view, power is increasingly centralized on the core executive, which has grown bigger, coordinates other networks, and often intervenes successfully to promote its own agenda.

Still, just as we should not exaggerate the decline of the state, so we should not ignore it. For a start, the growth of the core executive is often just the center's response to a realization of its own weakness. The center grabs desperately for new levers of control precisely because it finds its efforts at control are frustrated. In addition, there are clear limits to central steering. Often the center's levers are rubber ones—pulling them has little effect at the other end. The center is again left frustrated and increasingly finds its only recourse is the moral exhortation of a bully pulpit. Even within the core executive, ministerial or baronial government persists. The relationships among the barons and between the barons and the chief executive are characterized by power dependence. Thus, whether it is called strengthening central capability, joined-up government, or improving delivery, the recurrent theme of contemporary governance is the search for better coordination. Finally, surely the problems of coordinating an increasingly complex and disparate government machine through increasingly ineffectual levers of control is not evidence of the center's ability to intervene successfully. Intervention and control differ. The center clearly often intervenes, but its interventions rarely have the intended outcomes.

Brave New Democracy?

The new theories and new worlds of governance pose problems for the inherited account of a representative democracy overseeing a neutral bureaucracy. Consider the example of accountability. On one hand, we are increasingly aware of the private motives of public actors and the ways in which these may interfere with the pursuit of public goods, raising issues

[5] E.g., Marinetto, "Governing beyond the Centre"; and M. Smith, "Recentring British Government: Beliefs, Traditions, and Dilemmas in Political Science," *Political Studies Review* 6 (2008): 143–54.

[6] For a critical discussion see Bevir and Rhodes, *Governance Stories*, chap. 6.

about the moral hazards associated with citizens delegating decisions to elected politicians and especially public officials. On the other, we are increasingly aware of the limits to central control and coordination in systems where policymaking and service delivery are dispersed among a range of public, voluntary, and private organizations. In short, the new governance makes accountability look ever more important and yet ever more elusive.

Policy makers typically respond to contemporary democratic issues by trying to supplement representative institutions with an expertise based on the new theories of governance. It is helpful to distinguish here between two types of expertise. One type of expertise draws on the economic concept of rationality found in neoclassical economics and rational choice theory. This expertise inspires a whittling away of democracy that is evident in attempts to restrict the scope of democratic decision making in order to deal with collective irrationalities. Public affairs are given to nonmajoritarian institutions, including independent central banks as well as judges and the courts. Likewise, future democratic decisions are constrained by laws requiring that legislation, for example, balance budgets or respect legal rights.

A second type of expertise draws on the sociological concept of rationality found in institutionalism and related forms of social science. This expertise inspires a rethinking of democracy that is evident in new emphases on horizontal accountability and social inclusion. Bureaucratic hierarchies are to give way to joined-up networks. Policing, education, and other public services are increasingly to be based on partnerships that include private sector organizations and community groups.

Policy makers increasingly talk of a brave new world of decentralization, public involvement, and empowerment. It would be foolish to dismiss this talk. Policy makers often genuinely believe that network governance can and should promote democratic ideals. Nonetheless, their faith often derives at least implicitly from expert assertions that inclusive networks can support efficient and effective governance. As such, there is a possible tension within their brave new world. Are participation and dialogue means to efficient governance or democratic values? What would happen if the aim of promoting effective network governance came into conflict with that of extending social inclusion?

Challenging Modernism

Network governance may seem to promise participation and dialogue, but it also may be just another example of modernist rationalization. Modernist rationalization has arisen as social scientists and policy actors deployed economic and sociological concepts of rationality in order to promote a particular type of organization as uniquely efficient at least under specified circumstances associated with the contemporary age. Sometimes the rationalizers ignore history altogether. At other times they appeal to history to argue for the rational and perhaps inexorable rise of the relevant type of organization. Either way, they deploy formal concepts of rationality to analyze organizational structures as ideal types or reifications; they deploy much the same formal concepts of rationality to assess these organizational structures; they conclude that a particular organizational structure is peculiarly effective at least under certain conditions; and, perhaps most important, this conclusion inspires attempts to remake the social world so that public, voluntary, and private organizations embody the relevant structure.

We might schematically distinguish three forms of modernist rationalization. First, some social scientists—most famously Max Weber—present hierarchies with functional specialization and impersonal rules as uniquely efficient.[7] Second, social scientists inspired by neoclassical economics often present the competitive market as uniquely efficient especially in allocating scarce resources. Finally, yet other social scientists—often institutionalists responding to the perceived theoretical and practical failings of Weberian hierarchies—are increasingly presenting networks based on trust, reciprocity, and negotiation as uniquely efficient.

The conflict between these different forms of modernist rationalization may make us wary of taking any of them at face value. Of course, modernist social scientists might simply offer us yet another form of rationalization in which each organizational structure is presented as uniquely efficient under different conditions, thus leaving it to their formal expertise to define which structure we should adopt in any give case. Yet, recognition of the fallacy of expertise may lead us to reject the very idea of modernist rationalization, whatever form it takes.

If we reject modernist social science, what alternatives become available? What might come after modernism? It is to these questions that this chapter now turns. Table 11.1 provides an overview of the arguments. A concept of local rationality provides a counter to the reigning economic and sociological ones. It may lead to interpretive social science in contrast to rational choice and institutionalism. Equally, it may encourage us to rethink and remake democratic governance so as to allow greater space for pluralist citizenship, popular participation, and dialogic policymaking.

---

[7] In rejecting Weber's use of ideal types for social constructivism, I am suggesting that we think of him less as describing an inexorable process of objective rationalization, and more as contributing to the theoretical justification of a contingent process in which a particular concept of rationality came to dominate. See M. Weber, *The Theory of Social and Economic Organization*, trans. A. Henderson and T. Parsons (New York: Free Press, 1947).

TABLE 11.1
After Modernism

	Modernism		After modernism
Concept of rationality	Economic	Sociological	Local
Social science theory	Rational choice	Institutionalism	Interpretive theory
Citizenship	Consumerist	Communitarian	Pluralist
Democratic theory	Representative	Representative	Participatory
Policymaking	Expertise (markets)	Expertise (networks)	Dialogic

RETHINKING RATIONALITY

If we are to move beyond modernist social science, we must challenge the economic and sociological concepts of rationality that dominate it. These concepts of rationality arose as part of a general modernist culture in the late nineteenth and early twentieth centuries. The economic concept of rationality privileges utility maximization. It rose with neoclassical theorists and spread with rational choice theory. The sociological concept of rationality privileges adherence to appropriate social norms. It arose with functionalism and is now associated with institutionalism and communitarianism.

The economic and sociological concepts of rationality have fairly obvious theoretical flaws. Of course, much energy has been spent trying to overcome the flaws, or to defend them as necessary simplifications if we are to develop useful knowledge. Yet, the very need to address or justify these flaws just testifies to how obvious they are. The economic concept neglects ideas and, more particularly, local cultures. The sociological one neglects agency and, more particularly, local reasoning. The rest of this chapter is an attempt to defend and develop analyses of local reasoning and local cultures, and then to examine how they may lead us to rethink democratic governance.

A Presumption of Rationality

Social scientists who challenge the increasing dominance of the economic concept of rationality often do so on the grounds that actors are not always rational let alone self-interested. Choice is fallible, as psychologists and other social scientists often point out. People often do not have the necessary information to make informed choices. Even when they do have the relevant information, human judgment appears to exhibit systematic departures from rationality. Some writers have shown that people put more weight on minimizing loss than on maximizing gain.[8] Others have observed various inconsistencies over time and so introduced the idea of "myopic choice": what looks like a good choice today, may turn out to be a bad choice later on.[9]

Readers may welcome these challenges to the economic concept of rationality, but the challenges do not go far enough. Ultimately they remain within a broader universe of instrumental individual choice, however myopic or bounded such choice is considered to be. The resulting debate suffers from a failure properly to distinguish various concepts of rationality, and the various roles that these concepts might play in explanation.

There is a sense in which all explanations of action rely on attributing some sort of rationality to the actor. Typically, we explain an action by pointing to the reasons why an agent performed it, and these reasons explain the action precisely because they make it rational. Even if the reasons are unconscious, they still must have some kind of rational relationship to the action if they are to enable us to make the action intelligible. Because rationality appears in all social explanations, social scientists should rethink the debate on the validity of rational explanation. They should recast the debate as about the type of rationality that it is reasonable to presume in various forms of social explanation.

Let me suggest, as a starting point for such a debate, the conceptual priority of rationality defined as consistency.[10] The main argument in favor of a presumption of consistency concerns the prerequisites of ascribing meanings to statements. Crucially, language cannot exist unless saying one thing inherently rules out saying something else. Our ability to ascribe meaning to most statements depends on the fact that to assert them is to deny the contrary. For example, if saying that a chair was in a room did not rule out saying that it was not in the room, then to say it was there would typically have no meaning for us. The very existence of a language thus presupposes a norm of consistency governing its use. Even if there was a language that did not have a concept akin to ours of rationality, it still would have to embody attributes akin to those we equate with rationality, most notably a general consistency, and these attributes still would have to constitute norms in the language, since if its users did not presume consistency, they would not be able to ascribe meanings to statements. Now, because languages inevitably rely on a norm of consistency, they require us at least tacitly to grant conceptual priority to

[8] E.g., D. Kahneman and A. Tversky, eds., *Choices, Values, and Frames* (New York: Cambridge University Press, 2000).

[9] E.g., A. Offer, *The Challenge of Affluence: Self-Control and Well-Being in the United States and Britain since 1950* (Oxford: Oxford University Press, 2006).

[10] The following draws on the philosophical analysis in Bevir, *Logic of the History of Ideas*, 158–71.

consistent beliefs. We cannot treat people's use of language as governed by a norm of consistency unless we presume that they hold consistent beliefs. For example, if someone said that a chair was in a room, we could not take this statement to rule out their saying it was not there unless we presumed they did not believe it to be both there and not there. Our very ability to ascribe meanings to statements thus depends on our ascribing conceptual priority to consistent beliefs.

A second argument for a presumption of rationality as consistency is one about the prerequisites of action, and especially complex sets of actions guided by a plan. Because we cannot act in utterly incompatible ways at the same time, our beliefs must exhibit a degree of consistency at any given time in order for us to act on them. Again, because we act as we do, we must have a set of beliefs capable of sustaining such actions, so our beliefs must be fairly consistent. Successfully to go to the delicatessen and buy food, for example, we have to believe that the delicatessen exists, is open, and sells food; we cannot believe, say, that it is open but does not exist. Similarly, because our actions are often interlinked, sometimes according to complex plans, our beliefs must exhibit some stability over time. Because we can perform a series of actions in accord with an overall plan, we must have a set of beliefs capable of sustaining such actions, so our beliefs must be fairly stable. Successfully to plan a skiing holiday, for example, we must believe we are going to a place where there will be snow and where we will ski, and we must do so while we book the hotel, buy the tickets, pack, and so on. Our beliefs must cohere to the extent necessary to enable us to act in the world, and, indeed, to act over time in accord with complex plans. Our beliefs must be fairly consistent and fairly stable: in this sense, they must be fairly rational.

Two dangers await any presumption in favor of rationality no matter how it is defined: ethnocentrism and intellectualism. Consider first the danger that to presume beliefs are rational will be to translate them into our terms and so invalidate the self-understanding of other times and cultures. Most people who worry about ethnocentrism seem to have in mind the following: it would be ethnocentric to assume that all attempts to understand the world are self-critical in the sense that, for example, they entail a search for falsifying evidence. Yet, a presumption of rationality as consistency does not entail a presumption in favor of a self-critical stance toward one's beliefs. To be rational, a set of beliefs must be broadly consistent, but there is no reason to suppose it need be especially reflective, self-critical, or concerned with the evidence. Consider next the danger of intellectualism. It is important to emphasize here that a presumption of consistency does not involve any assertion about self-reflexivity on the part of those to whom it is applied: people accept a large number of beliefs on the authority of others, and many of their beliefs are subconscious. More generally, by equating rationality with consistency, we make rationality a feature of webs of belief rather than a disposition or a feature of actions. We thereby make it possible for beliefs to be rational no matter how they are reached and no matter how unreflectively they are held. Human societies can incorporate multiple beliefs instantiating diverse rationalities.

It is important, finally here, to be clear about the restricted range of a presumption of rationality as consistency. I am arguing for a presumption (not an axiom) of rationality conceived in terms of consistent belief (not utility-maximizing action). Unlike an axiom, a presumption does not preclude us from finding that some people may not be rational, and then looking for alternative forms of explanation for their behavior. A presumption merely encourages us to try to find a consistent pattern among people's beliefs before perhaps declaring them inconsistent and looking for explanations of their inconsistency. Indeed, because the set of consistent beliefs that people must hold depends on the actions that they perform, and because we cannot identify a set of actions that all people must perform, we cannot identify even a minimal way in which people's beliefs must be consistent. All we can say is that if someone performs a set of actions A, that person must hold beliefs possessing a minimal consistency B, where the content that we give to B will vary along with the content of A.

Local Reasoning

The restricted range of a presumption of rationality as consistency appears mainly, of course, in its applying only to rationality as consistent belief, not to rationality as utility-maximizing actions or perfect information. When neoclassical theorists adopt a concept of economic rationality that embraces these latter ideas, they elide the local and contingent nature of reasoning and decision making. Neoclassical theorists appear to presuppose that people are autonomous individuals whose preferences are formed and whose reasoning is secured outside of all particular cultures. In contrast, a presumption of consistency encourages us to emphasize the distinctly local nature of preferences, beliefs, and reason. To evoke local reasoning is, however, to say little about its nature or operation.

Reasoning is always local in that it occurs in the context of agents' existing webs of belief. The adjective "local" refers, in other words, to the fact that reasoning always takes place against the background of a particular subjective or intersubjective web of beliefs. While the content of the relevant web of beliefs varies from case to case, there is no possibility of reasoning outside of any such background. To insist on the local nature of reasoning is thus to preclude an autonomous and universal concept of reasoning and subjectivity associated with much economic theorizing. Where the concept of economic reasoning gestures at a view from nowhere—as if people could adopt beliefs and make decisions in ways that do not depend on the prior views they hold—local reasoning occurs in the specific context of just such prior views. Similarly, whereas the economic concept of rationality gestures at an assumption of perfect information, local reasoning recognizes that agents can use only the information they possesses, and they do just that even when the relevant information happens to be false.

While the adjective "local" captures the fact that reasoning only takes place against the background of prior beliefs, it need not have a spatial content. Local here means "local to a web of beliefs," not necessarily "local to a geographical area." Thus local reasoning differs importantly from the cognate concept of local knowledge.[11] Local knowledge refers to people's grasp of their own experiences, circumstances, and locality, and it is thus taken to be specific, concrete, and practical, rather than general, abstract, and theoretical. Usually local knowledge is thus contrasted less with an autonomous view from nowhere than with expert knowledge based on technical or professional training.

A concept of local reasoning applies to expert knowledge as much as to local knowledge. Local reasoning can occur against the background of highly specialized theories and academic practices: the neoclassical theorist who grapples with a technical issue so as to refine an equation or a model, and the sociological theorist who postulates a new correlation between network forms of organization and a particular rule of action, are themselves engaging in local reasoning against the background of established academic traditions and practices.

To anticipate the next section of this chapter, I will note here that the distinction between local reasoning and local knowledge can appear in different ways of conceiving interpretive social science. When interpretive social scientists champion local knowledge, they may take their task to be the recovery of local knowledge in its specific and concrete details, and they thus may conceive of interpretive social science primarily in terms of (ethnographic or qualitative) methods that appear to be conducive to thick descriptions of such knowledge as opposed to the (quantitative or large-N) methods that aim at broad generalizations.[12] In contrast, my concept of local reasoning implies that the primary task of interpretive social scientists is to recover the contingent webs of meaning that inform actions but not necessarily to do so at any particular level of specificity

[11] C. Geertz, *Local Knowledge* (New York: Basic Books, 1983).

[12] I take these to be recurring themes in much of Yanow and Schwartz-Shea, eds., *Interpretation and Method.*

or concreteness. It thus encourages us to conceive of interpretive social science in more philosophical and less methodological terms. Again, it encourages us to define interpretive social science in opposition not to broad generalizations but to formal concepts of rationality that neglect the holistic and contingent nature of belief and action.

Local reasoning operates through a capacity for creative if situated agency. Agency is creative in that there is no rule defining how people will modify their prior beliefs to make room for a newcomer. We can say only that the ways in which people reason reflect the content of their prior beliefs as well as the character of the idea with which they are grappling. Agency is situated in the same way as reasoning is local: it always takes place against an inherited background that influences it. Subjectivity may not be an illusion, but neither is it something completely within our control and immune from social influences; individuals are to a large extent what social traditions and practices make them.

Situated agents engage in local reasoning whenever they accommodate a new belief in an existing web of beliefs. Their local reasoning reflects both the character of the newcomer with which they are grappling and the content of their existing web of beliefs. If they are to make room for a newcomer, they have to modify their existing beliefs to accommodate it, so the particular modifications they make must reflect its character. Similarly, if they are to accommodate a new idea, they must attach it to aspects of their prior beliefs, where the content of these beliefs will make certain hooks available to them. The process of local reasoning thus typically involves people pushing and pulling at their existing beliefs and a new experience or idea in order to bring them into some kind of coherent relationship with one another. The new set of beliefs then appears in their situated agency, that is, their decisions and actions.

Just as local reasoning is not autonomous, so its operation need not necessarily be conscious and reflective. To the contrary, local reasoning often occurs tacitly, and it can occur in response to an experience of physical space or material objects as well as in response to novel arguments or ideas. Of course, local reasoning can be conscious and reflective, but we cannot reduce it to a conscious and reflective process, let alone one that can be reduced to a formal, deductive model.

RETHINKING GOVERNANCE

Just as modernist social science struggles to allow adequately for local reasoning, so it often inspires simplistic dichotomies between self-interest and altruism or modern and traditional societies. Social scientists often treat self-interest and social norms as both fixed and defined against each other.[13] The term "logic of appropriateness" is contrasted with "logic of consequences." Such dichotomies arise because many social scientists are committed to modernist modes of knowing that hide agency in monolithic and even reified concepts. Modernism encourages them to construct monolithic concepts defined by apparently fixed essences or properties that explain other features or effects of the objects to which the concepts refer by way of classifications or correlations. Modernism leads them to elide the different, contingent patterns of reasoning that lead people to act in overlapping ways that result in the social institutions and practices to which modernist concepts purport to refer.

A concept of local reasoning has the advantage of drawing attention to topics that are unsatisfactorily dealt with by the dichotomies of modernist social science: situated agency, change over time, and diversity.[14] The presence of multiple, shifting rationalities suggests, for example, that we need to think about the new governance not in terms of fixed institutions or clearly defined social trajectories, but in terms of contingent, diverse, and contested practices. We need more complex accounts of governance to challenge modernist dichotomies that pitch markets against collective action, consumerism against traditional societies, choice against community, and consumption against citizenship.

Rationality and Governance

An economic concept of rationality suggests that coordination and governance arise out of processes of bargaining and coalition building among utility-maximizing agents. It implies that collective practices and institutions are aggregations based on the fixed preferences of individuals. Sociological proponents of the logic of appropriateness suggest, in contrast, that institutions and so forms of governance are constituted by rules and norms that people take to be natural or at least legitimate. This

---

[13] I would like to emphasize that I am not arguing for a rejection of concepts such as interest and personal utility or institution and norm, but rather that these concepts should be analyzed and treated in ways that make it clear that they are forms of meaning and belief. Thus, it is an obvious mistake to treat my concern with meanings and beliefs as just adding a third term or variable to modernist dichotomies. Unfortunately, this mistake is an extremely common one. I can only assume that social scientists are so bewitched by modernism that they reflexively treat my arguments as if I too took modernism for granted. See, for just two clear examples of this mistake, C. Hay, "'Taking Ideas Seriously' in Explanatory Political Analysis," *British Journal of Politics and International Relations* 6 (2004): 142–48; and J. Hudson, G. Jin Hwang, and S. Kühner, "Between Ideas, Institutions, and Interests: Analysing Third Way Welfare Reform Programmes in Germany and the United Kingdom," *Journal of Social Policy* 37 (2008): 207–30.

[14] Compare Bevir, Rhodes, and Weller, eds., *Traditions of Governance*.

sociological approach allows that the rules can change over time, but it often explains change less in terms of choice than in terms of processes of selection and adaptation. To some extent, therefore, the dichotomy between economic and sociological concepts of rationality helps to sustain that between market and state as forms of social coordination. This latter dichotomy implies that social coordination requires either a market to aggregate the preferences of utility-maximizing agents or the state to establish norms and rules that individuals then follow in accord with a logic of appropriateness.

Of course, as social scientists crafted the new institutionalism, so they began to champion networks as an alternative to state and market forms of coordination. Once again, though, these social scientists still typically rely on modernist modes of knowing. Certainly the most widespread accounts of networks consciously draw on economic or sociological concepts of rationality. So, we find, on the one hand, neoclassical theory inspiring a rational choice analysis of networks as being composed of resource-dependent organizations.[15] This neoclassical approach postulates that the relationships between the organizations in a network are such that each depends on the others for resources and so has to exchange with them if it is to achieve its goals. As one would expect, it then argues that each organization rationally deploys its resources—whether these be financial, political, or informational—to maximize its influence on outcomes. In this view, networks are institutional settings that structure the opportunities for actors to realize their preferences, and actors then adopt strategies to maximize their satisfaction and their resources in the context of such settings. The emphasis thus falls on the use of formal game theory to analyze rule-governed networks. On the other hand, we find organizational theory, with its functionalist roots, inspiring a sociological approach to networks. In this approach, network is usually added as a third term alongside markets and hierarchies in classifications of organizations.[16] These classifications ascribe various characteristics to each type of organization and then seek to explain social outcomes by reference to these characteristics rather than situated agency and local reasoning.

A concept of local reasoning offers a new perspective outside of this dichotomy. To recover various traditions of belief and action is a reminder, first, that coordination and governance occur in civil society even in the absence of markets, and, second, that such coordination cannot be reduced to a reified concept of network but rather needs to be understood

---

[15] E.g., Scharpf, *Games Real Actors Play.*
[16] E.g., Powell, "Neither Market nor Hierarchy."

as the contingent product of the circulation of rationalities.[17] Situated agents intentionally and unintentionally create all kinds of formal and informal practices, and it is these practices that then coalesce into complex patterns of societal coordination and governance. It is important to stress that these practices are contingent, changing, and contested products of situated agency and local reasoning. This concept of a practice thus differs from the sociological concept of an institution as defined by fixed norms or rules, and also from those sociological ideal-types, such as networks, which are alleged to have fixed characteristics that explain their other features across time and space.[18]

Interpretive Theory

The concept of local reasoning may inspire an interpretive social science akin to that discussed in chapter 3. In particular, local reasoning challenges formal explanations based on economic and sociological concepts of rationality. If we take local reasoning seriously, we cannot reduce reasons, beliefs, and meanings to a universal rationality or to objective social factors such as institutional location. To the contrary, we must allow that reasons are intelligible only in the context of particular webs of belief. Recognition of local reasoning thus inspires contextualizing explanations. Social scientists properly explain actions (and so the practices to which they give rise) not by formal correlations, classifications, or models, but by explicating the web of beliefs that makes a reason for action intelligible.

An interpretive social science based on recognition of local reasoning typically leads to decentering, where to decenter is to analyze a practice in terms of the disparate beliefs of the actors. Interpretive social science concentrates on intentionality and so the meaningful nature of social life. Local reasoning draws attention to a creative if situated agency that suggests the beliefs or meanings held by any group, and even the ways in which they experience the world, are likely to be diverse and contested. Decentering thus consists in showing how an apparently monolithic institution actually embodies diverse, contested webs of belief informed by different traditions.

To decenter institutions or structures is to reveal them as composed of contingent and possibly competing webs of belief. Interpretive social sci-

---

[17] On the fortunes of voluntary associations and civil society before and in relation to modernism and the welfare state, see Harris, *Private Lives, Public Spirit*.

[18] For diverse examples of the turn to practices in the social sciences, see G. Spiegel, ed., *Practicing History: New Directions in Historical Writing after the Linguistic Turn* (New York: Routledge, 2005).

ence encourages us to think of institutions not as reified structures but in terms of traditions, practices, dilemmas, and other concepts that refer to beliefs. "Tradition" captures the idea that a social inheritance influences the beliefs people adopt and thus the actions they perform. "Practice" suggests that people act in social contexts: when they attempt to perform an action, their ability to succeed often depends on how others act. "Dilemma" captures the idea that people's experiences of the world can conflict with their beliefs, thereby forcing a change in their beliefs and actions.

Concepts such as tradition, practice, and dilemma stand as attempts to avoid the determinism, reification, and foundationalism that bedevil modernist social science. The term "tradition" recoils from determinism in order to allow for contingent agency. Social inheritances never fix the beliefs people might adopt and so the actions they might try to perform. A norm or rule does not determine how people will understand it, let alone respond to it. Similarly, the term "practice" recoils from reification in order to allow for intentionality. Practices are clusters of actions infused with the beliefs of the actors. Institutions or structures do not have a content or path of development that is fixed, independent of the agency of the relevant people. The term "dilemma" recoils from foundationalism in order to allow for the constructed nature of experience. Dilemmas are always subjective or intersubjective understandings of reality. We cannot assume that people experience the world as we take it to be.

Historicism

An interpretive social science based on recognition of local reasoning inspires a use of historical explanations. Crucially, because people can reason only against the background of an inherited web of beliefs, social scientists cannot explain why someone holds a particular web of beliefs solely by reference to his or her experiences, interests, or social location. To the contrary, even people's beliefs about their experiences, interests, and social location depend on their prior theories. Thus, social scientists can explain a particular web of beliefs only by reference to the historical tradition inherited by any particular person. Social explanation contains a historicist moment. Even concepts, actions, and practices that seem natural to us need to be explained as products of a contingent history.

While the new institutionalism has brought forth a chorus of "history matters," the members of the choir rarely pause to explain why or how history is important. Sometimes their silence occurs alongside an implicit treatment of history as little more than a source of illustrative cases. The more historically minded evoke a sense of time with metaphors such as path dependency, critical juncture, event, and sequencing. The more theoretically minded even appeal to history on the grounds that an adequate account of some social phenomena must refer to temporal mechanisms and processes.[19]

Unfortunately, institutionalists typically conceive of mechanisms and processes in modernist terms that are entangled with determinism, reification, and foundationalism. Their temporal mechanisms and processes come across as generalizations that operate either irrespective of agency or, more usually, through an agency that is fixed by norms or a universal rationality.[20] Mechanisms and processes are treated as reifications that operate irrespective of contingent agency. They are mistakenly given an objective content divorced from specific times and places. Again, when institutionalists reify processes and mechanisms, then far from treating history as a mode of explanation, they provide us with explanations that rely on the abstract logic of the mechanism or process. The mechanisms and processes may be temporal in that they unfold over time, but they are not historical: their operation is reduced to an abstract logic instead of being shown to be contingent on the particular beliefs and actions of people at a particular time.

If we are to avoid reifications and allow properly for agency, we need to treat history as a mode of explanation. Historical narratives explain social phenomena not by reference to a reified process, mechanism, or norm, but by describing contingent patterns of action in their specific contexts. Such narratives are not only temporal in that they move through time; they are also historical in that they locate the phenomena at a specific moment in time.

This book is, of course, an example of an interpretive social science that includes a historicist moment. It has explored governance as arising out of diverse actions infused by diverse beliefs or narratives including neoliberalism, institutionalism, the Third Way, and communitarianism. It decentered governance, showing how the relevant narratives have inspired varied, competing reform programs across states and policy sectors as well as up and down the policy chain. And it historicized governance, arguing that the relevant beliefs arose out of various traditions, most notably those associated with modernist social science and the dilemmas it poses for democracy.

---

[19] E.g., P. Pierson, *Politics in Time: History, Institutions, and Social Analysis* (Princeton: Princeton University Press, 2004).

[20] The main analyses of path dependency of which I am aware rely on assumptions about rational action. These assumptions sustain a model of the way in which an initial choice C can create extra costs for later attempts to depart from C such that rational individuals stick with C even though, in the absence of these extra costs, C would no longer be the optimal outcome for them.

RETHINKING DEMOCRACY

Once we recognize that governance consists of contingent, changing, and contested practices, we may rethink democratic ideals and practices. Neoliberals equate autonomy with participation in a market economy and a consumer society. They think of democracy as a way of protecting such freedom, while also expressing concern at the ways in which majoritarianism can interfere with the market economy. Institutionalists and communitarians often argue that an excess of autonomy results in dysfunctional communities. They call for homogenous communities, restricting personal choice in the name of a common citizenship. The broad thrust of this chapter has been, in contrast, to highlight alternative ideas of choice that might act as bases for diverse associations and communities. Local reasoning and situated agency constitute sites at which choice may promote civic goals. Choice can be about choosing ways of life in democratic communities. Citizens can engage one another, reflect on value systems, and modify their beliefs through deliberation and choice.

Citizenship

Recognition of local reasoning and situated agency highlights the diverse identities that people may hold even when they fall under common objective categories such as race, class, nation, or state. To respect such diversity, we may adopt notably more pluralist concepts of citizenship.

Pluralists advocate the devolution of aspects of governance to diverse associations in civil society. These associations can provide policy makers with information, voice the concerns of their members, and play an active role in devising and implementing a range of policies. A pluralist democracy of this sort may appeal as a way of improving public policy. It certainly seems likely that involving diverse groups and individuals in the policy process will bring more relevant information to bear on policies and also give those affected by policies a greater stake in making them work. A pluralist democracy also may appeal as a way of fostering opportunities for participation, deliberation, and collective choice. If we devolve aspects of governance to various groups in civil society, we will increase the number and range of organizations through which citizens can enter into democratic processes. Citizens could become involved through a diverse cluster of identities, concerns, and patterns of affiliation and consumption.

There is a danger that discussions of democratic pluralism will be too abstract to have any obvious purchase on contemporary governance. To counter this danger, I want to indicate how specific shifts in governance can be interpreted as steps toward pluralism and yet also as flawed. In Britain, New Labour embraces devolution and the involvement of voluntary and private partners alongside the public sector. Devolution and partnerships open up new, plural spaces for citizens to forge identities and act in consort. Nonetheless, they still remain tied primarily to the image of a representative democracy. Whereas New Labour's constitutional reforms consist mainly of devolution to national parliaments and doses of electoral reform, pluralism encourages us to invent and establish new sites at which citizens can deliberate, formulate policies, and connect with one another and the state. Similarly, whereas New Labour promotes partnerships in which the state plays an active role, even seeking to regulate and control outcomes, a pluralist democracy would hand aspects of governance over to associations other than the state.

Participation

Current responses to the democratic dilemmas posed by the new governance often buttress representative democracy with expertise based on modernist social science. But if such expertise is a fallacy—if modernist social science cannot deliver on its promises—then we cannot rely on it to supplement representative democracy. Perhaps we may turn instead to less formal, more participatory democratic practices. It is possible that we may turn to participatory practices to supersede representative ones. However, we should consider turning to participation instead as a supplement to representation. Formal representative democracy certainly embodies an equality that I would be reluctant to dismiss: an election can allow each citizen to have exactly one vote.

As we saw in chapter 5, radical democrats often advocate participatory practices as responses to the limits and failings of representative democracy. Participatory practices may well bring less formal equality and uniformity. Particular situations may give rise to different decision-making processes in which different people participate. The rules and manner of participating and reaching decisions may vary in large part with those who are actually involved. Legitimacy is thus less likely to derive from a kind of formal equality than from principles such as the openness of the process, the participation of relevant individuals, and the perceived fit between the process and the situation it is meant to address.

While many regimes are embracing participation, their endeavors remain flawed. To put the issue starkly, current initiatives typically pay lip service to participation while actually failing to go beyond consultation. For example, the Organisation for Economic Co-operation and Development advocates partnership and participation in policymaking, but it more or less restricts the role of citizens to being consulted on issues that are themselves selected by the state: "governments define the issues for consultation, set the questions and manage the process, while citizens are invited to contribute their views and opinions."[21]

Dialogic Policy

Current responses to the democratic dilemmas posed by the new governance often buttress representative democracy with expertise based on modernist social science. In contrast, recognition of local reasoning and situated agency highlights the failings of modernist social science and, indeed, the fallacy of expertise generally. Arguably it thus encourages us to experiment with more dialogic approaches to policy.

Modernist social science treats networks as both a structure to be managed and a tool for crafting greater central control.[22] This approach to networks is an increasingly prominent governing strategy, as we saw in examining the spread of evidence-based policymaking, whole of government approaches, and joined-up governance. Social scientists and policy actors alike often treat government departments, local authorities, markets, and networks as fixed structures that governments can manipulate using the right tools. They try to improve the ability of the state to manage the mix of hierarchies, markets, and networks that have flourished as part of the new governance.[23]

There are obvious difficulties with attempts to use networks as part of a control strategy. For a start, local networks cease to be local networks if they are directed from the center.[24] When networks are centrally manipulated, horizontal relationships often get transformed into vertical ones, and the results resemble exercises in official consultation more than sites of local discretion. Besides, my interpretive approach highlights a more general difficulty with expert strategies of network management. An emphasis on local reasoning undercuts the very idea of steering networks and the very idea of tools with which to manage governance. If governance is constructed differently, contingently, and continuously, there can be no tool kit for managing it.

---

[21] Organisation for Economic Co-operation and Development, *Citizens as Partners: Information, Consultation and Public Participation in Policy-Making* (Paris: OECD, 2001), 12.

[22] E.g., Kickert, Klijn, and Kooppenjan, eds., *Managing Complex Networks*; and Mandell, ed., *Getting Results through Collaboration.*

[23] E.g., L. Salamon, *The Tools of Government: A Guide to the New Governance* (New York: Oxford University Press, 2002).

[24] Compare J. Davies, "The Limits of Joined-up Governance: Bringing Politics Back In," *Public Administration* 87 (2009): 80–96.

Critics argue that this rejection of expertise means interpretive social science is descriptive, rather than evaluative or constructive, and thus cannot make a "positive contribution" to policy analysis.[25] But the critics are mistaken. As we saw in chapter 8, an interpretive approach may encourage us to adopt a more dialogic approach to policy. We may give up management techniques and strategies for a practice of learning by telling stories and listening to them. Instead of revealing policy consequences through insights into a social logic or lawlike regularities, stories enable policy makers to see things differently. Perhaps more important, storytelling is by no means the preserve of the policy wonk and the social scientist. Citizens too can tell stories about their world. Policy can arise out of dialogues and learning among citizens with the state playing a largely facilitative role.

Dialogic policy too appears to be spreading but in a severely limited form. States increasingly make their policy documents reader-friendly using bullet points, bold headings, pictures, side bars, and other such devices, as well as trying to avoid technical jargon. States sometimes also set up websites and other arenas in which citizens are invited to comment on proposed policies. But glossy brochures and the opportunity to comment scarcely constitute meaningful dialogue.

Conclusion

As the nineteenth century turned into the twentieth, two types of modernism arose and eventually came to dominate social theory. Neoclassical economics and its extension in rational choice theory inspired deductive models based on assumptions about utility maximization. Many sociological alternatives searched for correlations, classifications, and ideal types on the assumption that organizations, institutions, or norms fix patterns of reason and action. These two modernist approaches to social theory supported a series of dichotomies, including logic of consequences vs. logic of appropriateness, choice vs. community, market vs. state, and consumption vs. citizenship.

This chapter has tried to chart a course beyond modernism and the false dichotomies it inspired. I challenged neoclassical economics for its neglect of culture; a presumption of rationality should extend only to consistency of belief, not to utility-maximizing behavior. Likewise, I challenged much modernist sociology for its neglect of agency; the possibility of local reasoning and situated agency entail a creativity that means

---

[25] D. Bobrow and J. Dryzek, *Policy Analysis by Design* (Pittsburgh: Pittsburgh University Press, 1987), 171.

rules, norms, and institutional and social trajectories are contingent and contested. An emphasis on culture and agency encourages us to explore the diverse meanings and traditions embodied in governance, revealing its contingent, contested, and complex trajectories. Perhaps more important, it may facilitate more imaginative responses to the democratic issues raised by the new governance. It may free us from an increasingly obsolete faith in representative democracy buttressed by expertise. It may give us hope for a pluralist and participatory democracy built around diverse openings and support for citizens to develop voice, enter dialogues, and rule themselves.

Bibliography

NEWSPAPERS AND PERIODICALS

Constitutional Update (London)
Economist (London)
Governing (Washington, DC)
Guardian (London)
Independent (London)
Monitor (London)
Observer (London)
Sunday Times (London)

OFFICIAL PUBLICATIONS

Australia. Australian Public Service Commission. *Connecting Government: Whole of Government Responses to Australia's Priority Challenges.* 2004.
———. *Tackling Wicked Problems: A Public Policy Perspective.* 2007.
Australia. Department of Human Services. *Centrelink Annual Report 2006–2007.*
Commission of the European Communities. *European Governance: A White Paper.* COM(2001) 428.
International Monetary Fund. *Lessons of the Financial Crisis for Future Regulation of Financial Institutions and Markets and for Liquidity Management.* February 4, 2009.
New Zealand. State Service Commission and the Treasury. *The Spirit of Reform: Managing the New Zealand State Sector in a Time of Change,* by A. Schick. Wellington: State Services Commission, 1996.
Organisation for Economic Cooperation and Development. Citizens as Partners: Information, Consultation and Public Participation in Policy-Making. Paris: OECD, 2001.
———. *Whole of Government Approaches to Fragile States.* Paris: OECD, 2006.
United Kingdom. *Royal Commission on the Depression of Trade and Industry, Final Report.* C. 4893. 1886.
———. *The Royal Commission on the Reform of the House of Lords.* Cm. 4534. 2000.
United Kingdom. Cabinet Office. *Ministerial Code: A Code of Conduct and Guidance on Procedures for Ministers.* 1997.
———. *Modernising Government.* Cm. 4310. 1999.
United Kingdom. Department of Health. *The New National Health Service: Modern, Dependable.* Cm. 3807. 1997.
United Kingdom. Department of Social Security. *New Ambitions for Our Country: A New Contract for Welfare.* Cm. 3805. 1998.

United Kingdom. Department of Trade and Industry. *Our Competitive Future: Building the Knowledge Driven Economy*. Cm. 4176. 1998.

United Kingdom. H.M. Treasury. *Modern Public Services for Britain: Investing in Reform*. Cm. 4011. 1998.

United Kingdom. Home Office. *Building Communities, Beating Crime: A Better Police Service for the 21st Century*. Cm. 6360. 2004.

————. *Confident Communities in a Secure Britain*. Cm. 6287. 2004.

————. *Inquiry into Police Responsibilities and Rewards* Cm. 2280. 1993.

————. *National Policing Plan 2005–08: Safer, Stronger Communities*. 2004.

————. *Police Reform: A Police Service for the 21st Century*. Cm. 2281. 1993.

————. *Policing: Building Safer Communities Together*. 2004.

————. *The Report of the Independent Commission on the Voting System*. Cm. 4090. 1998.

————. *Review of Police Core and Ancillary Tasks: Final Report*. 1995.

United Kingdom. Ministry of Justice. *The Governance of Britain*. Cm. 7170. 2007.

United Kingdom. National Assembly for Wales. *Report of the Richard Commission on the Powers and Electoral Arrangements of the National Assembly for Wales*, by Lord Richard of Ammanford. Cardiff: National Assembly for Wales, 2004.

United Kingdom. Scottish Executive. *Choosing Scotland's Future: A National Conversation: Independence and Responsibility in the Modern World*. 2007.

United Kingdom. Social Exclusion Unit. *Bringing Britain Together: A National Strategy for Neighbourhood Renewal*. Cm. 4045. 1998.

United States. Department of Homeland Security. *Securing our Homeland: Department of Homeland Security Strategic Plan*. Washington, DC: DHS, 2004.

United States. Department of Justice. *Community Policing: A Practical Guide for Police Officials*, by L. Brown. Washington, DC, 1989.

World Bank. *Social Accountability in the Public Sector: A Conceptual Discussion and Learning Module*. Washington, DC: World Bank, 2005.

————. *Sub-Saharan Africa: From Crisis to Sustainable Growth*. Washington, DC: World Bank, 1989.

COURT CASES

A & Others v. Secretary of State for the Home Department [2004] UKHL 56.

Costa v. ENEL, case 6/64, ECR 585 et seq., ECJ 1964.

Francovich & Bonifaci v. Italy, case 6/90 and 9/90, ECR 5357, ECJ 1991.

M v. Home Office [1993] 3 *All ER* 537 (HL).

R v. Secretary of State for Transport, ex p. Factortame Ltd (No. 2) [1991] 1 AC 603.

Van Duyn v. Home Office, case 41/74, ECR 1337, ECJ 1974.

Von Colson v. Land Nordrhein-Westfalen, case 14/83, ECR 1891, ECJ 1984.

Van Gend en Loos v. Nederlandse Administratie der Belastingen, case 26/62, ECR 1, ECJ 1963

BOOKS AND ARTICLES

Acemoglu, D., and J. Robinson. *Economic Origins of Dictatorship and Democracy*. New York: Cambridge University Press, 2005.

Adcock, R. "Interpreting Behavioralism." In *Modern Political Science: Anglo-American Exchanges since 1880*, edited by R. Adcock, M. Bevir, and S. Stimson, 180–208. Princeton: Princeton University Press, 2007.

Adcock, R., M. Bevir, and S. Stimson. "Historicizing the New Institutionalism(s)." In *Modern Political Science: Anglo-American Exchanges since 1880*, edited by R. Adcock, M. Bevir, and S. Stimson, 259–89. Princeton: Princeton University Press, 2007.

Adcock, R., M. Bevir, and S. Stimson, eds. *Modern Political Science: Anglo-American Exchanges since 1880*. Princeton: Princeton University Press, 2007.

Albert, M. "Governance and Democracy in European Systems: On Systems Theory and European Integration." *Review of International Studies* 28 (2002): 293–309.

Allan, T. *Law, Liberty and Justice: The Legal Foundations of British Constitutionalism*. Oxford: Clarendon, 1993.

Allingham, A. *Theory of Markets*. London: Macmillan, 1989.

Amadae, S. *Rationalizing Capitalist Democracy: The Cold War Origins of Rational Choice Liberalism*. Chicago: University of Chicago Press, 2003.

Ansell, C. "The Networked Polity: Regional Development in Western Europe." *Governance* 13 (2000): 303–33.

Arganoff, R., and M. McGuire. "Managing in Network Settings." *Policy Studies Review* 16 (1999): 18–41.

Armstrong, K. "Rediscovering Civil Society: The European Union and the White Paper on Governance." *European Law Journal* 8 (2002): 102–32.

Bagehot, W. *The English Constitution*. London: Oxford University Press, 1963.

Bang, H., ed. *Governance as Social and Political Communication*. Manchester: Manchester University Press, 2003.

Bang, H., and E. Sørensen. "The Everyday Maker: A New Challenge to Democratic Governance." *Administrative Theory & Praxis* 21 (1999): 325–41.

Barnett, A. *This Time: Our Constitutional Revolution*. London: Vintage, 1997.

Barnett, A., C. Ellis, and P. Hirst, eds. *Debating the Constitution: New Perspectives on Constitutional Reform*. Cambridge: Polity, 1993.

Barrow, L., and I. Bullock. *Democratic Ideas and the British Labour Movement 1880–1914*. Cambridge: Cambridge University Press, 1996.

Bayley, D., ed. *What Works in Policing*. Oxford: Oxford University Press, 1998.

Bayley, D., and C. Shearing. "The Future of Policing." *Law and Society Review* 30 (1996): 585–606.

Beer, S. *Britain Against Itself*. London: Faber, 1982.

Bell, D. *The Idea of Greater Britain: Empire and the Future of World Order, 1860–1900*. Princeton: Princeton University Press, 2007.

Bellamy, R. *Political Constitutionalism: A Republican Defence of the Constitutionality of Democracy*. Cambridge: Cambridge University Press, 2007.

Benson, J. "Organizational Dialectics." *Administrative Science Quarterly* 22 (1977): 1–22.

Bentley, A. *The Process of Government.* Chicago: University of Chicago Press, 1908.

Berle, A., and G. Means. *The Modern Corporation and Private Property.* New York: Macmillan, 1993.

Bernstein, R. *The Restructuring of Social and Political Theory.* Philadelphia: University of Pennsylvania Press, 1976.

Bevir, M. "A Decentered Theory of Governance." In *Governance as Social and Political Communication*, edited by H. Bang, 200–21. Manchester: Manchester University Press, 2003.

———. "Democratic Governance: Systems and Radical Perspectives." *Public Administration Review* 66 (2006): 426–36.

———. *The Logic of the History of Ideas.* Cambridge: Cambridge University Press, 1999.

———. *New Labour: A Critique.* London: Routledge, 2005.

———. "Political Studies as Narrative and Science, 1880–2000." *Political Studies* 54 (2006): 583–606.

———. "Prisoners of Professionalism." *Public Administration* 79 (2001): 469–89.

Bevir, M., and R. Rhodes. *Interpreting British Governance.* London: Routledge, 2003.

———. *Governance Stories.* London: Routledge, 2006.

Bevir, M., R. Rhodes, and P. Weller, eds. "Traditions of Governance: History and Diversity." Special issue, *Public Administration* 81/1 (2003).

Bevir, M., and D. Richards, eds. "Decentring Policy Networks." Special issue. *Public Administration* 87/1 (2009).

Bevir, M., and F. Trentmann, eds. *Governance, Consumers, and Citizens: Agency and Resistance in Contemporary Politics.* Basingstoke: Palgrave, 2007.

Birch, A. "The Theory and Practice of Modern British Democracy." In *The Changing Constitution*, edited by J. Jowell and D. Oliver, 87–111. Oxford: Clarendon Press, 1989.

Black, B., K. Reinier, and A. Tarassova. "Russian Privatization and Corporate Governance: What Went Wrong?" *Ekonomski Anali* 44 (2000): 29–117.

Blair, T. *New Britain: My Vision of a Young Country.* London: Fourth Estate, 1996.

Blichner, L., and A. Molander. "What Is Juridification?" *Northwestern Journal of International Law and Business* 97 (1996): 354–97.

Bobrow, D., and J. Dryzek. *Policy Analysis by Design.* Pittsburgh: Pittsburgh University Press, 1987.

Bogdanor, V., ed. *The British Constitution in the Twentieth Century.* Oxford: Oxford University Press, 2003.

———. "Constitutional Reform." In *The Blair Effect: The Blair Government 1997–2001*, edited by A. Seldon, 139–56. London: Little Brown, 2001.

Börzel, T. "Organizing Babylon: On the Different Conceptions of Policy Networks." *Public Administration* 76 (1998): 253–73.

Bouckaert, G., and S. van de Walle. "Comparing Measures of Citizen Trust and User Satisfaction as Indicators of 'Good Governance': Difficulties in Linking

Trust and Satisfaction Indicators." *International Review of Administrative Sciences* 69 (2003): 329–43.

Bovaird, T. "Public-Private Partnerships: From Contested Concept to Prevalent Practice." *International Review of Administrative Sciences* 70 (2004): 199–215.

Bowerman, M., H. Raby, and C. Humphrey. "In Search of the Audit Society: Some Evidence from Health Care, Police, and Schools." *International Journal of Auditing* 4 (2000): 71–100.

Box-Steffensmeier, J., H. Brady, and D. Collier, eds. *The Oxford Handbook of Political Methodology*. Oxford: Oxford University Press, 2008.

Boyer, R. *The Regulation School: A Critical Introduction*, translated by C. Charney. New York: Columbia University Press, 1990.

Boyne, G., C. Farrell, J. Law, M. Powell, and R. Walker. *Evaluating Public Management Reform: Principles and Practice*. Buckingham: Open University Press, 2003.

Brady, H. "Causation and Explanation in Social Science." In *The Oxford Handbook of Political Methodology*, edited by J. Box-Steffensmeier, H. Brady, and D. Collier, 217–70. Oxford: Oxford University Press, 2008.

Braithwaite, V., and M. Levi, eds. *Trust and Governance*. New York: Russell Sage Foundation, 1998.

Brans, M., and S. Rossbach. "The Autopoiesis of Administrative Systems: Niklas Luhmann on Public Administration and Public Policy." *Public Administration* 85 (1997): 417–39.

Brereton, M., and M. Temple. "The New Public Service Ethos: An Ethical Environment for Governance." *Public Administration* 77 (1999): 455–74.

Brook, D., and C. King. "Civil Service Reform as National Security: The Homeland Security Act of 2002." *Public Administration Review* 67 (2007): 399–407.

Brown, M. *Working the Street: Police Discretion and the Dilemmas of Reform*. New York: Russell Sage Foundation, 1981.

Burke, T. *Lawyers, Lawsuits, and Legal Rights*. Berkeley: University of California Press, 2002.

Campbell, J., and O. Pederson, eds. *The Rise of Neoliberalism and Institutional Analysis*. Princeton: Princeton University Press, 2001.

Chan, J. "Governing Police Practice: Limits of the New Accountability." *British Journal of Sociology* 50 (1999): 251–70.

Clarke, J., J. Newman, N. Smith, E. Vidler, and L. Westmarland. *Creating Citizen-Consumers: Changing Publics and Changing Public Services*. London: Sage, 2006.

Cole, G. "Conflicting Social Obligations." *Proceedings of the Aristotelian Society* 15 (1914–15): 159.

———. *Guild Socialism Restated*. London: Leonard Parsons, 1920.

Collini, S., D. Winch, and J. Burrow. *That Noble Science of Politics: A Study in Nineteenth Century Intellectual History*. Cambridge: Cambridge University Press, 1983.

Conklin, J. *Dialogue Mapping: Building Shared Understanding of Wicked Problems*. Chichester: Wiley, 2006.

Considine, M. "The End of the Line? Accountable Governance in the Age of Networks, Partnerships, and Joined-up Services." *Governance* 15 (2002): 21–40.

Cope, S., F. Leishman, and P. Starie. "Globalization, New Public Management and the Enabling State: Futures of Police Management." *International Journal of Public Sector Management* 10 (1997): 444–60.

Cox, T. "The Implementation of Cultural Diversity in Police Organizations." *Journal of Police and Criminal Psychology* 10 (1994): 41–46.

Crick, B. *The Reform of Parliament: The Crisis of Government.* London: Weidenfeld and Nicolson, 1964.

Crick, B., and A. Hanson, eds. *The Commons in Transition.* London: Fontana, 1979.

Dahl, R. *Pluralist Democracy in the United States.* Chicago: Rand McNally, 1967.

Davidson, D. *Essays on Actions and Events.* Oxford: Clarendon Press, 1980.

Davies, A., and R. Thomas, "Talking Cop: Discourses of Change and Policing Identities." *Public Administration* 81 (2003): 681–99.

Davies, J. "The Limits of Joined-up Governance: Bringing Politics Back In." *Public Administration* 87 (2009), 80–96.

Davis, K. "The Future of Judge-Made Public Law in England: A Problem of Practical Jurisprudence." *Columbia Law Review* 61 (1961): 201–20.

De la Porte, C., P. Pochet, and G. Room. "Social Benchmarking, Policy Making and New Governance in the EU." *Journal of European Social Policy* 11 (2001): 291–307.

DeLeon, L. "Accountability in a 'Reinvented Government.'" *Public Administration* 76 (1998): 539–58.

DeLeon, L., and R. Denhardt. "The Political Theory of Reinvention." *Public Administration Review* 60 (2000): 89–97.

Denhardt, R., and J. Denhardt. "The New Public Service: Serving Rather than Steering." *Public Administration Review* 60 (2000): 549–59.

Dicey, A. *Introduction to the Study of the Law of the Constitution.* London: Macmillan, 1902.

Donahue, J. *The Privatization Decision: Public Ends, Private Means.* New York: Basic Books, 1989.

Doombos, M. "'Good Governance': The Rise and Decline of a Policy Metaphor." *Journal of Development Studies* 37 (2001): 93–108.

Dowding, K. "Model or Metaphor? A Critical Review of the Policy Network Approach." *Political Studies* 43 (1995): 136–58.

———. "There Must Be an End to the Confusion: Policy Networks, Intellectual Fatigue, and the Need for Political Science Methods Courses in British Universities." *Political Studies* 49 (2001): 89–105.

Dowding, K., P. Dunleavy, D. King, H. Margetts, and Y. Rydin. "Understanding Urban Governance: The Contribution of Rational Choice." In *Power and Participation: The New Politics of Local Governance*, edited by G. Stoker, 91–116. London: Macmillan, 2000.

Dryzek, J. "Policy Analysis and Planning: From Science to Argument." In *The Argumentative Turn in Policy Analysis and Planning*, edited by F. Fischer and J. Forester, 213–32. Durham: Duke University Press, 1993.

Dubnick, M. "Accountability and the Promise of Performance: In Search of the Mechanisms." *Public Performance and Management Review* 28 (2005): 376–417.

Dunleavy, P. "The Westminster Model and the Distinctiveness of British Politics." In *Developments in British Politics*, edited by P. Dunleavy, R. Heffernan, P. Cowley and C. Hay, 8th series. Basingstoke: Palgrave Macmillan, 2006.

Dunsire, A. *Control in a Bureaucracy*. Oxford: St Martin's Press, 1978.

———. *Implementation in a Bureaucracy*. Oxford: Martin Robertson, 1978.

Eisenhardt, K. "Agency Theory: An Assessment and Review." *Academy of Management Review* 14 (1989): 57–74.

Emsley, C. *The English Police: A Political and Social History*. London: Longman, 1996.

Esping-Andersen, G. *Three Worlds of Welfare Capitalism*. Princeton: Princeton University Press, 1990.

Etzioni, A. *The Spirit of Community: Rights, Responsibilities, and the Communitarian Agenda*. New York: Crown, 1993.

Evans, M. *Charter 88: A Successful Challenge to the British Political Tradition?* Aldershot: Dartmouth, 1995.

———. *Constitution-making and the Labour Party*. Basingstoke: Palgrave Macmillan, 2003.

———. "Understanding Dialectics in Policy Network Analysis." *Political Studies* 49 (2001): 542–50.

Everdell, W. *The First Moderns*. Chicago: University of Chicago Press, 1997.

Fearon, J. "Electoral Accountability and the Control of Politicians: Selecting Good Types versus Sanctioning Poor Performance." In *Democracy, Accountability, and Representation*, edited by A. Przeworski, S. Stokes, and B. Manin, 55–97. New York: Cambridge University Press, 1999.

Fenwick, H. *Civil Rights: New Labour, Freedom, and the Human Rights Act*. London: Longman, 2000.

Field, F. *Reforming Welfare*. London: Social Markets Foundation, 1997.

Finer, S., ed. *Adversary Politics and Electoral Reform*. London: Anthony Wigram, 1975.

Fleming, J. "Working through Networks: The Challenge of Partnership Policing." In *Fighting Crime Together: The Challenges of Policing and Security Networks*, edited by J. Fleming and J. Wood, 87–115. Sydney: University of New South Wales Press, 2006.

Forester, J. *The Deliberative Practitioner: Encouraging Participatory Planning Processes*. Cambridge: MIT Press, 1999.

Francis, M., and J. Morrow. *A History of English Political Thought in the 19th Century*. London: Duckworth, 1994.

Fraser, N., and A. Honneth. *Redistribution or Recognition? A Political-Philosophical Exchange*, translated by J. Golb and C. Wilke. London: Verso, 2003.

Freeden, M. *Liberalism Divided*. Oxford: Clarendon Press, 1986.

Fukuyama, F. *State-Building: Governance and World Order in the 21st Century*. Ithaca: Cornell University Press, 2004.

Fung, A. "Deliberation before the Revolution: Toward an Ethic of Deliberative Democracy in an Unjust World." *Political Theory* 33 (2005): 397–419.

———. *Empowered Participation: Reinventing Urban Democracy*. Princeton: Princeton University Press, 2004.

Fung, A., and E. Wright. "Deepening Democracy: Innovations in Empowered Participatory Governance." *Politics & Society* 29 (2001): 5–41.

Gamble, A. "Theories of British Politics." *Political Studies* 38 (1990): 404–20.

Geddes, M. "Tackling Social Exclusion in the European Union? The Limits to the New Orthodoxy of Local Partnership." *International Journal of Urban and Regional Research* 24 (2000): 782–800.

Geertz, C. *The Interpretation of Cultures*. New York: Basic Books, 1973.

———. *Local Knowledge*. New York: Basic Books, 1983.

Gerring, J. "Case Selection for Case-Study Analysis." In *The Oxford Handbook of Political Methodology*, edited by J. Box-Steffensmeier, H. Brady, and D. Collier, 645–84. Oxford: Oxford University Press, 2008.

Gramsci, A. *Selections from the Prison Notebooks*, edited and translated by Q. Hoare and G. Nowell Smith. London: Lawrence and Wishart, 1971.

Granovetter, M. "Business Groups." In *Handbook of Economic Sociology*, edited by N. Smelser and R. Swedberg, 453–75. Princeton: Princeton University Press, 1994.

———. "Economic Action and Social Structure: The Problem of Embededness." *American Journal of Sociology* 78 (1973): 1360–80.

———. *Getting a Job: A Study of Contacts and Careers*. Cambridge: Harvard University Press, 1974.

Greene, J. "Community Policing in America: Changing the Nature, Structure, and Function of the Police." In *Policies, Processes, and Decisions of the Criminal Justice System*, edited by J. Horney, 299–370. Washington, DC: National Institute of Justice, 2000.

Greener, I. "Understanding NHS Reform: The Policy-Transfer, Social-Learning, and Path Dependency Perspectives." *Governance* 15 (2002): 161–83.

Grindle, M. "Good Enough Governance: Poverty Reduction and Reform in Developing Countries." *Governance* 17 (2004): 525–48.

Gruening, G. "Origin and Theoretical Basis of the New Public Management." *International Public Management Review* 4 (2001): 1–25.

Gunnell, J. *Imagining the American Polity: Political Science and the Discourse of Democracy*. University Park: Pennsylvania State University Press, 2004.

Gyford, J., S. Leach, and C. Game. *The Changing Politics of Local Government*. London: Unwin Hyman, 1989.

Habermas, J. "Law as Medium and Law as Institution." In *Dilemmas of Law in the Welfare State*, edited by G. Teubner. Berlin: W. de Gruyter, 1986.

Hailsham, Lord. *The Dilemma of Democracy*. London: Collins, 1978.

Hall, P., and R. Taylor. "Political Science and the Three Institutionalisms." *Political Studies* 44 (1996): 936–57.

Haque, M. "The Diminishing Publicness of Public Service under the Current Mode of Governance." *Public Administration Review* 61 (2001): 65–82.

Harden, I., and N. Lewis. *The Noble Lie: The British Constitution and the Rule of Law*. London: Hutchinson, 1986.

Hardin, G. *Collective Action*. Baltimore: Johns Hopkins University Press, 1982.

———. "The Tragedy of the Commons." *Science* 162 (1968): 1243–48.

Harlow, C., and R. Rawlings, *Law and Administration*. London: Butterworths, 1997.

Harris, J. *Private Lives, Public Spirit: A Social History of Britain, 1870–1914*. Oxford: Oxford University Press, 1993.

Harvey, D. *A Brief History of Neoliberalism*. Oxford: Oxford University Press, 2005.

Hay, C. "Narrating Crisis: The Discursive Construction of the Winter of Discontent." *Sociology* 30 (1996): 253–77.

———. "'Taking Ideas Seriously' in Explanatory Political Analysis." *British Journal of Politics and International Relations* 6 (2004): 142–48.

———. "The Tangled Webs We Weave: The Discourse, Strategy, and Practice of Networking." In *Comparing Policy Networks*, edited by D. Marsh, 33–51. Buckingham: Open University Press, 1998.

Hayward J., and V. Wright. *Governing from the Centre: Core Executive Coordination in France*. Oxford: Oxford University Press, 2002.

Hazlehurst, C., and J. Nethercote, eds. *Reforming Australian Government: The Coombs Report and Beyond*. Canberra: ANU Press, 1977.

Healy, P. *Collaborative Planning: Shaping Places in Fragmented Societies*. London: Macmillan, 1997.

Heastfield, J. "Brand New Britain." *LM Magazine* 11 (1997).

Henderson, A. "A Porous and Pragmatic Settlement: Asymmetrical Devolution and Democratic Constraint in Scotland and Wales." In *Reinventing Britain: Constitutional Change under New Labour*, edited by A. McDonald, 151–69. London: Politico's, 2007.

Hennart, J-F. "Explaining the Swollen Middle: Why Most Transactions Are a Mix of Market and Hierarchy." *Organization Science* 4 (1993): 529–47.

Hill, C., and L. Lynn, "Is Hierarchical Governance in Decline? Evidence from Empirical Research." *Journal of Public Administration Research and Theory* 15 (2005): 173–96.

Hindmoor, A. "The Importance of Being Trusted: Transaction Costs and Policy Network Theory." *Public Administration* 76 (1998): 25–43.

Holmes, M., and D. Shand, "Management Reform: Some Practitioner Perspectives on the Past Ten Years." *Governance* 8 (1995): 551–78.

Hood, C. "A Public Management for All Seasons." *Public Administration* 69 (1991): 3–19.

Hood, C., O. James, and C. Scott. "Regulation of Government: Has It Increased, Is It Increasing, Should It be Diminished?" *Public Administration* 78 (2000): 283–304.

Hood, C., and B. Peters, "The Middle Aging of New Public Management: Into the Age of Paradox?" *Journal of Public Administration Research and Theory* 14 (2004): 267–82.

Hudson, J., G. Jin Hwang, and S. Kühner. "Between Ideas, Institutions, and Interests: Analysing Third Way Welfare Reform Programmes in Germany and the United Kingdom." *Journal of Social Policy* 37 (2008): 207–30.

Hutchison, T. *A Review of Economic Doctrines, 1870–1929*. Oxford: Clarendon Press, 1953.

Huxham, C. "The Challenge of Collaborative Governance." *Public Management* 2 (2000): 337–57.

Jennings, I. *Cabinet Government*. Cambridge: Cambridge University Press, 1936.

———. *The Law and the Constitution*. London: University of London Press, 1933.

———. *Parliament*. Cambridge: Cambridge University Press, 1939.

Jessop, B. *The Future of the Capitalist State*. Cambridge: Polity, 2002.

———. "Governance and Meta-Governance: On Reflexivity, Requisite Variety, and Requisite Irony." In *Governance as Social and Political Communication*, edited by H. Bang, 101–16. Manchester: Manchester University Press, 2003.

———. "The Regulation Approach: Implications for Political Theory." *Journal of Political Philosophy* 5 (1997): 287–326.

———. *State Theory: Putting the Capitalist State in Its Place*. Cambridge: Polity, 1990.

Jessop, B., and N-L. Sum. *Beyond the Regulation Approach: Putting the Capitalist State in Its Place*. Cheltenham: Edward Elgar, 2006.

Johnson, N. *Reshaping the British Constitution: Essays in Political Interpretation*. Basingstoke: Palgrave Macmillan, 2004.

Johnston, L. "Private Policing in Context." *European Journal on Criminal Policy and Research* 7 (1999): 175–96.

Jones, B., and M. Keating. *Labour and the British State*. Oxford: Oxford University Press, 1985.

Jones, N. *The Control Freaks: How New Labour Gets Its Own Way*. London: Politico's, 2001.

Jordan, A., R. Wurzel, and A. Zito. "The Rise of 'New' Policy Instruments in Comparative Perspective: Has Governance Eclipsed Government?" *Political Studies* 53 (2005): 477–96.

Jordana, J., and D. Levi-Faurr, eds. *The Politics of Regulation: Institutions and Regulatory Reforms for the Age of Governance*. Cheltenham: Edward Elgar, 2004.

Kagan, R. *Adversarial Legalism: The American way of Law*. Cambridge: Harvard University Press, 2001.

Kahneman, D., and A. Tversky, eds. *Choices, Values, and Frames*. New York: Cambridge University Press, 2000.

Kamensky, J. "Role of the 'Reinventing Government' Movement in Federal Management Reform." *Public Administration Review* 56 (1996): 247–55.

Kerley, K., and M. Benson, "Does Community-Orientated Policing Help Build Stronger Communities?" *Police Quarterly* 3 (2000): 46–69.

Kettl, D. "The Global Revolution in Public Management: Driving Themes, Missing Links." *Journal of Policy Analysis and Management* 16 (1997): 446–62.

Kettner, P., and L. Martin. "Performance, Accountability, and the Purchase of Service Contracting." *Administration in Social Work* 17 (1993): 61–79.

Kickert, W. E-H. Klijn, and J. Koppenjan, eds. *Managing Complex Networks: Strategies for the Public Sector*. London: Sage, 1997.

Kiewiet, R., and M. McCubbins. *The Logic of Delegation: Congressional Parties and the Appropriations Process*. Chicago: University of Chicago Press, 1991.

Kilcullen, D. "Three Pillars of Counterinsurgency." Paper presented to the U.S. Government Counterinsurgency Conference, Washington, DC, September 2006.

King, A. "Overload: Problems of Governing in the 1970s." *Political Studies* 23 (1975): 284–96.

Klijn, E-H., and G. Teisman. "Managing Public-Private Partnerships: Influencing Processes and Institutional Context of Public-Private Partnerships." In *Governance in Modern Societies: Effects, Change and Formation of Government Institutions*, edited by O. van Heffen, W. Kickert, and J. Thomassen, 329–48. Dordrecht: Kulwer, 2000.

Knoke, D. *Policy Networks: The Structural Perspective*. Cambridge: Cambridge University Press, 1990.

Kooiman, J., ed. *Modern Governance: New Government-Society Interactions*. London: Sage, 1990.

———. "Societal Governance: Levels, Modes and Orders of Political Interaction." In *Debating Governance: Authority, Steering, and Democracy*, edited by J. Pierre, 138–64. Oxford: Oxford University Press, 2000.

Kooiman, J., and M. van Vliet. "Self-Governance as a Mode of Societal Governance." *Public Management* 2 (2000): 359–77.

Labour Party. *Labour Party Manifesto 2005: Britain Forward not Back*. London: Labour Party, 2005.

Lanni-Reus, E., and F. Lanni. "Street Cops and Management Cops." In *Control in the Police Organisation*, edited by M. Punch. Cambridge: MIT Press, 1983.

Laws, J. "The Constitution: Morals and Rights." *Public Law* 73 (1996): 622–35.

———. "Law and Democracy." *Public Law* 72 (1995): 73–93.

Leadbeater, C. *Britain: The California of Europe?* London: Demos, 1999.

——— *Living on Thin Air*. Harmondsworth: Penguin, 1999.

Leadbeater, C., and S. Goss. *Civic Entrepreneurship*. London: Demos, 1998.

Leadbeater, C., and G. Mulgan. *Mistakeholding: Whatever Happened to Labour's Big Idea?* London: Demos, 1996.

Leonard, M. *Britain: Renewing Our Identity*. London: Demos, 1997.

Lipsky, M. *Street Level Bureaucracy: Dilemmas of the Individual in Public Services*. New York: Russell Sage Foundation, 1980.

Lindblom, C. "The Science of 'Muddling Through.'" *Public Administration Review* 19 (1959): 79–88.

Loader, I. "Policing and the Social: Questions of Symbolic Power." *British Journal of Sociology* 48 (1997): 1–18.

Lombardi, M., and S. Sahota. "International Financial Institutions and the Politics of Structural Adjustment: The African Experience." In *Handbook of Global Economic Policy*, edited by S. Nagel, 65–92. New York: Marcel Dekker, 2000.

Lord, C., and D. Beetham. "Legitimizing the EU: Is There a 'Post-Parliamentary Basis' for Its Legitimation?" *Journal of Common Market Studies* 39 (2001): 443–62.

Loughlin, M. "Law, Ideologies and the Political-Administrative System." *Journal of Law and Society* 16 (1989): 21–41.

Loveday. B. "Reforming the Police: From Local Service to State Police?" *Political Quarterly* 66 (1995): 141–56.

Lowndes, V., and C. Skelcher. "The Dynamics of Multi-Organisational Partner-ships: An Analysis of Changing Modes of Governance." *Public Administration* 76 (1998): 313–33.

Luhmann, N. "Limits of Steering." *Theory, Culture, and Society* 14 (1997): 41–57.

———. *Social Systems*, translated by J. Bednarz Jr. with D. Baecker. Stanford: Stanford University Press, 1995.

Lynn, L. "The Myth of the Bureaucratic Paradigm: What Traditional Public Administration Really Stood For." *Public Administration Review* 61 (2001): 144–60.

MacDonald, R. *Socialism and Society*. London: Independent Labour Party, 1905.

McDonough, F. "Whole of Government: Visions, Strategies, and Challenges." Paper presented to the 40th Conference of the International Council for Information Technology in Government Administration, Guadalajara, Mexico, September 12 –14, 2006.

McGuire, J. "A Dialectical Analysis of Interorganizational Networks." *Journal of Management* 14 (1988): 109–24.

MacIntyre, D. *Mandelson: The Biography*. London: Harper Collins, 1999.

McLaughlin, K., S. Osborne, and E. Ferlie, eds. *New Public Management: Current Trends and Future Prospects*. London: Routledge, 2002.

MacLeod, R., ed. *Government and Expertise: Specialists, Administrators, and Professionals, 1860–1919*. Cambridge: Cambridge University Press, 1988.

Madison, J., A. Hamilton, and J. Jay. *The Federalist*, edited by T. Ball. Cambridge: Cambridge University Press, 2003.

Majone, G. "From the Positive to the Regulatory State: Causes and Consequences of Changes in the Mode of Governance." *Journal of Public Policy* 17 (1997): 139–67.

———. "Nonmajoritarian Institutions and the Limits of Democratic Governance: A Political Transaction-Cost Approach." *Journal of Institutional and Theoretical Economics* 157 (2001): 57–78.

Malone, T. "Modelling Coordination in Organizations and Markets." *Management Science* 33 (1987): 1317–32.

Mandell, M., ed. *Getting Results Through Collaboration: Networks and Network Structures for Public Policy and Management*. Westport, CT: Quorum Books, 2001.

Mandelson, P., and R. Liddle. *The Blair Revolution*. London: Faber and Faber, 1996.

March, J., and J. Olsen. "The New Institutionalism: Organisational Factors in Political Life." *American Political Science Review* 78 (1984): 734–49.

———. *Rediscovering Institutions: The Organizational Basis of Politics*. New York: Free Press, 1989.

Marinetto, M. "Governing beyond the Centre: A Critique of the Anglo-Governance School." *Political Studies* 51 (2003): 592–608.

Marsh, D., and R. Rhodes, eds. *Implementing Thatcherite Policies: Audit of an Era*. Buckingham: Open University Press, 1992.

———. *Policy Networks in British Government*. Oxford: Clarendon Press, 1992.

Marsh D., and M. Smith. "Understanding Policy Networks: Towards a Dialectical Approach." *Political Studies* 48 (2000): 4–21.

———. "There Is More than One Way to Do Political Science: On Different Ways to Study Policy Networks." *Political Studies* 49 (2001): 528–41.

Mayntz, R., and B. Marin, eds. *Policy Networks: Empirical Evidence and Theoretical Considerations.* Frankfurt: Campus, 1991.

Megginson, W., and J. Netter. "From State to Market: A Survey of Empirical Studies of Privatization." *Journal of Economic Literature* 39 (2001): 321–89.

Mill, J. S. *Collected Works of J.S. Mill.* Toronto: University of Toronto Press, 1963–91.

———. "Considerations on Representative Government." In *The Collected Works of John Stuart Mill,* vol. 19. Toronto: University of Toronto Press, 1963–91.

———. "Thornton on Labour and its Claims." In *The Collected Works of J.S. Mill,* vol. 5. Toronto: University of Toronto Press, 1963–91.

Miller, G. *Managerial Dilemmas: The Political Economy of Hierarchy.* Cambridge: Cambridge University Press, 1992.

Minow, M. "Public and Private Partnerships: Accounting for the New Religion." *Harvard Law Review* 116 (2003): 1229–70.

Moran, M. *The British Regulatory State: High Modernism and Hyper-Innovation.* Oxford: Oxford University Press, 2003.

Moravcsik, A. "In Defence of the 'Democratic Deficit': Reassessing Legitimacy in the European Union." *Journal of Common Market Studies* 40 (2002): 603–24.

———. "Is There a 'Democratic Deficit' in World Politics? A Framework for Analysis." *Government and Opposition* 39 (2004): 336–63.

Mulgan, G. *Connexity.* London: Jonathon Cape, 1997.

Mulgan, R. "Accountability: An Ever Expanding Concept." *Public Administration* 78 (2000): 555–73.

Nairn, T. *After Britain: New Labour and the Return of Scotland.* London: Granta, 1999.

Nellis, J. *Time to Rethink Privatization in Transition Economies?* International Finance Corporation Discussion Paper No. 38.

Newman, J. "Introduction." In *Remaking Governance,* edited by J. Newman, 1–15. Bristol: Policy Press, 2005.

Newman, P., and A. Thornly. *Urban Planning in Europe: International Competition, National Systems and Planning Projects.* London: Routledge, 1996.

Nicol, D. *EC Membership and the Judicialization of British Politics.* Oxford: Oxford University Press, 2002.

Nutley, S., H. Davies, and P. Smith, eds. *What Works? Evidence Based Policy and Practice in Public Services.* Bristol: Policy Press, 2000.

O'Donnell, G. "Horizontal Accountability in New Democracies." In *The Self-restraining State: Power and Accountability in New Democracies,* edited by A. Schedler, L. Diamond, and M. Plattner, 29–52. Boulder: Lynne Rienner, 1999.

Offer, A. *The Challenge of Affluence: Self-Control and Well-Being in the United States and Britain since 1950.* Oxford: Oxford University Press, 2006.

Olson, M. *The Logic of Collective Action.* Cambridge: Harvard University Press, 1965.

Osborne, D., and T. Gaebler. *Reinventing Government: How the Entrepreneurial Spirit Is Transforming the Public Sector.* Reading, MA: Addison-Wesley, 1992.

O'Toole, L. "Treating Networks Seriously: Practical and Research-Based Agendas in Public Administration." *Public Administration Review* 57 (1997): 45–52.

Paquet, G. *Governance through Social Learning*. Ottawa: University of Ottawa Press, 1999.

Patrick, S., and K. Brown. *Greater than the Sum of its Parts? Assessing 'Whole of Government' Approaches to Fragile States*. New York: International Peace Academy, 2007.

Penty, A. *The Restoration of the Gild System*. London: Swan Sonnenschein, 1906.

Perri 6. *Escaping Poverty: From Safety Nets to Networks of Opportunity*. London: Demos, 1997.

———. *Holistic Government*. London: Demos, 1997.

Perri 6, D. Leat, K. Seltzer, and G. Stoker. *Governing in the Round: Strategies for Holistic Government*. London: Demos, 1999.

Peters, B. *The Politics of Bureaucracy*. New York: Longman, 1995.

Peters, B., and J. Pierre, eds. *Politicians, Bureaucrats, and Administrative Reform*. London: Routledge, 2001.

Peters, B., R. Rhodes, and V. Wright, eds. *Administering the Summit: Administration of the Core Executive in Developed Countries*. Basingstoke: Macmillan, 2000.

Pierre, J., ed. *Debating Governance: Authority, Steering and Democracy*. Oxford: Oxford University Press, 2000.

Pierre, J., and B. Peters. *Governance, Politics, and the State*. Basingstoke: Macmillan, 2000.

Pierson, P. *Politics in Time: History, Institutions, and Social Analysis*. Princeton: Princeton University Press, 2004.

Pierson, S. *Marxism and the Origins of British Socialism*. Ithaca: Cornell University Press, 1973.

———. *British Socialism: The Journey from Fantasy to Politics*. Cambridge: Harvard University Press, 1979.

Pollitt, C., and G. Bouckaert. *Public Management Reform: A Comparative Analysis*. Oxford: Oxford University Press, 2000.

Porter, T. *Trust in Numbers: The Pursuit of Objectivity in Science and Public Life*. Princeton: Princeton University Press, 1995.

Posner, R. "The Social Costs of Monopoly and Regulation." *Journal of Political Economy* 83 (1975): 807–28.

Powell, W. "Neither Market nor Hierarchy: Network Forms of Organization." *Research in Organizational Behaviour* 12 (1990): 295–336.

Powell, W., K. Koput, and L. Smith-Doerr. "Interorganizational Collaboration and the Locus of Innovation: Networks of Learning in Biotechnology." *Administrative Science Quarterly* 41 (1996): 116–45.

Power, M. *The Audit Explosion*. London: Demos, 1994.

Putnam, R. *Bowling Alone: The Collapse and Revival of American Community*. New York: Simon and Schuster, 2000.

Redwood, J. *The Death of Britain?* London: Palgrave Macmillan, 1999.

Rentoul, J. *Tony Blair*. London: Little Brown, 1995.

Rhodes, R. "From Marketization to Diplomacy: It's the Mix That Matters." *Australian Journal of Public Administration* 56 (1997): 40–53.

————. "Policy Network Analysis." In *The Oxford Handbook of Public Policy*, edited by M. Moran, M. Rein, and R. Goodin, 425–47. Oxford: Oxford University Press, 2006.

————. *Understanding Governance: Policy Networks, Governance, Reflexivity, and Accountability.* Buckingham: Open University Press, 1997.

Rhodes, R., S. Bender, and B. Rockman, eds. *The Oxford Handbook of Political Institutions.* Oxford: Oxford University Press, 2006.

Rhodes, R., and P. Dunleavy, eds. *Prime Minister, Cabinet, and Core Executive.* London: Macmillan, 1995.

Richards, D., and M. Smith. "The Tensions of Political Control and Administrative Autonomy: From NPM to a Reconstituted Westminster Model." In *Autonomy and Regulation: Coping with Agencies in the Modern State*, edited by T. Christensen and P. Laegreid, 181–201. Cheltenham: Edward Elgar, 2006.

Richardson, J., ed. *Policy Styles in Western Europe.* London: Allen and Unwin, 1982.

————. "Government, Interest Groups, and Policy Change." *Political Studies* 48 (2000): 1006–25.

Rittel, H., and M. Webber. "Dilemmas in a General Theory of Planning." *Policy Sciences* 4 (1973): 155–69.

Room, G. *The European Challenge: Innovation, Policy Learning, and Social Cohesion in the New Knowledge Economy.* Bristol: Policy Press, 2005.

Ross, D. *The Origins of American Social Science.* Cambridge: Cambridge University Press, 1991.

Routledge, P. *Gordon Brown: The Biography.* London: Simon and Schuster, 1998.

Rutherford, M. *Institutions in Economics: The Old and New Institutionalism.* Cambridge: Cambridge University Press, 1994.

Salamon, L. *The Tools of Government: A Guide to the New Governance.* New York: Oxford University Press, 2002.

Sandel, M. *Democracy's Discontent.* Cambridge: Harvard University Press, 1996.

Sanders, L. "Against Deliberation." *Political Theory* 25 (1997): 347–76.

Sanderson, I. "Evaluation, Policy Learning, and Evidence-based Policy Making." *Public Administration* 80 (2002): 1–22.

Sappington, D. "Incentives in Principal-Agent Relationships." *Journal of Economic Perspectives* 5 (1991): 45–66.

Savoie, D. *Thatcher, Reagan, Mulroney: In Search of a New Bureaucracy.* Pittsburgh: Pittsburgh University Press, 1995.

Schabas, M. *A World Ruled by Number: William Stanley Jevons and the Rise of Mathematical Economics.* Princeton: Princeton University Press, 1990.

Scharpf, F. "Co-ordination in Hierarchies and Networks." In *Games in Hierarchies and Networks: Analytical and Empirical Approaches to the Study of Governance Institutions*, edited by F. Scharpf, 125–65. Frankfurt: Campus, 1993.

————. *Games Real Actors Play: Actor-Centered Institutionalism in Policy Research.* Boulder: Westview, 1997.

————. "Politische Steuerung und Politische Institutionen." *Politisches Vierteljahresschrift* 30 (1989): 10–21.

Schattschneider, E. *The Semisovereign People: A Realists' View of Democracy in America*. New York: Holt, Rinehart, and Winston, 1960.

Schick, A. "Why Most Developing Countries Should Not Try New Zealand's Reforms." *The World Bank Research Observer* 13 (1998): 123–31.

Schmitter, P. and G. Lehmbruch. *Patterns of Corporatist Policy Making*. London: Sage, 1982.

———, eds. *Trends towards Corporatist Intermediation*. Beverly Hills: Sage, 1979.

Shapiro, M. "The Giving Reasons Requirement." In *On Law, Politics and Judicialization*, edited by M. Shapiro and A. Sweet, 228–58. New York: Oxford University Press, 2002.

Shapiro, M., and A. Sweet, eds. *On Law, Politics and Judicialization*. New York: Oxford University Press, 2002.

Sheplse, K. "Studying Institutions: Some Lessons from the Rational Choice Approach." In *Political Science in History: Research Programs and Political Traditions*, edited by J. Farr, J. Dryzek, and S. Leonard, 276–95. New York: Cambridge University Press, 1995.

Silverman, E. "Community Policing: The Implementation Gap." In *Issues in Community Policing*, edited by P. Kratcoski and D. Dukes. Cincinnati: Anderson, 1995.

Sklansky, D. "Police and Democracy." *Michigan Law Review* 103 (2005): 1699–1743.

———. "Private Police and Democracy." *American Criminal Law Review* 43 (2006): 89–105.

Skogan W., and S. Hartnett. *Community Policing, Chicago Style*. New York: Oxford University Press, 1999.

Slater, D. "Other Domains of Democratic Theory: Space, Power, and the Politics of Democratization." *Environment and Planning D: Society and Space* 20 (2002): 255–76.

Slaughter, A-M. *A New World Order*. Princeton: Princeton University Press, 2004.

Slaughter, A-M., A. Sweet, and J. Weiler, eds. *The European Court and National Courts—Doctrine and Jurisprudence: Legal Change in its Social Context*. Oxford: Hart, 2000.

Smith, M. *The Core Executive in Britain*. Basingstoke: Palgrave, 1999.

———. "Recentring British Government: Beliefs, Traditions, and Dilemmas in Political Science." *Political Studies Review* 6 (2008), 143–54.

Snowdon, P. "The Socialist Budget 1907," in *From Serfdom to Socialism*, edited by J. Hardie, 7–37. Hassocks: Harvester, 1974.

Sørensen, E. "Democratic Theory and Network Governance." *Administrative Theory and Praxis* 24 (2002): 693–720.

Spiegel, G., ed. *Practicing History: New Directions in Historical Writing after the Linguistic Turn*. New York: Routledge, 2005.

Steinheider, B., and T. Wuestewald. "From the Bottom Up: Sharing Leadership in a Police Agency." *Police Practice and Research* 9 (2008): 145–63.

Stewart, J., and R. Ayres. "Systems Theory and Policy Practice: An Exploration." *Policy Sciences* 34 (2001): 79–94.

Stiglitz, J. "Principal and Agent." In *The New Palgrave: Allocation, Information, and Markets*, edited by J. Eatwell, M. Milgate, and P. Newman, 241–53. London: Macmillan, 1989.

Stoker, G. "Introduction: The Unintended Costs and Benefits of New Management Reform for British Local Governance." In *The New Management of British Local Governance*, edited by G. Stoker, 1–21. London: Macmillan, 1999.

———. "Urban Political Science and the Challenge of Urban Governance." In *Debating Governance*, edited by J. Pierre, 98–104. Oxford: Oxford University Press, 2000.

Sweet, A. "The European Court and Integration." In *On Law, Politics and Judicialization*, edited by M. Shapiro and A. Sweet, 1–45. New York: Oxford University Press, 2002.

Sweet, A., and M. Thatcher. "Theory and Practice of Delegation to Non-Majoritarian Institutions." *West European Politics* 25 (2002): 1–22.

Taylor, A. "Hollowing Out or Filling In? Task Forces and the Management of Cross-cutting Issues in British Government." *British Journal of Politics and International Relations* 2 (2000): 46–71.

Terry, L. "Administrative Leadership, Neo-Managerialism, and the Public Management Movement." *Public Administration Review* 58 (1998): 194–200.

Thelen, K., and S. Steinmo. "Historical Institutionalism in Comparative Politics." In *Structuring Politics: Historical Institutionalism in Comparative Analysis*, edited by S. Steinmo, K. Thelen, and F. Longsttreth, 1–32. New York: Cambridge University Press, 1992.

Thompson, G., J. Francis, R. Levacic, and J. Mitchell, eds. *Markets, Hierarchies, and Networks: The Coordination of Social Life*. London: Sage, 1991.

Tomaney, J. "End of the Empire State? New Labour and Devolution in the United Kingdom." *International Journal of Urban and Regional Research* 24 (2000): 672–88.

Trägardh, L., and M. Carpini. "The Juridification of Politics in the United States and Europe: Historical Roots, Contemporary Debates and Future Prospects." In *After National Democracy: Rights, Law and Power in America and the New Europe*, edited by L. Trägardh, 41–78. Oxford: Hart, 2004.

Van Waarden, F. "Persistence of National Policy Styles: A Study of Their Institutional Foundations." In *Convergence or Diversity? Internationalisation and Economic Policy Response*, edited by B. Unger and F. van Waarden, 333–72. Dartmouth: Ashgate, 1995.

Verney, D. "Westminster Model." In *The Blackwell Encyclopaedia of Political Science*, edited by V. Bogdanor, 637. Oxford: Blackwell, 1991.

Vigoda, E. "From Responsiveness to Collaboration: Governance, Citizens, and the Next Generation of Public Administration." *Public Administration Review* 62 (2002): 527–40.

Vincent-Jones, P. "The Limits of Near Contractual Governance: Local Authority Internal Trading Under CCT." *Journal of Law and Society* 21 (1994): 214–37.

Wadman, R., and S. Bailey. *Community Policing and Crime Prevention in America and England*. Chicago: Office of International Criminal Justice, 1993.

Wallace, W., and J. Smith. "Democracy or Technocracy? European Integration and the Problem of Popular Consent." *West European Politics* 18 (1995): 137–57.

Wallington, P. "Policing the Miners Strike." *Industrial Law Journal* 14 (1985): 145–59.

Watson, J. *Behaviorism*. New York: Norton, 1924.

Weber, M. *The Theory of Social and Economic Organization*, translated by A. Henderson and T. Parsons. New York: Free Press, 1947.

Weller, P., H. Bakvis, and R. Rhodes, eds. *The Hollow Crown: Countervailing Trends in Core Executives*. Basingstoke: Macmillan, 1997.

Wheen, F. *Karl Marx*. London: Fourth Estate, 1999.

Wiener, M. *Between Two Worlds: The Political Thought of Graham Wallas*. Oxford: Clarendon Press, 1971.

Williams, D., and T. Young. "Governance, the World Bank, and Liberal Theory." *Political Studies* 42 (1994): 84–100.

Williamson, O. "Transaction-cost Economics: The Governance of Contractual Relations." *Journal of Law and Economics* 22 (1979): 233–61.

Wittgenstein, L. *Philosophical Investigations*, translated by G. Anscombe. Oxford: Basil Blackwell, 1972.

Wright, A. *G.D.H. Cole and Socialist Democracy*. Oxford: Clarendon Press, 1979.

Yanow, D., and P. Schwartz-Shea, eds. *Interpretation and Method: Empirical Research Methods and the Interpretive Turn*. Armonk, NY: M. E. Sharpe, 2006.

Index

accountability: and bureaucracy, 34–36,
255–56; of European Union (EU),
110–12; and institutionalism, 107–10,
121; and juridification, 166–67; and
leadership, 182; and marketization,
102–4, 109, 110; and modernism, 34;
performance, 36–38, 75; and rational
choice theory, 35–36, 120–21; v. responsibility, 33–34. *See also* democracy
actions, 6, 7, 10, 23, 58–60, 85–87, 88,
228–29, 260, 265. *See also* situated
agency
Adam Smith Institute, 200
administrative law, 152, 166–67
Administrative Procedures Act, 167
adversarial legalism, 159–60
Africa Conflict Prevention Pool, 223
African Development Bank, 222–23
agency, 23, 268. *See also* situated agency
Aktivierender Staat, 75
Anglo-governance school, 81–85
Anson, William, 148
antiessentialism, 60–61
antirealism, 60–61
Armstrong, Kenneth, 114
Asian Development Bank, 223
auditing, 33, 187–91
Australia, whole of government approach
in, 218–20

Bagehot, Walter, 148, 151
Bang, Henrik, 196
Beetham, David, 111
behavioralism, 20, 62
beliefs, 3, 8, 10, 23, 58–60, 85–87, 228–29,
260, 262–63, 265–67
benchmarking, 192
Bentley, Tom, 200
best practices, 72
Blair, Tony, 123, 130, 136, 141, 165, 200,
203, 207, 208, 209, 210, 216, 255
Blichner, Lars, 154
Blunkett, David, 165, 200
Bourdieu, Pierre, 22

Brans, Marleen, 52
Brown, Gordon, 123, 130, 136, 173–74,
200, 216
Brown v. Board of Education of Topeka,
166
bureaucracy: and accountability, 34–36,
255–56; bureaucratic narrative, 25–27,
35, 36; and democracy, 25–26, 255–56;
and the police, 230–31, 239, 240; and
rational choice theory, 28–29, 30–31

Cameron, David, 174
Campbell, Alastair, 141
Canada, 223–24
Carpini, Michael, 155, 173
case studies, 8–9
centralization, 214, 217
Centre for Policy Studies, 200
Centrelink, 219
choice, 258–59, 269
citizenship, 103, 196–97, 246–49, 269–70
civil liberties, 165
civil society, 99, 108, 113–14, 126, 153–54,
252, 265
coercion, 43, 44
Cole, G.D.H., 129
collaboration, 185
common law, 150
communication, 182
communitarianism, 23, 236, 258
community policing, 228, 236–38, 239–40,
241–42, 247–48
competition, 72. *See also* contracting out;
marketization
Comte, Auguste, 18, 23
Connecticut, Griswold v., 166
Connolly, James, 128
Considine, Mark, 109
consistency, 259–61
constitution, Dicey on, 149–53
constitutional conventions, 151
constitutional reform: constitutional statutes under New Labour, 132–34; debates
about content of, 140–43; devolution,

DATE DUE

FEB 1 0 2011	
SEP 1 0 2011	
OCT 2 1 2013	
NOV 0 3 2014	